TOW

Thoughts Of Waid

Thoughts Order Wisdom

Written By

Waid Sainvil

PREFACE

In the vast tapestry of existence, humanity often finds itself adrift, caught in the turbulent currents of chaos and disharmony. Despite the noise and confusion of the external world, hidden within each individual is a profound and eternal source of wisdom, a guiding energy that can illuminate the path toward balance and peace.

Life is a journey where we are both the traveler and the force that TOWs us forward. Sometimes, we pull the weight of our past, our burdens, and our doubts. Other times, we are guided by unseen hands, lifted by faith, purpose, and the energy of the universe. True spiritual growth comes when we recognize that we are never alone in our struggles, there is always a force, whether within or beyond, that helps us move forward.

Thoughts of Waid (TOW) is far more than a simple collection of teachings. It is a beacon of light for those who seek clarity, purpose, and harmony in the journey of life.

Texitur Ordo Worldi, "The Order of the World is Woven," embodies the profound interconnection between all things in creation. existence is not random but part of an intricate design, a tapestry woven with intention and meaning. Indeed, life, the cosmos, and all natural laws follow an unseen order, bound together in a continuous process of formation and evolution. This perspective aligns with ancient philosophical and metaphysical traditions, which view the universe as a harmonious structure rather than a chaotic accident.

T - exitur represents the act of weaving, a metaphor for the dynamic process of creation. Just as a weaver interlaces threads to create a unified fabric, existence unfolds through countless interwoven forces, energy, consciousness, and matter, forming the reality we perceive. This truth reflects both spiritual and scientific understandings, where natural laws govern the fabric of space-time while deeper, unseen forces shape existence beyond what is immediately observable.

O - rdo, meaning order, signifies the underlying structure that maintains balance in the universe. From the cycles of nature to the principles of mathematics, order ensures stability and continuity. Without it, creation would be formless and without purpose. Ancient thinkers like Pythagoras and Plato recognized this order as a divine principle, while modern physics continues to unveil the mathematical elegance of the cosmos. Truly, everything, from galaxies to the smallest organisms, follows a path aligned with an overarching design.

W - orldi, though a Latinized form of "world, " expands the meaning beyond just Earth. It signifies the entirety of existence, both the material and immaterial realms. In many traditions, the world is not merely a physical space but a manifestation of deeper realities. Whether through religious doctrines, philosophical insights, or scientific discoveries, humanity has long sought to understand how the world functions as part of a greater cosmic order. This word, within the phrase, emphasizes the unity of all creation under a singular woven pattern.

The significance of Texitur Ordo Worldi lies in its universal applicability. It speaks to those who seek meaning in life, guiding them to recognize that they are part of something greater. It encourages individuals to embrace the interconnectedness of existence, to see beyond personal struggles, and to understand that their actions contribute to the greater weave of reality. Whether through spirituality, science, or philosophy, this truth reminds us that everything is part of an ongoing process of creation.

Ultimately, this phrase serves as a reminder that we are not separate from the universe but integral threads in its vast, unfolding tapestry. Just as a single thread contributes to the strength and beauty of a woven fabric, each life and event plays a role in shaping the order of the world. By understanding and embracing this truth, we can align ourselves with the natural harmony of existence, living with purpose, wisdom, and a sense of connection to the infinite.

Thoughts of Waid reminds us that:

T-houghts shape our reality. Every thought we create carries the energy to build or destroy, to heal or harm. Through conscious awareness, we can align our thoughts with the principles of peace and love.

O-rder within leads to order without. A balanced mind and heart create a ripple effect, fostering harmony in our relationships, communities, and ultimately, the planet.

W-isdom is the cornerstone of evolution. True wisdom is not bound by time or culture, it is universal and accessible to all who seek it with sincerity and patience.

This book draws its essence from the timeless Creation Energy Teachings presented by Billy Meier, a body of ancient wisdom that transcends cultures and eras. TOW is a call to reconnect with universal truths, encouraging a journey inward, toward thought, reflection, and understanding. Inner harmony is the seed from which external balance grows, creating a ripple effect that extends to others and, ultimately, to the world around us.

At its core, Thoughts of Waid highlights the power of thoughts. Thoughts are the architects of our reality, each one carrying energy that can either build or destroy, heal or harm. By cultivating conscious awareness, we gain the ability to align our thoughts with the principles of peace, love, and understanding. This alignment is not just a mental exercise, it is a transformative process that shapes the quality of our lives and the world we share.

Another fundamental truth presented in TOW is that order within leads to order without. When the mind and heart find balance, this inner stability radiates outward, influencing our relationships, communities, and even the broader environment. A harmonious inner world creates a foundation for a harmonious external existence, enabling individuals to become catalysts for positive change.

Wisdom is a cornerstone of evolution, and TOW emphasizes that true wisdom is not confined by time, culture, or personal experience. Instead, it is universal and accessible to all who seek it with sincerity and patience. By embracing wisdom, we not only evolve individually but contribute to the collective growth of humanity.

This book is not a promise of instant solutions or fleeting happiness. Instead, it offers tools to cultivate long-lasting harmony and fulfillment. It invites readers to align their lives with the natural laws of creation, laws that govern the universe with precision and balance. By doing so, we empower ourselves to live purposefully, embracing lives of meaning and contentment.

As you turn the pages of Thoughts of Waid, you are encouraged to embark on a deeply personal journey of self-discovery. The courage to look inward, the strength to embrace growth, and the serenity to live in harmony with all beings are the qualities this book seeks to inspire. True change begins within, and as we transform ourselves, the world around us transforms in kind.

Ultimately, the key to peace in the world lies in the peace we nurture within ourselves. When we choose to harmonize our thoughts, actions, and intentions with the principles of unity and love, we become part of the solution to the world's disharmony. In this way, TOW serves as both a guide and a companion on the journey to a more peaceful existence.

May you approach this work with an open heart and a willing mind. Allow its teachings to resonate within you, planting seeds of clarity and understanding that grow with time. This journey is not just about individual transformation but about fostering unity and balance in a world that so desperately needs it.

In wisdom and unity, Thoughts of Waid is offered as a gift, a pathway to living in harmony with yourself, others, and the universal truths that connect all of existence. As you begin this journey, may you find inspiration, empowerment, and the profound serenity that comes from aligning with the natural rhythm of creation.

TABLE OF CONTENTS

SATIRE

Conversation between God and Jesus before he was sent to Earth

God:

Yo, Son, we need to talk.

Jesus:

Technically, you could just talk to yourself. What did I do now?

God:

Don't start with that. It's

not you. It's the Earth humans. They screwed up.

Jesus:

Alright, alright. What's up?

(Gives himself a high five)

Jesus:

Again? What is it this time? Are they building a tower to heaven?

God:

Worse.

1

Jesus:

Worse than a tower?

God:

They ate an apple.

Jesus:

Wait... an apple? That's it? You're freaking out over fruit?

God:

Not just any fruit. The one fruit I told them not to eat. It's like the one rule I gave them, and they still blew it.

Jesus:

I mean... you did make it look delicious. Wasn't that, like, entrapment?

God:

Excuse me? I'm God. I don't entrap. I test. Big difference.

Jesus:

Okay, so what's the punishment?

God:

Oh, you know, the usual: eternal suffering, fire raining from the sky, the whole "wrath of God" package.

Jesus:

Dad, I mean me, we can't just nuke humanity over a snack!

God:

Watch me.

Jesus:

Wait, wait, wait! What if... hear me out... I go down there, take the blame, and you spare them?

God:

Hmm. Interesting. Go on.

Jesus:

I'll let them kill me, dramatic, emotional, real tearjerker vibes. Then you can forgive them, and we all move on.

God:

(stroking his beard)

Full-on execution. It's gotta be big. Crucifixion, like, nails and everything. You know how much I love theater.

Jesus:

Fine. But after this, I'm taking a serious vacation.

God:

Deal. But the furnace stays. You know, just in case.

Jesus:

"Just in case"? Dad, you're supposed to be forgiving!

God:

I am. But I also like options.

Jesus:

Unbelievable. Okay, when do I leave?

God:

Oh, don't worry. I already sent Gabriel with the memo. You're booked for a virgin birth next week.

Jesus:

A virgin birth? Seriously? You just had to make it weird.

God:

Hey, go big or go home. Now get ready. Humanity isn't going to save itself.

Jesus:

Yeah, yeah. But I'm bringing this up at the next family meeting.

TRUE JOY

Whatever path you choose in life, always remember that your journey is ultimately your own.

Your actions, decisions, and pursuits should come from a place of personal fulfillment rather than a desire for external approval.

True joy is not something granted by the world around you.

It is something that arises from within, independent of recognition or validation.

Even when you dedicate yourself to helping others, the deepest satisfaction should stem from the act itself, not from the gratitude you receive.

If your happiness is tied to how others react, it becomes fragile, constantly shifting based on circumstances beyond your control.

Seeking acknowledgment, praise, or validation may bring temporary satisfaction, but it leaves you vulnerable to disappointment.

What happens if your efforts go unnoticed? What if your kindness is met with indifference? When external approval dictates your sense of joy, you risk feeling empty when that approval fades.

True joy, however, is different. It does not rely on applause, appreciation, or acknowledgment.

It comes from acting in alignment with your values, from knowing that what you do is meaningful to you, regardless of how others perceive it.

This kind of joy is deeply rooted, unshaken by the fleeting opinions of others.

It is not selfish, it is self-sustaining.

When your motivation comes from within, you are free.

Free from the weight of expectations, free from the need for validation, free from the constant search for approval.

You no longer depend on others to tell you that you are enough.

You simply are.

This freedom brings a sense of peace, allowing you to live authentically, without fear of judgment or disappointment.

Acting for yourself does not mean ignoring others, rather, it means that your kindness, generosity, and efforts come from a place of true sincerity.

When you act out of obligation or a need for recognition, your actions lose their purity.

But when you act because it aligns with who you are, the fulfillment is real and lasting.

The world may not always reward you.

People may not always notice the good you do.

But when your joy is independent of external validation, it remains steady.

You no longer feel let down when your kindness is unacknowledged or when your hard work goes unnoticed.

You find satisfaction in the act itself, in knowing that you stayed true to your principles.

In the end, the key to lasting happiness is inner peace.

It is the quiet confidence of knowing that your actions reflect your truest self.

It is the ability to stand firm in your decisions without needing reassurance from others.

It is the understanding that your worth is not defined by recognition but by your own sense of purpose.

True joy is not something that comes and goes with the approval of others, it is a state of being, a deep-rooted contentment that remains, no matter what the world says.

And when you cultivate that joy from within, you will find that it is the most unshakable, enduring happiness of all.

WISDOM

In every moment, strive to cultivate peace and harmony.

Life constantly presents challenges, situations that test your patience, interactions that push your understanding, and disagreements that can either divide or strengthen bonds.

The way you respond shapes not only your experiences but also the world around you.

Choosing calmness over conflict, understanding over judgment, and balance over chaos creates a ripple effect that inspires others to do the same.

When you seek peaceful resolutions, you contribute to a more harmonious world, one interaction at a time.

Wisdom begins with the ability to listen.

Allow others the space to express themselves fully, even when their words challenge your beliefs. Everyone has the same right to voice their thoughts and feelings as you do.

When you listen with patience instead of immediately forming a rebuttal, you offer respect and validation.

True wisdom is not about proving oneself right but about understanding different perspectives.

When you wait for your turn to speak, you cultivate empathy, which strengthens the bonds between you and those around you.

Conversations should not be competitions.

The goal of a discussion is not to dominate but to learn.

If you argue only to assert dominance or force agreement, you miss the deeper purpose of communication. Instead, approach disagreements as opportunities for growth.

Every interaction holds a lesson, it is up to you to uncover and embrace it.

Viewing discussions as exchanges of ideas rather than battles to be won allows for genuine understanding and mutual respect.

Your treatment of others reflects the level of wisdom you carry.

Treat people with the same kindness and patience that you wish to receive.

At the same time, recognize that people will often treat you in the way you permit them to.

If you accept disrespect, it may continue.

If you establish healthy boundaries, you teach others how you deserve to be treated.

Carry yourself with dignity, and let your actions set the standard for the way others engage with you.

Honesty is a cornerstone of wisdom.

Speak your truth with sincerity, but always with kindness.

Holding back your true sentiments out of fear or discomfort creates distance between you and others, as well as within yourself.

When you express yourself openly and authentically, you experience a profound sense of freedom.

Living truthfully invites deeper connections, greater self-respect, and a more meaningful existence.

Beyond personal interactions, wisdom extends to how you view the world.

Recognizing the love of Creation within all people and all things fosters deep compassion and appreciation.

When you begin to see the world through this lens, your perspective shifts. You become more patient, more understanding, and more at peace.

You recognize that everyone is on their own journey, learning and growing in their own way.

Instead of judging, you empathize.

Instead of reacting impulsively, you reflect.

This shift not only transforms your relationships but also enriches your own life in ways you never imagined.

To walk the path of wisdom is to embrace the art of balance, between speaking and listening, between standing firm and being open-minded, between expressing yourself and considering the feelings of others.

It is to approach life with curiosity rather than assumption, with patience rather than frustration, and with love rather than fear.

Wisdom is not found in knowing everything but in the willingness to continue learning.

It is in choosing peace when faced with conflict, understanding when confronted with ignorance, and authenticity when tempted by conformity.

When you live with wisdom, you do not merely exist, you inspire, uplift, and contribute to a world where harmony is not just an ideal but a reality.

CONTROL

One of the greatest challenges facing humanity is the persistent desire to control how others think, act, or live.

This need to impose personal beliefs onto others has fueled division, conflict, and suffering throughout history.

Many people cling to the notion that their perspective is the only correct one, leading them to judge, criticize, and even attempt to regulate the lives of those who choose a different path.

This mindset fails to acknowledge one of the most fundamental truths of existence, that each person is a unique individual with the right to their own choices, experiences, and beliefs.

The impulse to control often comes from fear, the fear that if others live differently, it somehow threatens our own way of life.

But in reality, diversity in thought and action does not diminish us. It strengthens us.

When we attempt to force others into our mold, we rob them of their authenticity, and in doing so, we diminish the richness of human existence.

Instead of allowing people the freedom to grow in their own way, we create restrictions that stifle creativity, innovation, and personal evolution.

The consequences of control are evident everywhere.

Political divisions, religious conflicts, social unrest, many of these issues stem from an unwillingness to accept differing viewpoints.

When one group insists that their way is the only way, oppression inevitably follows. Control is not just about imposing rules or laws.

It manifests in the way we interact daily.

It appears in the judgments we pass, the expectations we set, and the limitations we impose on others based on our own beliefs and fears.

By trying to control how others live, we create unnecessary tension and disharmony.

Instead of fostering an environment of mutual respect, we breed resentment, resistance, and division.

The more we attempt to enforce conformity, the further we push people away from genuine understanding and connection.

The irony is that control does not bring security or order, it brings resistance and chaos.

History has shown time and again that societies built on excessive control eventually collapse under the weight of their own rigidity.

If humanity is to move forward, we must embrace the concept of true freedom.

Peace and harmony will only emerge when we collectively acknowledge the importance of allowing others to live as they see fit.

True freedom is not just about having rights on paper.

It is about creating a world where individuals are not pressured to conform to someone else's ideals.

It means respecting the personal journey of every human being, even when it does not align with our own beliefs.

This does not mean we should abandon our values or accept harmful behaviors.

There is a difference between allowing freedom and permitting injustice.

True wisdom lies in knowing when to stand up for what is right and when to let go of the need to control others.

It is possible to live by our own principles while still allowing others the space to live by theirs.

The beauty of humanity lies in its diversity.

No two people are the same, and that is a strength, not a weakness.

When we embrace differences instead of fearing them, we open the door to deeper understanding and stronger connections.

Every person has their own unique perspective, shaped by their experiences, upbringing, and personal insights.

By learning from one another rather than trying to control each other, we expand our awareness and enrich our own lives.

I know wholeheartedly that when humanity learns to let go of the need to control others, a profound shift will take place.

Instead of trying to force the world to fit a singular mold, we will begin to see the beauty in allowing life to unfold naturally.

When people are free to be themselves without fear of judgment or coercion, they flourish. Creativity thrives, relationships deepen, and societies grow stronger.

This realization, the understanding that true peace comes from embracing freedom, marks the first step toward a better world.

If we can move beyond the compulsion to control and instead focus on cultivating respect, empathy, and acceptance, we will lay the foundation for a future where harmony is not just an ideal but a reality.

Only by relinquishing control can we truly experience the boundless potential of human existence.

THE "WHY"

The urge to share excessive information about ourselves often stems from a deeper, unrecognized insecurity.

Many of us feel compelled to express our thoughts, experiences, and emotions in ways that go beyond simple communication, we overshare, seeking validation from others as if their approval can somehow solidify our worth.

This tendency is not always conscious.

It operates in the background, subtly influencing our interactions, leading us to believe that if others understand or affirm us, we will finally feel whole.

But why?

Why do we feel this need?

Why do we look to others for reassurance instead of finding it within ourselves?

These are questions we rarely ask, yet they hold the key to breaking free from patterns of excessive self-disclosure and dependence on external validation.

The moment we begin to understand the "why" behind our actions, we gain the power to change them.

Awareness is the first step to transformation.

When we recognize that our impulse to overshare is rooted in self-doubt or an unspoken need for connection, we can begin to reshape our approach, ensuring that what we share is intentional rather than compulsive.

Understanding the "why" does not mean silencing ourselves or withdrawing from meaningful conversations.

It means learning to differentiate between authentic self-expression and the need for external reassurance.

It means developing a sense of internal stability, where we no longer feel driven to seek approval, but instead, we share because we truly want to, not because we need validation to feel secure.

When we pause to reflect on our motives, we can reframe our actions with greater awareness.

The need to impress, to be understood, or to feel seen loses its urgency.

Instead, we become comfortable with silence, knowing that our worth is not dependent on how much we reveal or how others respond.

The ability to exist without seeking validation is a form of liberation, one that brings true peace and confidence.

The Creation Energy Teachings provide profound wisdom that goes beyond superficial understanding.

They guide us to look inward, to explore the deeper truths of existence, and to recognize the interconnectedness of all things.

Like a flower that blooms in the unexpected chill of autumn, these teachings illuminate what was once obscured, revealing clarity where there was confusion.

They offer insights that transform the way we see ourselves and the world, helping us move beyond the need for constant reassurance and into a space of self-assurance.

Through this wisdom, life takes on a new level of clarity.

We begin to see not only the external patterns that shape our experiences but also the internal forces that drive us.

The motives, fears, and unspoken desires that once dictated our behavior become visible, allowing us to shift our perspective and break free from unhealthy cycles.

This awareness empowers us to embrace authenticity, to be at peace with ourselves, and to interact with the world from a place of strength rather than insecurity.

When we no longer rely on external validation, we develop a sense of calm confidence.

We no longer feel the need to prove ourselves, explain every aspect of our lives, or seek constant affirmation.

Instead, we cultivate inner certainty, knowing that who we are does not require justification.

We become more present, more deliberate in our words and actions, and more capable of forming genuine connections, ones that are based not on need, but on mutual understanding and respect.

Ultimately, understanding the "why" behind our actions is a journey of self-discovery.

It is about recognizing the unconscious patterns that dictate our behavior and replacing them with intentional choices.

It is about learning to trust ourselves, to embrace silence when words are unnecessary, and to find fulfillment from within rather than from external sources.

When we internalize these truths, our relationship with the world transforms.

We no longer chase approval because we no longer need it.

We no longer overshare because we no longer feel incomplete.

Instead, we move forward with quiet confidence, secure in the knowledge that our worth is inherent, unshaken by the fleeting opinions of others.

And in this state of self-awareness, we find something even greater than validation, we find peace.

WE ARE NOT ALONE

Humanity is not the only intelligent life in existence, not on this planet, not within this galaxy, and certainly not in the vast, immeasurable expanse of the Universe.

The idea that Earth is the singular cradle of life is not only illogical but also deeply limiting.

The Universe is teeming with life, and beyond what is visible to us, there exist other dimensions, planes of existence, and even seven universes interconnected within the vastness of Creation.

Recognizing this reality is not just an exercise in speculation. It is a necessary evolution of human understanding.

For far too long, Earth humans have lived under the illusion of being alone, shaped by restrictive beliefs that deny the greater truths of existence.

Many cling to the notion of a singular, omnipotent deity, a belief that has been ingrained into societies for millennia, despite its foundation resting on nothing but myth and human invention.

But the sooner humanity accepts the truth, that we are part of an expansive, intelligent, and evolving cosmos, the sooner it will be able to move beyond these self-imposed limitations.

Releasing the belief in a deity that does not exist is not a loss. It is a liberation.

It is an essential step toward the growth of human consciousness, one that will allow individuals to embrace their true origins and their profound potential.

Once humanity sheds these illusions, it will have the opportunity to perceive something far greater, the reality of oneness.

This oneness is not an abstract concept. It is the fundamental truth of existence.

All life is interconnected, woven together by the intricate forces of Creation itself.

The divisions that currently define human societies, religion, nationality, culture, and ideology, are illusions sustained by ignorance.

These constructs, while deeply ingrained, are not eternal truths but temporary obstacles that hinder the realization of our shared existence.

The recognition of this interconnectedness has the power to unify humanity in a way that has never been seen before.

If people understood that they are not separate from one another, nor separate from the vast community of life beyond this planet, their entire perception of existence would shift.

Fear would give way to understanding.

Conflict would lose its foundation.

The endless divisions that fuel suffering and strife would dissolve in the light of a greater awareness.

Although I do not yet see this unity manifest in my fellow human beings,

I feel it deeply within myself.

This inner sense of oneness fills me with a peace that cannot be shaken by the turbulence of the world.

It is a knowing that transcends what the eyes perceive, a connection that extends beyond the limitations of human thought.

This understanding is not something that can be forced upon others, it is something that must awaken naturally within them.

But when it does, it transforms not only the individual but the collective.

This realization brings with it immense joy, for it reveals the boundless potential that humanity holds.

The ability to recognize and embrace our place within the greater expanse of life across the Universe is the key to our evolution.

It is a shift from fear to wisdom, from division to unity, from limitation to boundless possibility. But this transformation requires willingness.

It requires a conscious effort to let go of falsehoods and embrace the truth.

The path forward for humanity is clear.

It lies in awakening to the reality of existence beyond the narrow scope of earthly perception.

It lies in the courage to release old beliefs, to question deeply, and to seek truth with an open heart and mind.

Letting go of false doctrines and embracing the true nature of life will not only elevate human consciousness but will also open the doors to direct contact and understanding with our cosmic neighbors, those who have long observed, guided, and, at times, even intervened in human affairs.

We are not alone, nor have we ever been.

The Universe is vast, abundant, and filled with life in forms beyond our current comprehension.

To deny this is to remain in darkness, trapped in an illusion of isolation.

But to accept it is to step into the light of truth, to recognize our place in the grand design of Creation.

The choice remains with humanity: to cling to outdated beliefs that limit growth or to embrace the knowledge that will lead to true understanding, unity, and an era of enlightenment unlike anything we have known before.

The time to awaken is now.

LYING

Lying, in my view, is one of the most disrespectful acts a person can commit against another.

At its core, deception is an act of control, an attempt to manipulate reality in a way that benefits the liar while diminishing the autonomy of the one being lied to.

When you lie to someone, you are essentially making a decision on their behalf, deciding what they should and shouldn't know, as if they are incapable of handling the truth.

This is both condescending and unfair, as it denies them the right to respond to reality with their own strength and judgment.

Honesty is the foundation of any meaningful relationship, whether personal or professional.

When you lie, you introduce an element of falsehood that distorts trust, making genuine connection impossible.

Even small lies can erode the integrity of a relationship over time, leading to suspicion, doubt, and an inability to fully trust the other person.

Every time you lie, you create a false version of yourself in someone else's mind, forcing them to interact with an illusion rather than the real you.

In doing so, you rob them of the opportunity to know and understand you as you truly are.

Beyond damaging relationships, lying also takes away people's ability to make informed decisions.

Every action we take is based on the information we have, and when that information is false, our choices become compromised.

This means that a person who is lied to is not only deceived but also manipulated.

They are forced to operate under a false premise, making decisions that may not align with their best interests or true intentions.

This violation of personal autonomy is deeply unethical, as it prevents individuals from living authentically and taking responsibility for their own lives.

Furthermore, lying weakens the liar just as much as it deceives the victim.

Dishonesty often stems from fear, fear of consequences, fear of judgment, fear of losing something valuable.

But giving in to this fear only reinforces feelings of inadequacy and cowardice.

It takes far more strength to tell the truth and face the consequences than to construct a web of deception.

Every time a person chooses dishonesty over truth, they chip away at their own self-respect, and with each lie, their integrity becomes more fragile.

Lying also creates a cycle of deception that is difficult to escape.

One lie often leads to another, as maintaining the illusion requires additional falsehoods to cover up previous ones.

This cycle becomes exhausting, forcing the liar to constantly remember what they said, to whom, and how to keep their story consistent.

In contrast, honesty requires no such effort.

The truth remains steady and unchanging, while lies demand constant upkeep.

In the end, maintaining deception is far more difficult than simply telling the truth in the first place.

Eventually, the truth has a way of surfacing, no matter how carefully it has been concealed.

When it does, the consequences of the lie are often far greater than if the truth had been told from the beginning.

The sense of betrayal felt by those who were deceived can be profound, and the damage to relationships, whether personal, professional, or societal, can be irreparable.

Lies breed mistrust, and once trust is broken, it is incredibly difficult to rebuild.

Choosing honesty, even in difficult situations, is a sign of respect, not just for others, but for yourself.

Speaking the truth, no matter how uncomfortable, fosters relationships rooted in authenticity and mutual understanding.

It allows for open communication, the resolution of conflicts, and the development of deeper connections based on genuine trust.

The world would be a much better place if people valued truth over convenience, if they chose honesty over deception, even when it was difficult.

THE POWER OF TRUTH

When you first begin speaking the truth, you may find that people instinctively turn away, much like the early cavemen who fled in fear at the sight of fire.

The truth, in its raw and unfiltered form, is a powerful force, one that challenges perceptions, disrupts comfort, and demands a confrontation with reality.

Most people are conditioned to embrace familiar narratives, even if they are built on illusions.

When truth enters their world, it shakes the foundation of their beliefs, often triggering resistance or denial.

This reaction, however, is not necessarily a rejection of truth's value but rather a natural response to the unfamiliar.

Change is unsettling, and truth carries with it the weight of transformation.

It forces individuals to see beyond the illusions they have accepted, requiring them to question long-held assumptions.

This can be an uncomfortable process, leading some to withdraw or even react with hostility.

But their initial fear does not mean they will never return to what they have heard.

Just as those early cavemen eventually returned to the fire, drawn not only by its warmth but by its undeniable utility, people, too, will find their way back to the truth.

The mind, despite its resistance, has a natural inclination toward clarity.

Once a person has been exposed to the truth, a seed is planted, and that seed will continue to grow, even if they try to ignore it.

Curiosity, reflection, and the undeniable pull of truth will eventually guide them back.

Truth is not about immediate acceptance or instant validation.

When you speak the truth, it may not always be met with open arms.

Some may challenge it, some may dismiss it, and others may quietly absorb it while saying nothing.

This does not mean your words have no impact.

Many people listen from the shadows, processing what they've heard in silence, much like those cavemen who observed fire from a distance before daring to step closer.

Therefore, continue to speak the truth, even when it seems like no one is listening.

Do not measure the value of your words by the number of visible supporters.

Just because people do not immediately respond does not mean they are not affected.

The truth has a way of lingering in the minds of those who hear it, slowly unraveling falsehoods and leading them toward deeper understanding.

The path of truth is not one of instant gratification, it is one of patience and persistence.

There will be moments when doubt creeps in, when it feels as if your voice is echoing into emptiness.

But remember that truth, much like fire, is a force of change that cannot be ignored.

Even when it seems like your message is going unnoticed, trust that its energy is reaching the right people in the right time.

Truth is a beacon, illuminating the darkness of ignorance and deception.

Its warmth, once feared, will eventually become a source of comfort and guidance.

So, stand firm in your commitment to truth, knowing that every word spoken in honesty has the power to ignite a transformation, both in yourself and in those who, whether now or later, will be drawn to its undeniable light.

RESPECT

Every human being possesses the undeniable right to believe, think, and live in a manner that aligns with their own values.

This fundamental freedom is the cornerstone of individuality and personal growth.

As long as a person's beliefs and actions cause no harm to others, they should be respected without judgment or interference.

Respecting this right is not just a moral obligation but a necessary step toward fostering harmony in a world rich with diverse perspectives.

People come from different backgrounds, experiences, and traditions.

Their beliefs are shaped by personal journeys, cultural influences, and deep introspection.

No two paths are exactly the same, and it is this very diversity that makes humanity so vibrant.

When we recognize and honor each person's right to think and live as they choose, we contribute to an atmosphere of acceptance and understanding.

In contrast, attempting to impose one's own beliefs onto others only leads to division, conflict, and unnecessary suffering.

No one should be ridiculed, condemned, or attacked for the way they live or what they believe, provided that their choices do not bring harm to others.

Agreement is not a requirement for respect.

You do not have to share someone's viewpoint to acknowledge their right to hold it.

True respect means allowing people to walk their own path without interference, even if their choices differ from your own.

At the same time, respect does not mean blind acceptance of all ideas.

It is not about silencing your own thoughts or avoiding discussion.

You have the right to think critically, to analyze, and to express your perspective.

Engaging in thoughtful conversations about different viewpoints can lead to greater awareness and understanding.

However, it is essential that such exchanges be approached with care and consideration.

Truth can be shared without hostility, and differences can be explored without conflict.

The way we communicate matters.

Respectful dialogue encourages open-mindedness and growth. When ideas are shared in a spirit of mutual understanding, even opposing perspectives can coexist peacefully.

Every meaningful conversation is an opportunity to learn, to reflect, and to expand one's understanding of the world.

Disagreements do not have to result in division, rather, they can serve as stepping stones to deeper connections.

By embracing respect in our interactions, we help create a world where freedom of thought and peaceful coexistence flourish.

A world where people feel safe to express their beliefs without fear of hostility.

A world where understanding replaces judgment, and unity triumphs over division.

Respect is not just about tolerance, it is about recognizing the dignity of every human being.

It is about understanding that true harmony is not achieved through conformity but through the acceptance of diversity.

When we treat one another with respect, we pave the way for a more enlightened, compassionate, and united world.

LET THEM BE

It is essential to recognize that questioning another person's choices too often can lead to unintended judgment and interference.

While curiosity and discussion can foster understanding, there is a fine line between seeking knowledge and imposing personal opinions.

Every individual has the right to navigate life according to their own values, experiences, and aspirations, provided their actions do not cause harm to others.

Allowing people the freedom to live authentically is a fundamental pillar of mutual respect and societal harmony.

Human beings are shaped by countless factors, cultural background, personal experiences, emotional struggles, and inner convictions.

No two people walk the same path, and it is neither practical nor fair to expect uniformity in thoughts, actions, or beliefs.

Instead of trying to alter another's journey to fit our own expectations, we must practice acceptance and allow them to be who they are.

This does not mean we must always agree, but rather that we must respect the right of each person to make their own choices.

However, there are situations where intervention is necessary.

When an individual's behavior directly harms others or disrupts the balance of society, allowing them to continue unchecked can lead to chaos and suffering.

Protecting the well-being of the collective sometimes requires addressing actions that threaten peace, security, or fundamental human rights.

In such cases, intervention should be guided by wisdom, fairness, and the intention to restore balance rather than exert control.

Balancing individual freedom with social responsibility requires careful thought.

While everyone deserves autonomy, that freedom should not come at the expense of another's safety or dignity.

It is a delicate equilibrium, requiring societies to establish fair guidelines that preserve both personal liberties and collective harmony.

This is where the importance of governance, justice, and ethical decision-making comes into play.

For those who repeatedly refuse to respect the principles of peaceful coexistence, who reject the fundamental rights of others and create persistent harm, alternative solutions may need to be considered.

If a person or group continually disrupts the peace and refuses to live within the boundaries of mutual respect, then perhaps the best course of action is to grant them a space where they can govern themselves, free from the interference of others and without imposing on the wider community.

A humane and balanced solution could involve relocating such individuals to an environment where they can function independently, a self-sustaining area, perhaps even an isolated island, where they are given the opportunity to build their own society according to their beliefs and rules.

This approach is not about exile or punishment but about ensuring both personal autonomy and social stability.

Such an arrangement would need to be executed with fairness and compassion.

It should prioritize the preservation of basic human rights while maintaining a peaceful resolution for the greater society.

Rather than forcing conformity, it would offer a space for those unwilling to integrate with others to create their own way of life, free from external influence.

In the end, the goal is coexistence, finding ways to live together peacefully while respecting the freedom of each individual.

True harmony is achieved not by forcing everyone into the same mold, but by allowing space for diversity while maintaining a foundation of respect, fairness, and responsibility.

By letting people be, while ensuring justice and accountability when necessary, society can foster an environment of peace, balance, and progress.

DISCUSSING PEOPLE

The more you focus on the lives and affairs of others, the more you weigh down your mind with information that does not serve your growth or well-being.

Constantly analyzing or discussing other people's choices, behaviors, or circumstances creates unnecessary distractions, diverting your energy from matters that truly impact your own life.

Every moment spent fixating on someone else's journey is a moment lost in building your own.

When you allow your attention to linger on the personal affairs of others, your mind absorbs a flood of details that have no real significance to your personal evolution.

These details, opinions, judgments, speculations, slowly accumulate, occupying valuable mental space that could otherwise be used for constructive thought.

Over time, this excess clutter can lead to mental fatigue, making it harder to focus on your own aspirations and responsibilities.

An overloaded mind is a clouded mind.

When your thoughts are tangled in the lives of others, your ability to think logically and make sound decisions diminishes.

The more external noise you allow in, the harder it becomes to sift through what truly matters.

Instead of using your intellect to solve problems, generate ideas, or make strategic life choices, you find yourself drowning in irrelevant details that serve no purpose in your personal growth.

Moreover, excessive focus on other people's lives often leads to misplaced emotions, jealousy, frustration, unnecessary comparison.

These emotions drain your energy, leaving you mentally and emotionally exhausted.

Instead of nurturing your own ambitions, you become entangled in someone else's reality, reacting to their successes, failures, and choices as if they directly impact your own path.

This pattern can create unnecessary stress and hinder your ability to pursue your own goals with clarity and determination.

If you wish to preserve your mental energy and cultivate clear thinking, you must be selective about where you place your focus.

Filtering out distractions and limiting your attention to what is genuinely relevant to your own journey allows for deeper concentration and a more logical approach to life.

By redirecting your mental resources toward self-improvement, creativity, and personal fulfillment, you unlock the ability to engage with life in a way that is both meaningful and productive.

This is not to say that we should ignore others completely, empathy and awareness are valuable qualities.

However, there is a distinct difference between offering support or learning from others and obsessively analyzing or discussing their lives.

A healthy balance allows you to maintain strong relationships without losing sight of your own path.

When you shift your focus inward, toward your own growth, knowledge, and aspirations, you regain control of your mental space.

Your thoughts become clearer, your decisions more intentional, and your overall sense of well-being significantly improved.

Instead of being a spectator in the lives of others, you become the architect of your own destiny, channeling your energy into pursuits that elevate and enrich your existence.

YOUR MIND

Your mind is one of the most precious resources you possess, and you must guard it with care.

Never allow anyone to alter your perspective or shift your convictions without first seeking the truth for yourself.

Your thoughts, your beliefs, and your knowledge are yours alone, and they should remain as such unless you have a clear and personal reason to adjust them.

When someone presents a new idea, a different belief, or an alternative viewpoint, take the time to consider it thoughtfully and thoroughly.

Only after you have examined it with your own reason and experience should you allow it to influence your beliefs.

It is vital to remain grounded in your own understanding, for your mind is the lens through which you see the world.

Allowing others to impose their opinions on you without thoughtful evaluation can result in a loss of personal clarity and self-direction.

Be cautious of those who seek to change your mind without offering you the space to explore the truth on your own terms.

Every belief, every piece of knowledge, and every conclusion you reach should be a product of your own inquiry and reasoning, not simply a belief adopted from someone else.

Trust in your ability to discern the truth. Doubting yourself without a valid reason only leads to confusion and instability.

You must have confidence in your own capacity for thought and understanding.

While it is natural to seek guidance and learn from others, the ultimate responsibility for forming your beliefs and making decisions lies within you.

You have the power to critically analyze, to reflect, and to come to your own conclusions.

The confidence to trust in your reasoning is the foundation for genuine understanding.

Taking the time to deeply contemplate a subject or idea opens the door to discovering the truth firsthand.

Thoughtful reflection and inquiry allow you to move beyond surface-level assumptions and uncover the core of any matter.

When you devote yourself to learning and seeking truth through your own experiences, you develop a deeper and more meaningful understanding that cannot be swayed easily by external pressures.

This process of intellectual inquiry transforms uncertainty into clarity, and confusion into knowledge.

Only through personal effort and reflection can your understanding evolve into true knowledge, grounded not just in facts or theories, but in your own lived experience and thoughtful exploration.

If you simply accept what others say without question, what you hold will only be a belief, shaped more by external influences and doubt than by your own understanding.

A belief adopted from someone else, or accepted without contemplation, may not carry the strength or conviction that genuine knowledge holds.

On the other hand, knowledge that is built on your own observations, your critical thinking, and your personal experiences will always be more valuable and enduring.

It becomes a solid foundation that cannot easily be shaken by the opinions of others.

When you engage deeply with a subject, allowing your mind to wrestle with ideas and seek the truth, you build a framework of understanding that is both reliable and empowering.

Remember, the process of learning and forming beliefs should be ongoing. Your mind is not static, and neither should your beliefs be.

The key is to approach new ideas with an open mind, but one that is also discerning and capable of questioning.

Let your thoughts evolve through careful reflection and consideration, always returning to the core of your own understanding and experience.

Only then can you truly own your knowledge, confidently stand by them, and continue to grow in wisdom and insight.

MEANING OF LIFE

To live truly, one must seek and understand the profound meaning of life.

Without this understanding, life can often feel like a random series of events, one after another, with no deeper significance.

Too many people move through their days as though they are on autopilot, caught in the grind of routine, unaware of the spiritual journey that underlies every moment of their existence.

They are like chickens running in every direction, aimlessly flapping about without a clear sense of direction or purpose, and their awareness is consumed by the constant distractions of the surface world.

They chase after fleeting pleasures and scramble to resolve struggles, but they fail to see that these experiences are merely the outer layers of a deeper, more meaningful existence.

They are so absorbed in the trivial that they miss the essence of life itself.

True life begins with the recognition that life is not simply a series of random occurrences or unimportant experiences.

It starts when one becomes aware of the greater purpose that lies behind everything.

To understand life, one must first understand the energy that moves through and connects all of existence, the Creation Energy.

This energy is not just a force of the universe, it is the very essence of every human being, the spiritual current that links humanity to the universal consciousness.

It is through this energy that we grow, evolve, and reach higher states of awareness.

Understanding this energy is key to unlocking the deeper meaning of life and to aligning ourselves with the true purpose of our existence.

The essence of life is found in the continuous evolution of the Creation Energy within each person.

This evolution is not a random process, but one that is deeply connected to our spiritual growth.

Each human being is a vessel through which this energy can expand, and each person's life is part of a greater, ongoing process of spiritual evolution.

Life is not just about what happens on the surface, it is a deeply spiritual journey that takes place within, where every experience, no matter how insignificant it may seem at the time, holds the potential for growth and transformation.

To live without an understanding of this purpose is to live in ignorance of the most fulfilling and meaningful aspect of existence.

Every moment of life, whether joyful or filled with hardship, has a purpose in the greater scheme of things.

These moments are not just random or meaningless, they are opportunities.

Opportunities to learn, to grow, and to develop the Creation Energy within us.

Life's challenges are not meant to defeat us, rather, they are stepping stones on our path to higher consciousness.

Every lesson we encounter, every joy we embrace, and every struggle we endure is a part of the greater process of spiritual evolution.

These experiences push us toward greater awareness, allowing us to reflect, learn, and transform in ways we could never have anticipated.

To embrace life fully, we must approach every moment with an open heart and a reflective mind. By doing so, we become more attuned to the deeper lessons embedded in our experiences.

This kind of awareness allows us to align with the true purpose of life, the spiritual evolution of our being.

It is only when we see life through this lens that we begin to experience real growth, real fulfillment, and real transformation.

Living with this awareness brings clarity and meaning to everything we encounter.

Rather than getting lost in the chaos of daily life, we begin to see life as a harmonious progression of moments, each one guiding us closer to spiritual enlightenment.

Ultimately, life is about progress, about the continual development of the self in harmony with the universe.

Our purpose is to grow, to evolve, and to expand our consciousness in alignment with the greater cosmic order.

The journey of life, when understood in this way, is not just about individual achievement or personal success, but about the intentional unfolding of one's spiritual self.

By committing to this journey, we rise above the superficial distractions of modern existence and embrace a life filled with meaning, clarity, and purpose.

It is in this pursuit of evolution and spiritual growth that we fulfill our true role in the grand design of existence, contributing to the expansion and enrichment of universal consciousness.

By aligning with this higher purpose, we participate in the eternal cycle of growth, not just as individuals, but as part of the collective consciousness of humanity.

Through this understanding, we experience life in its fullest form, with the knowledge that our existence is far more than it appears on the surface, it's a sacred journey of connection, growth, and transformation.

THE LITTLE MOMENTS

The little moments in life, though they may seem small or insignificant at first glance, are anything but.

They are, in fact, the very threads that weave the intricate fabric of our existence, gently shaping our days and giving us a sense of grounding in an otherwise chaotic world.

Each of these moments, no matter how brief, carries its own unique essence, offering a quiet yet profound beauty that often goes unnoticed amid the whirlwind of our busy lives.

To truly see and appreciate these moments is to tap into the very rhythm of life itself, connecting with its ebb and flow in ways we rarely stop to consider.

Whether it's the sound of laughter shared with friends, the soft golden glow of a sunset casting its warmth upon the earth, or the feeling of a gentle breeze brushing against our skin, these seemingly simple experiences hold a deeper power.

They have the ability to remind us of the richness, the depth, and the subtle wonder of everything that surrounds us.

These moments are not just fleeting events to be quickly forgotten but are opportunities, small, quiet invitations to pause, to reflect, and to truly embrace the wonder of simply being alive.

When we take the time to notice and savor these little pockets of time, we awaken to the extraordinary within the ordinary.

We begin to realize that the true beauty of life is not found in the grand, sweeping gestures or the monumental achievements we often chase after, but rather in the countless small encounters that fill our days in ways we might overlook.

Each of these moments carries with it a quiet, unspoken magic, waiting patiently to be recognized, appreciated, and cherished for the treasure it is.

Ultimately, life is nothing more than a series of these little moments, strung together like pearls on a necklace, each one significant in its own right.

They are not distractions or interruptions in the flow of life, but rather the very essence of our journey.

By choosing to see them, to honor them, and to celebrate them, we open our hearts to the beauty that surrounds us in every waking moment.

And in doing so, we discover that life's greatest treasures are often not far off or hidden away but lie waiting for us, quietly, in plain sight, just waiting for us to notice.

PAST LIFE

You don't remember your past lives because the weight of such knowledge would be far too heavy to bear, making it nearly impossible to live fully in this one.

The memories and experiences from countless previous lifetimes would flood your mind, overwhelming it in ways that would leave you in a state of confusion or, worse, madness.

Those who claim to recall their past lives, to possess vivid memories of who they were, are only fooling themselves, allowing their imaginations to run wild in the absence of true understanding.

In truth, the only exception to this rule is Billy, his consciousness is advanced enough to access and comprehend the profound and intricate truths of his past experiences across time.

But for most of us, the veil between our current life and our previous ones remains firmly closed.

Still, let me assure you, this is not your first time in a human body, and it certainly will not be your last.

Each life you live is a unique chapter in the journey of your Creation Energy, an opportunity for growth, transformation, and evolution.

Every lifetime brings with it different lessons, different circumstances, different opportunities to learn and expand in ways you never could have in any other form.

Yet, in this moment, this life is the one you are living.

It is your only life, this is the one you are meant to embrace fully, with open arms and a grateful heart.

This moment, with all its challenges and joys, is a gift, one that can only be appreciated when you surrender to its beauty and depth.

Instead of yearning for the past or worrying about the future, it is far more important to focus on the here and now.

It's in this present moment where your true power lies, waiting to be tapped into.

In my own life, I have discovered a powerful truth: inner peace creates outer peace.

When you cultivate a calm and balanced state within yourself, it becomes a force that radiates outward, influencing your relationships, your environment, and your reality in ways that are both subtle and profound.

This inner tranquility has allowed me to reach a deep contentment with my life, an acceptance and fulfillment that drives me to share what I have learned with others.

It is my way of passing on the joy and harmony I have found, offering a piece of this peaceful existence to those who may need it most.

I wish for everyone to experience life's beauty as I have, to see the world not as a place of hardship and strife, but as a vast landscape filled with wonder and possibility.

The world, when seen with the right perspective, is a place brimming with magic and delight, but it requires a shift in perception, a deeper way of seeing and experiencing things.

Life is fleeting. It is fragile, precious, and full of boundless possibilities, but it is also incredibly short.

This moment, this breath, this heartbeat, it's yours to live, to treasure, and to savor.

The richness of life lies not in waiting for some future event or lamenting past mistakes, but in fully embracing and appreciating the now, for it is in the now that all potential exists.

So, I encourage you to take a step back and recognize the beauty that already surrounds you. It is waiting, quietly and patiently, for you to notice it and claim it as your own.

DIFFERENT VIEWS

Don't let differences in views lead to the loss of loved ones.

The world is full of varying perspectives, and it's all too easy to become entrenched in the belief that only your own point of view is the "right" one.

But the truth is, everyone has the right to think, feel, and act according to their own beliefs, values, and experiences.

These are shaped by their upbringing, culture, and personal journey, and they can differ greatly from your own.

Respecting this free will, the ability to form and express individual thoughts and beliefs, is absolutely vital, even when their perspectives don't align with yours.

At the core of every healthy relationship is the ability to honor one another's right to be different.

Love and relationships should not be overshadowed by disagreements over opinions or beliefs, as losing someone you care about over differing views often causes more harm than you might initially realize.

In the heat of disagreement, it's easy to forget that the person you are arguing with is still the same person you love. It's important not to take other people's views personally.

Their beliefs and opinions are not an attack on you.

They are simply an expression of their unique experiences and understanding of the world.

It's essential to remember that, whether their opinions are admirable or troubling to you, they are still the same person you care for.

Rejecting them or distancing yourself from them because of their beliefs creates unnecessary gaps in the relationship and hinders the possibility of understanding, growth, and reconciliation.

When people feel attacked, criticized, or judged for their views, they tend to cling more fiercely to their beliefs.

This is a natural human response, defensiveness often rises when someone feels that their core identity is being questioned or rejected.

Confrontation, especially if it's charged with judgment, rarely leads to positive change.

In fact, it often only serves to reinforce divisions and solidify the opposing stances, making it harder to engage in meaningful conversations or find common ground.

In contrast, when individuals are allowed to express themselves freely without the fear of being ridiculed or dismissed, it creates an environment where openness thrives.

The freedom to express one's thoughts without judgment encourages vulnerability and fosters a sense of mutual respect, even when perspectives differ.

This doesn't mean you have to agree with everything someone says, but it does mean that you acknowledge and respect their right to hold those beliefs.

By respecting others' freedom to express their thoughts, we are, in turn, promoting peace, empathy, and harmony in our relationships.

This approach is not about tolerating harmful ideologies or practices, but rather about choosing connection and understanding over alienation.

When we understand that people are more than their opinions, that their worth is not defined by what they believe in the moment, we open the door to deeper connections.

The beauty of human relationships lies in our ability to grow together, to challenge one another, and to share in the learning process.

By embracing and valuing each other despite differences, we create the space for love, understanding, growth, and meaningful dialogue.

The relationships that thrive are the ones where both parties feel seen, heard, and respected, even when they stand in opposition.

In these moments of difference, we are given the chance to learn more about ourselves and one another, and to become better versions of who we are as individuals and as part of a greater whole.

THE HERALD

Billy, a name simple in its sound, steps forward as the Herald, embodying something much greater than the sum of his words.

His presence alone speaks volumes, carrying a message of hope and understanding.

He does not seek confrontation, nor will he engage in a battle against the ignorance that surrounds him.

Unlike those who are quick to react in anger or frustration, Billy takes a different approach.

His method is not to fight but to offer something far more powerful, the gift of patience and understanding.

Billy's role is not to engage in meaningless arguments or to assert his own perspective over others.

Instead, he simply presents himself, his quiet strength and calm demeanor serving as a beacon in the storm of misconceptions and false beliefs.

His very being is the message.

His actions, his way of living, and his presence are all a testament to the truth he carries.

Through the way he lives and the way he interacts with the world, Billy shows what is true. He lets his actions speak louder than any spoken word could.

While Billy remains calm, composed, and unshaken by the chaos around him, the weight of responsibility is not solely his to bear.

He is not alone in this mission.

There are others, those who stand beside him, walking in the same light, who share in the task of bringing clarity to a world clouded by ignorance.

Together, they form a united front, a collective strength bound by a shared purpose.

These are the ones who will rise, with Billy at their side, to confront the misconceptions that have taken root and challenge the falsehoods that obscure the truth.

The battle against ignorance, though it may seem like a daunting struggle, is not one of anger or violence.

It is a battle fought not with weapons but with persistence, patience, and unwavering dedication.

The Herald, in his wisdom, understands that true change does not come from shouting or force.

He does not need to raise his voice or his fists to make a difference.

Instead, he allows the power of knowledge, the weight of truth, and the force of wisdom to speak for themselves.

Over time, those who are willing to listen, who are open to hearing beyond their own limited perceptions, will begin to see.

The truth will become clear, and the light of understanding will illuminate the path that leads to clarity.

The truth is not hidden and nor elusive.

It is simply waiting to be recognized, to be embraced by those who are ready to see it.

The message Billy carries is both clear and simple, much like Billy himself.

His purpose is not to complicate or confuse but to offer a straightforward, honest reflection of what is real. The truth does not require embellishment or grandiosity.

It stands firm in its simplicity, needing no adornment or explanation.

What Billy offers is something anyone can understand, should they be willing to open their hearts and minds to it.

And though this journey may seem solitary at times, the struggle against ignorance will not be fought alone.

There are many who, like Billy, understand the power of love, unity, and understanding.

Those who truly care about the future of humanity and the possibility of a world built on truth and compassion will carry the fight forward.

With love as their guide and unity as their strength, they will challenge the darkness of ignorance and spread the light of wisdom wherever they go.

Together, they will forge a path toward a more enlightened world, one where understanding replaces judgment, and where truth triumphs over the noise of falsehoods.

And through it all, Billy will continue to stand, unwavering, as the Herald, not by raising his voice, but by simply being the truth in a world that so desperately needs to see it.

TRUE FRIEND

A true friend is someone with whom you should feel completely at ease, a person who allows you to be your truest, most authentic self without fear of judgment or rejection.

They are the ones you can turn to when you are feeling vulnerable, knowing that they will listen without criticism and understand without reservation.

In their presence, you are free to express your innermost thoughts, your deepest fears, and your most heartfelt dreams, without the concern of being misunderstood or dismissed.

A true friend creates an environment where you feel seen, heard, and accepted for exactly who you are.

This level of openness, where both people can share their raw selves, is the cornerstone upon which genuine friendship is built.

But friendship, like any meaningful connection, is not just about the moments of shared joy or the laughs you share together.

The true strength of a friendship lies in the trust that binds it.

Trust is the invisible thread that holds the relationship together, allowing it to withstand the inevitable challenges and changes life throws your way.

Without trust, however, the foundation of friendship crumbles.

If you cannot confide in someone or share your authentic self with them, then the relationship lacks the depth necessary for it to truly flourish.

It may appear strong on the surface, but the truth is that a friendship without trust is like a house built on shaky ground, it may stand for a while, but over time it will begin to crack and falter, and eventually, it will collapse under its own weight.

Love and affection, though important, are not enough to sustain a friendship without trust.

While shared memories and a bond of care can create a sense of connection, the absence of honesty, vulnerability, and genuine emotional exchange creates a void that cannot be filled.

Friendship, at its core, is not about simply being around someone who is kind to you.

It is about sharing your lives in a way that is authentic, vulnerable, and real.

When you feel you cannot trust your friend with your truth, the very foundation of that bond begins to erode.

Without the space to be vulnerable, to express your real feelings and thoughts, there can be no growth, no depth, no true connection.

True friendship thrives on the freedom to be yourself and the assurance that your feelings are safe with the other person.

It is a relationship where both individuals feel comfortable letting down their walls, knowing that the other will meet them with compassion and understanding.

A true friend does not judge you for your mistakes or shortcomings but instead offers a hand of support and empathy, encouraging you to be your most authentic self.

They stand beside you, not because they have to, but because they choose to, valuing the bond of trust and the sincerity of your shared experiences.

In the end, a relationship without trust is destined to fail.

It is not a matter of love or care, it is a matter of connection and authenticity.

No matter how much affection is present, the lack of genuine trust will inevitably cause the relationship to break down.

Without the ability to be vulnerable and open, without the assurance that your feelings are safe and that your friend values your truth, the relationship will slowly wither.

A true friend is someone who not only loves and cares for you, but who also creates a safe space for you to express your deepest truths.

They provide a foundation upon which trust can grow, offering you the comfort and security to be yourself, flaws and all.

This is what makes a true friend so invaluable, they are not just a companion for the good times, but a steadfast presence in your life who helps you navigate the challenges with unwavering support and understanding.

They are the ones who help you grow, help you heal, and help you become the best version of yourself, all while honoring the person you are right now.

True friendship is built on trust, and without it, the bond simply cannot thrive.

PEACE OF MIND.

Peace of mind is undoubtedly the most valuable gift a human being can possess.

It is the bedrock upon which all true happiness and contentment are built, providing us with the foundation to navigate life with clarity, grace, and ease.

When we are at peace within ourselves, we are freed from the weight of unnecessary stress and distractions that so often cloud our judgment and steal our focus.

In this state of inner calm, we become fully present in each moment, able to embrace life's simple joys without being overshadowed by worries, anxieties, or the constant pull of external demands.

True peace of mind allows us to step back from the noise of the world and find the quiet space within where clarity resides.

However, as human beings, we often complicate our lives in ways that undermine our peace of mind.

Many people chase after material possessions, societal validation, or an endless list of tasks, believing that these pursuits will bring them fulfillment and happiness.

While some of these things may appear important or desirable on the surface, they are often distractions that prevent us from recognizing the true sources of peace and contentment within.

In striving for "more," more things, more approval, more achievements, we risk losing sight of the very thing that sustains our well-being: our mental and emotional balance.

The constant pursuit of external validation can leave us feeling restless, unfulfilled, and disconnected from our true selves.

It can create a cycle of striving and yearning that is never quite satisfied, leading us to miss out on the deeper peace that comes from within.

In the process, we forget that the most precious resource we all have is time.

Time is the one thing that is universally shared, no matter who we are or where we come from.

Each of us is given the same 24 hours in a day, and no matter our circumstances, we all have a finite number of days in our lives.

How we choose to spend that time can determine the quality of our lives.

Time spent chasing after superficial goals or chasing after "more" only contributes to our stress and dissatisfaction.

But time spent nurturing peace, cultivating simplicity, and focusing on the things that truly matter, our relationships, our well-being, our personal growth, enriches our experience and brings lasting joy.

The more we value peace and simplicity, the more we are able to make the most of our time, finding satisfaction in the everyday moments that often go unnoticed in the rush of life.

At its core, inner peace is the most rewarding state of being because it allows us to experience life in its truest form.

When we cultivate peace within ourselves, we create a space where we can truly enjoy each moment, free from the chaos and clutter that so often surround us.

In this peaceful state, we can hear our own thoughts more clearly, make decisions with wisdom, and approach challenges with a calm demeanor.

We are better able to connect with others, offer kindness, and approach the world with compassion.

Life becomes richer and more meaningful when we choose peace over complexity, when we allow ourselves the space to simply be.

The more we embrace peace within ourselves, the more life unfolds in ways that are genuinely fulfilling.

We find joy in the simplest of moments, a quiet cup of coffee in the morning, a walk in nature, a conversation with a friend.

These small, ordinary experiences become profound when we are at peace, for we are able to truly savor them without being distracted by the constant noise of our minds.

Our relationships deepen, our creativity flows more freely, and our overall sense of well-being improves when we choose peace as our foundation.

By choosing peace over complexity, we create a harmonious existence that nurtures not only our minds but also our Creation Energy.

The energy we put into the world is a reflection of the energy we cultivate within.

When we are at peace, we naturally radiate that peace to those around us, creating an environment of calm and understanding.

This ripple effect enhances not only our own lives but the lives of those we interact with, fostering a world where peace and harmony can grow.

Truly, peace of mind is not just a personal journey, it is the foundation of a more balanced and compassionate world.

SUCCESS.

Success is not defined by material wealth, status, or possessions.

In fact, these external markers often obscure the true meaning of success, creating a false narrative that leads many down paths of constant striving without ever reaching fulfillment.

True success, in its purest form, is found in the simple act of being alive.

To live, to breathe, and to face each new day with resilience and hope is a profound form of success in itself.

Every moment we wake up to and every breath we take are reminders that we have the power to continue, to endure, and to rise in the face of life's challenges.

Simply existing, experiencing life in its entirety, is a reflection of our innate ability to persevere against all odds.

Success, then, is not something we need to chase or measure by worldly standards.

It is something that is inherently present in our being, woven into the very fabric of our existence.

Life, in all its complexity, offers us endless opportunities to grow, to evolve, and to learn.

The fact that we are here, alive and aware, is proof of the incredible potential we carry within us.

Each new day presents a fresh chance to better understand ourselves, to connect with others, and to deepen our relationship with the world around us.

In this sense, success begins and ends within us.

It is not something dictated by external circumstances or the judgments of others.

It is not dependent on how much we own, how far we climb in our careers, or how many accolades we collect along the way.

True success is a reflection of our internal state, our peace of mind, our growth, and our ability to adapt to life's twists and turns.

At its core, success is about the lessons we learn from mistakes and how we embrace the wisdom they bring.

Mistakes are not defeats, as many may perceive them to be.

They are stepping stones, critical moments that guide us toward growth and self-awareness.

Every failure, no matter how painful, holds valuable insights that shape our future actions.

When we allow ourselves to learn from these experiences, we develop resilience, emotional intelligence, and an ever-deepening understanding of who we are and what we are capable of.

Success, therefore, is not about avoiding failure but about how we rise after we fall. It's about how we transform setbacks into opportunities for self-improvement.

The true essence of success is found in our willingness to reflect, adapt, and keep moving forward, even when the path is uncertain.

Importantly, success is a deeply personal journey. It has nothing to do with others' achievements or standards.

It resides within the individual, independent of external validation or comparison.

We are often taught to measure ourselves against others, whether it's by social media, societal expectations, or peer pressure, but true success cannot be found by following someone else's path.

No one else's definition of success can define our own.

Our worth is not determined by the achievements of others or by how closely we match their milestones.

True success comes from staying authentic to ourselves, listening to our inner voice, and walking the path that resonates with our deepest values.

When we focus inward, recognizing our unique worth and talents, we unlock a sense of accomplishment that is unshaken by outside influences.

We become free from the trap of comparison and instead celebrate the beauty of our own journey.

Success, ultimately, is the triumph over our own inner battles.

It is the courage to confront our fears, doubts, and insecurities, and to emerge stronger and more self-aware on the other side.

We all face internal struggles, moments when we question our worth, our decisions, and our place in the world.

These challenges are not signs of weakness but opportunities for profound growth.

Each time we overcome a fear, no matter how small, we claim a victory against the "demons" within.

Each moment we stand up to our doubts and push through feelings of inadequacy, we reinforce our inner strength and resilience.

These battles, though often invisible to the outside world, are the true tests of our character.

The more we conquer them, the more we become the individuals we were always meant to be.

This personal growth, this development of inner strength and emotional maturity, is the ultimate measure of success.

It proves that success is not about what we have or what we accomplish externally, but about who we become in the process.

The journey to success is not linear or neatly defined by milestones and achievements.

It is messy, full of challenges, and deeply personal.

But each step we take, each lesson we learn, and each victory we win against our own fears and limitations bring us closer to the truest form of success: the realization of our full potential.

Success is the evolution of the self, the unfolding of our true nature, and the courage to become who we are meant to be, without compromise or fear.

INNER PEACE.

Maintaining inner peace is a delicate art, but it can be achieved through two primary approaches: either by walking away from conflicts or by confronting them head-on and expressing your authentic feelings.

Each individual possesses the innate ability to assess the dynamics of any situation and determine whether it is likely to push them toward losing control or help them maintain composure.

This self-awareness is paramount in making the right decision in challenging circumstances, as it allows you to act from a place of understanding and emotional intelligence.

Without this level of mindfulness, we risk reacting impulsively, which can lead to regret and emotional turmoil.

Therefore, cultivating self-awareness and tuning into your emotional state is the first step in protecting your peace.

When you choose to confront a conflict, it is vital to approach the situation with a calm and composed demeanor.

It's easy to let emotions take over in the heat of the moment, but this often exacerbates the issue and leads to further misunderstanding.

Instead, take a moment to breathe, assess the situation, and collect your thoughts before speaking.

Express your emotions and viewpoints logically, without allowing anger or frustration to cloud your judgment.

By doing so, you ensure that your perspective is communicated clearly and that your intentions are understood without the distortion of heightened emotions.

This method of clear and measured communication not only helps prevent unnecessary escalation, but it also allows you to maintain control over your reactions.

When you are in control of your emotions, you are more likely to resolve the situation peacefully and with mutual respect.

Furthermore, confronting a conflict calmly requires the ability to listen attentively. It's not just about expressing your feelings but also about hearing the other person's perspective.

Active listening fosters empathy and helps you understand where the other person is coming from.

This mutual exchange of thoughts can diffuse tension and lead to more constructive conversations.

It is also a reminder that inner peace isn't about always getting your way, but about creating an environment where both parties feel heard, respected, and understood.

Such an approach not only resolves conflict but strengthens relationships, as it builds trust and promotes emotional maturity.

Ultimately, when you approach conflict with calmness, respect, and understanding, you reinforce your inner tranquility while fostering a deeper connection with others.

On the other hand, sometimes the wisest choice is to walk away from a conflict.

This does not mean avoiding the issue forever, but rather recognizing when a situation has escalated beyond productive dialogue.

If you feel that engaging in the conflict will only lead to emotional turmoil or further aggression, it may be better to step away.

However, it is important that once you decide to disengage, you make a firm commitment to let go of the situation mentally.

Simply removing yourself from a conflict physically does not guarantee that your peace will be restored if you continue to dwell on it in your mind.

Resentment, anger, or lingering thoughts about the issue can disrupt your emotional equilibrium and lead to unnecessary stress.

Walking away with intention means giving yourself the space to process your emotions, allowing them to dissipate naturally without holding on to them.

It's about finding a mental distance from the conflict so that you can regain your balance.

This act of mental detachment frees your mind from negativity and allows you to reconnect with your peace of mind.

By choosing to mentally let go of a conflict, you create a protective barrier against the emotional turbulence that can arise when unresolved issues continue to weigh heavily on your heart and mind.

This act of self-care ensures that you do not carry the burden of someone else's behavior or the emotional fallout of the situation with you.

Ultimately, the path to inner peace is about making conscious, intentional choices that align with your values, emotional state, and overall well-being.

Whether you decide to confront a conflict directly or step away from it, the key is to remain grounded in your sense of self.

When you are mindful of your emotions and thoughtful in your responses, you maintain a sense of stability, no matter what external chaos may surround you.

Being aware of the consequences of your actions, both immediate and long-term, allows you to navigate conflicts with assurance, knowing that your peace is always within reach.

The ability to maintain inner peace, therefore, is not about avoiding conflict altogether or suppressing emotions, but about knowing when to engage and when to step back.

It's about choosing the best course of action based on your emotional capacity and ensuring that your peace remains intact throughout.

By practicing this awareness, you cultivate a steady, unwavering calmness that serves as the foundation for a balanced, fulfilling life.

With each conflict you face, whether you confront it or walk away, you grow more confident in your ability to protect your inner peace and live with greater emotional clarity.

THE HUMAN BODY.

The human body is more than just a physical entity.

It is a vessel uniquely crafted to carry each person on their individual journey, shaped by their experiences, challenges, and the lessons life has to offer.

Every body, regardless of its form or appearance, is a living testament to the beauty of diversity and the intricate design of existence itself.

This beauty is not confined to the external, fleeting qualities we often focus on, but is woven deep within the essence of every human being.

It serves as a powerful reminder that our worth is not determined by the physical form we inhabit, but by the depth of who we are.

Beneath the skin, beyond the structure of bones and flesh, lies something far more significant, the unique and untouchable soul that gives each person life and meaning.

True beauty is not something that can be defined by the standards of society, nor can it be validated by external sources.

It is an innate quality, rooted deeply in our spirit, character, and the way we express our unique existence.

The radiance of this beauty shines from within, and it takes many forms, reflected in the way a person loves, cares, and interacts with the world around them.

Each individual, no matter their appearance, carries a unique expression of this beauty, shaped by their inner light, their values, and the way they move through the world.

To recognize this beauty in others is to honor the profound value of every human life, regardless of its outward form.

We are not solely defined by our physical appearance, but by the intentions, actions, and energy we bring into the world.

Our bodies are mere temporary expressions of our existence, fleeting, fragile, and imperfect, while the true essence of who we are lies far beyond the surface.

True beauty, in its most authentic form, flourishes not through physical perfection but through qualities like kindness, empathy, authenticity, and the courage to act with integrity.

It is revealed not in how we look, but in how we choose to live, how we interact with others, and the love we share.

In all my years, I have never seen an ugly human being, until they betray their own inner goodness through harmful actions, cruelty, or dishonesty.

It is through these choices that a person's essence becomes obscured, clouded by negativity, deceit, or malice.

But conversely, those who embody compassion, love, and sincerity radiate a beauty that far surpasses the superficial qualities we so often idolize.

This truth is a reminder that it is not our physical features that define us, but the actions we take and the energy we bring into the world that shape the beauty we share with others.

THE CREATION ENERGY.

The human Creation Energy, also known as the spirit form, is an eternal force that transcends the limitations of our physical existence.

It is a force that is destined for an ongoing journey of growth and evolution.

The Creation Energy ceases reincarnating into human bodies once it has reached a pivotal point in its spiritual development, when it achieves a 100% Brain Quotient in its final reincarnation.

This point of evolution is marked by the attainment of self-awareness and the formation of an ego, a transformation so profound that it unfolds over a span of 40 to 60 million years.

Upon reaching this advanced stage, the Creation Energy enters a new phase of spiritual evolution, culminating in its ascent to the High Council level, where it spends millions of years refining its knowledge and expanding its consciousness.

During this period, the Creation Energy becomes further attuned to the intricacies of the universe and begins preparing for its eventual progression to the first spiritual realm of Arahat Athersata.

This represents the pinnacle of spiritual development before it advances to even higher realms of existence.

The journey of the Creation Energy, therefore, is not a quick process but one that requires patience, introspection, and growth through countless cycles of life.

While the human Creation Energies on Earth are relatively young, with an average age of approximately 4.5 million years, there are beings whose Creation Energies are far older and have experienced much more profound cycles of reincarnation.

For example, Nokodemion, whose Creation Energy is the oldest known, is 9.6 billion years old. Nokodemion's spiritual energy serves as a beacon to humanity, as well as to the Plejaren, demonstrating a level of wisdom and experience that few other Creation Energies have reached.

This vast age difference between various Creation Energies illustrates the differing stages of spiritual evolution across the universe, with some energies having walked many more paths of enlightenment than others.

Understanding the concept of the immortality of our Creation Energy profoundly alters our perception of life and its challenges.

It brings into focus the idea that life is not a finite journey, but rather an ongoing, never-ending process of growth and learning.

Each incarnation offers us the opportunity to refine our consciousness, expand our awareness, and ultimately fulfill our spiritual objectives over many lifetimes.

The recognition that we are eternal beings who never truly die allows us to embrace each life as an important part of a much larger, infinite cycle.

This knowledge provides solace, knowing that even in times of difficulty, our growth is part of a greater process that spans countless lifetimes.

Creation itself, which embodies the Universal Consciousness, is an expression of infinite love.

Through this Universal Consciousness, we are granted the profound ability to experience life as an integral aspect of the larger whole.

While human beings are material entities, our experience on Earth exists within a world that was specifically designed to allow us to grow and learn through the unique lens of material consciousness.

This material consciousness manifests in each lifetime, and once it has fulfilled its purpose, it recedes.

However, the Creation Energy within us transcends this material existence, existing beyond time and space.

It is immortal and is eternally connected with the universal essence, remaining an inseparable part of Creation itself.

The realization that we are not created by a higher deity, but instead are beings of inherent power, created from and within the Universal Consciousness, offers us a liberating truth.

It reveals that we have always possessed the divine power within ourselves, and we are not subjugated to any external force.

This understanding empowers us to live our lives with a sense of purpose, confidence, and harmony, knowing that we are eternal beings on a sacred journey of self-discovery, spiritual evolution, and enlightenment.

We are not merely at the mercy of the world around us, but are active participants in the creation of our own spiritual destiny.

This knowledge invites us to live fully, knowing that every experience, every challenge, and every moment is part of a profound journey of growth and transformation.

THE DISCONNECT.

The majority of Earth's people operate primarily on the level of belief, a state that governs much of human thought and decision-making.

Belief, in essence, is rooted in the lack of certainty.

To believe in something inherently means to accept it without definitive proof or understanding, relying instead on assumptions, personal interpretations, or external assertions that have not been conclusively demonstrated.

Belief leaves room for doubt, as it arises from a position of uncertainty and is, therefore, always subject to change or revision.

A human being, however, should not live by belief alone, but by truth and certainty.

The pursuit of truth is what should guide an individual, for it provides a stable foundation upon which to build knowledge and understanding.

When one is confined to holding beliefs, they remain disconnected from their deeper, innate potential for genuine comprehension.

This disconnect is subtle yet profound, arising from the fact that belief, by its very nature, is an imprecise, provisional concept.

It creates an invisible barrier between the conscious mind and the deeper layers of understanding that lie beneath the surface.

This barrier prevents the mind from aligning with the deeper wisdom that resides within the subconscious.

The subconscious mind, a powerful reservoir of boundless potential and insight, cannot fully connect with a consciousness that is clouded by belief.

The subconscious thrives on truth and knowledge, and it is only when the conscious mind embraces these elements that true harmony can be established between the two.

When belief takes precedence, it creates confusion and dissonance within the psyche, preventing the subconscious from harmonizing with the conscious mind.

This fragmentation disrupts the flow of clear thought, insight, and intuitive understanding.

The consequence of this is that many individuals remain trapped in a state of superficial awareness, unable to tap into the full potential of their consciousness.

This is why belief, while it may provide comfort or a sense of security, is ultimately limiting.

The individual who operates purely on belief is caught in a cycle of uncertainty, never fully aligning with the clarity that comes from direct knowledge.

The subconscious, which holds the key to deeper understanding, is unable to share its vast knowledge because it requires the conscious mind to first embrace the certainty of truth.

Without this, the connection remains obscured, and the individual's growth is stunted.

Humanity, therefore, must strive to transcend the reliance on belief and instead pursue a path of truth and knowledge.

Only by seeking truth can one truly understand the nature of existence and the self.

Knowledge allows individuals to see beyond the surface and tap into the profound wisdom that lies dormant within their subconscious.

As this wisdom is unlocked, the individual's consciousness expands, leading to a more holistic understanding of reality and a deeper connection with themselves and the world around them.

In this state of truth and understanding, doubt is replaced by certainty, and belief, often based on assumption or external influence, gives way to the clarity of direct knowledge.

When one fully embraces truth, there is no room left for uncertainty, as certainty arises naturally from an informed, clear-minded perspective.

This shift from belief to truth is the key to unlocking the full potential of the human mind, allowing individuals to live with purpose, direction, and profound insight.

Only by transcending belief can humanity achieve the clarity necessary for real growth and fulfillment, both as individuals and as a collective.

This transformation represents the next step in human evolution, where understanding replaces assumption, and knowledge replaces belief, leading to a world where clarity and truth reign.

THE UFO SIGHTINGS.

The UFO sightings that have captured the curiosity of many are not, in fact, connected to the Plejaren.

These advanced beings, known for their extraordinary wisdom and technology, have ships that are always shielded from view, designed to remain invisible to human detection.

Their vessels are cloaked in such a way that no ordinary human technology can perceive them, keeping their presence hidden from our eyes.

Despite this, Earth is not a lonely planet. It is home to three distinct groups of extraterrestrial beings: the Blue People, the Ocean Dwellers, and the Long Skulls.

These beings have coexisted with humanity for centuries, existing alongside us, often unseen, but present in subtle ways that challenge our understanding of life on this planet.

The Blue People, the Ocean Dwellers, and the Long Skulls are among the many groups that quietly share Earth with us, each of them carrying their own unique history, culture, and wisdom.

They have maintained a low profile, choosing to remain outside of the human spotlight, but their existence is an undeniable reality.

They are not interlopers. Rather, they are an integral part of the complex web of life that defines our world.

Their presence and influence on human history and evolution are often overlooked, yet they have always been here, participating in the shared experience of life on Earth.

These beings serve as a reminder that humanity is not the sole occupant of this planet, nor are we the only advanced species to call it home.

Moreover, Earth is occasionally visited by another group: visitors from the future, our very own descendants.

These time travelers are a further complication to the already intricate and mysterious narrative of life on Earth.

They bring with them knowledge and perspectives from a time far ahead of our own, further expanding our understanding of existence and pushing us to rethink the very nature of time, space, and human potential.

The arrival of future humans offers profound insights into the evolution of consciousness, technology, and society, and invites us to consider the infinite possibilities that lie ahead.

This influx of extraterrestrial and time-traveling visitors raises profound questions about humanity's spiritual and moral framework.

For example, one cannot help but wonder: Did the sacrifice and teachings of Jesus Christ extend to these extraterrestrial beings?

If these beings have coexisted with us for centuries, what role do they play in the larger spiritual narrative of the Universe?

Are they also recipients of the divine messages of love, compassion, and redemption that Jesus imparted to humanity?

These are not merely theoretical questions.

They challenge us to expand our perspective on spirituality, urging us to see beyond the confines of human-centered beliefs and embrace a more universal understanding of life.

Such questions call for a reimagining of spirituality, one that transcends Earthly boundaries and includes all life forms, whether they are from this planet or beyond.

The realization that humanity is not alone in the Universe forces us to reconsider our place in it.

We are not the sole sentient beings on this planet, nor are we the only intelligent life forms in the cosmos.

The presence of these extraterrestrial beings serves as a reminder of the vastness of life beyond our comprehension, a life that spans across not just different planets but also different dimensions and times.

Rather than viewing this revelation with fear or suspicion, we are called to embrace it with wonder and a sense of connection.

We are part of something far greater than ourselves, a shared existence that links us to other species, other worlds, and even the future.

Rather than allowing fear to dictate our response to this greater reality, we should see it as an opportunity for growth.

The unknown is not something to shy away from, but rather something to explore with courage and an open mind.

We stand on the brink of a new age, a transformative phase in human evolution, one that promises to expand our consciousness and challenge our understanding of reality.

This is a time for exploration, curiosity, and openness to new ideas that will shape the future of humanity.

It is a time to embrace change, not with trepidation but with a sense of purpose and excitement.

There is no reason to fear the changes that lie ahead. These changes are not threats, but opportunities, opportunities for unity, for greater understanding, and for the expansion of consciousness.

The dawn of this new era invites us to recognize the vast, interconnected web of life that binds us to all other forms of existence in the Universe.

It calls us to expand our consciousness and embrace the reality that we are all part of a greater cosmic tapestry that spans not just across space, but also across time.

This is our moment to step forward, to embrace the unknown, and to take our place in the ever-expanding Universe with a sense of awe, wonder, and responsibility.

FREE WILL.

Free will is one of humanity's greatest gifts, yet it remains widely misunderstood by many.

At its core, free will is not simply the ability to make choices, it is an expression of love, a profound and unconditional freedom to live your life as you choose.

It is the opportunity to embrace your innermost desires, to carve your unique path, and to trust in the divine unfolding of everything that happens.

True freedom, then, lies in the deep understanding that, no matter what challenges or twists life may bring, all will be well.

This knowledge offers comfort, even in the face of adversity, because you recognize that every experience is part of the greater flow of life and your growth.

Life, in its essence, asks you to be authentic. It invites you to show up in the world as your true self, to live without fear, hesitation, or shame.

This is your one life in this form, and it is yours to live fully and with intention.

The beauty of free will is that it gives you permission to embrace your individuality without feeling the need to conform to the expectations of others.

There is no need to hide who you are or suppress your truth in order to fit in.

This world needs your unique expression, and it is through this authenticity that you contribute your deepest gifts to the world around you.

Too often, fear of the unknown keeps people from fully embracing the life they are meant to live.

Fear of what might come after this life, fear of judgment, and fear of failure can create an overwhelming sense of anxiety that holds them back.

Yet, the truth is, you are eternal. Your existence does not end with this lifetime, and there is nothing to fear.

Your Creation energy's journey extends beyond the physical realm, continuing to grow and evolve in ways beyond what the limited human mind can comprehend.

This awareness frees you from the weight of worrying about others' opinions, as their judgments hold no power over your true self.

What others think of you is not your concern.

You are not here to live up to someone else's expectations but to honor your own path, your own truth.

Your task in this life is simple, though profound: to be yourself, fully and unapologetically.

To present yourself as you truly are, without fear of rejection or judgment.

This is the only life you have in this form, and it is yours to experience and shape.

Living in this way honors the essence of free will and grants you a deep sense of fulfillment and peace.

When you choose to step into your power, to express yourself authentically, you align with the truth of your being and with the flow of the universe.

To live with free will is to recognize and honor the connections and experiences that shape your journey.

It is not just about individual freedom, it is about the relationships you cultivate and the love you share.

The bonds you create with others, the moments you treasure, and the lessons you learn along the way are eternal.

These connections do not end when this life does, they are woven into the very fabric of your being, echoing through the infinite expanse of your existence.

Every act of kindness, every moment of love, every shared smile or tear becomes a part of who you are.

And when you embrace your true self, free of the limitations of fear or expectation, those relationships can flourish in their purest and most fulfilling form.

In truth, free will is an invitation to live courageously and truthfully.

It is not merely the ability to choose, but the invitation to live from the heart, to express your deepest truths, and to trust the flow of life as it unfolds.

It is the power to be yourself, to love openly and without reservation, and to embrace the present moment with an open heart.

By living authentically and rejecting the influence of fear, you honor the precious gift of existence.

You create a life that is filled with meaning, connection, and an eternal love that transcends time and space.

I've never done anything I regretted because when I live from a place of truth and authenticity, my actions align with my highest self.

There is no room for regret when you trust yourself fully and embrace the journey with all its twists and turns.

Every step you take in alignment with your true self is a step toward deeper understanding, greater peace, and a life lived in harmony with the universal flow.

This is the power of free will, freedom to be, to love, and to trust in the unfolding of life with a heart full of gratitude and purpose.

MASK.

Many people carry a deep fear of judgment, which often prevents them from expressing their true feelings.

This fear can be paralyzing, causing them to mold their personalities and behavior to fit societal expectations.

They construct elaborate masks that hide their authentic selves, thinking that by doing so, they will gain acceptance, respect, or freedom.

In reality, these masks are cages. The person behind the mask may convince themselves that they are living freely, but beneath the surface, they feel a constant, subtle dissonance.

They know, deep down, that they are not truly living as their authentic selves.

This internal conflict creates a barrier to genuine self-expression, stifling the full potential of their being and limiting their ability to form meaningful, honest connections with others.

Every person, regardless of background, has the inherent right to live authentically.

This means being true to oneself, to one's feelings, and to one's beliefs, as long as those actions do not cause harm to others.

Unfortunately, many people are denied the freedom to express themselves honestly due to societal pressures, resulting in a fundamental disruption of harmony.

When this freedom is suppressed, unnecessary tension builds within both the individual and society.

The fear of judgment breeds silence, forcing individuals to shrink back, censoring themselves to avoid confrontation or rejection.

But this silence often comes at the cost of personal growth and meaningful relationships.

For example, I stand against the idea of forbidding white people from using the word "nigga."

I understand the weight of the term and its historical context, and I acknowledge its controversial nature.

However, I feel that people should have the freedom to express themselves, even if their words expose ignorance or prejudice.

The truth is, it's better to have open, uncomfortable conversations with someone who is willing to express their true beliefs, even if those beliefs are misguided or offensive, than to engage with someone who hides their prejudices behind politeness or masks of conformity.

When people are transparent about their views, even when those views are flawed or offensive, it opens the door for genuine dialogue and understanding.

Transparency reveals the truth, and only through truth can real change begin.

When individuals choose to reveal who they truly are, it removes the potential for misunderstandings and creates opportunities for meaningful, sometimes difficult, conversations.

Pretending to be something one is not only leads to confusion and distrust. It is the walls of pretense that cause division, not the honest expression of who we are.

Authenticity, no matter how uncomfortable it may be or how it may challenge social norms, is essential for mutual respect and open communication.

Only when people are willing to speak from their hearts, to express their true beliefs, can society truly thrive.

It is in these honest interactions that we find common ground, even when that ground is rocky or uncertain.

I choose to live my life unapologetically, fully embracing who I am. I do not hide my thoughts or sugarcoat my knowledge to fit the expectations of others.

To me, freedom is not merely the absence of restrictions, it is the ability to live in full alignment with one's true self, without fear of judgment or rejection.

This kind of authenticity brings power, clarity, and purpose to every aspect of life.

I present myself exactly as I am, because I know that this is the path to a life that is both liberated and meaningful.

In the end, it is authenticity that provides the foundation for real connection and understanding.

We may not always agree, and sometimes our truths may challenge one another, but it is through these challenges that we grow, learn, and evolve as individuals and as a society.

I firmly think that a life lived honestly, in full alignment with one's values and beliefs, is the only life worth living.

We owe it to ourselves and to others to be as honest and transparent as possible, because only then can we truly build the connections that matter, and create a world that respects and celebrates authenticity in all its forms.

RIP.

The common notion of "resting in peace" after death is, in fact, not entirely accurate or representative of the true nature of existence beyond the physical realm.

While the material consciousness and personality that defined a person's life cease to exist, the journey does not end at the moment of physical death.

Life, in its essence, is a continuous cycle, and death is merely a transition.

When a person passes, all the accumulated wisdom, experiences, and knowledge from that lifetime are not lost but instead are transferred into the individual's Creation Energy.

This Creation Energy serves as a vast, dynamic repository of everything learned and experienced during that lifetime.

It ensures that nothing is truly gone, preserving the essence of one's growth and understanding.

This accumulated energy is the core of one's true self, and while the personality and individual identity dissolve, the wisdom gained remains intact within the energetic imprint.

Once the transfer of knowledge and experience is complete, the former personality, who once occupied the physical body, disappears. It is erased, transforming into pure energy.

This marks the end of its existence as an individual entity with a separate identity.

However, this pure energy is far from inert.

It is not a passive force but an active and vital part of the universal flow of consciousness.

This energy now becomes the foundation upon which a new material consciousness will emerge.

Over time, this new consciousness will reincarnate, carrying with it the Creation Energy that has been refined and enriched through the previous lifetime.

The Creation Energy will accompany this new consciousness into a new life, continuing the cycle of learning and evolution.

This intricate cycle of transformation reveals that life and death are not separate, isolated events, but interconnected stages of a much larger process.

While the physical form, identity, and personality dissolve, the essence of the individual, what truly defines them, continues its journey.

This ensures that growth and continuity are maintained through successive lifetimes.

Death, then, is not an end but a necessary phase that leads to the next step in the ongoing evolution of consciousness.

The death of one form is but the beginning of another, with each phase contributing to the larger tapestry of existence.

Even after death, the process of learning and growth does not cease.

The Creation Energy, which now holds the wisdom of the past life, remains active and engaged in refining and absorbing knowledge.

This phase is not one of rest, slumber, or inactivity, but a time of transformation and development.

In the energetic realm beyond physical existence, the essence of the being is continuously evolving.

It is an ongoing journey where the Creation Energy prepares for its next incarnation.

This preparation is not a passive state, rather, it is a dynamic, active process, as the being adapts, refines, and integrates the lessons from the past in order to face the challenges and opportunities of the new life awaiting it.

In this sense, no one truly "rests" after death. There is no eternal pause in the grand cycle of existence.

Instead, the cycle of energy and consciousness remains in constant motion. It evolves and transforms, as each lifetime builds upon the one that came before it.

The end of one life is not a period of peace or stillness, but rather the beginning of a new chapter in the ever-continuing flow of existence.

This perpetual interplay between the material world and the eternal nature of energy ensures that consciousness is always evolving, ever-changing, and ever-expanding.

The true nature of existence, therefore, is not limited by physical life, it stretches beyond the confines of the material world, with infinite potential for growth, understanding, and transformation.

Even beyond physical death, the journey continues, fueled by the energy of the Creation, the endless source from which all life emerges and to which it ultimately returns.

FREE.

The day I truly understood that nothing I do could change or delay the year 3999 was the day I became a free human being in the fullest sense.

It wasn't just a passing thought, it was a moment of absolute clarity, a profound realization that lifted the heavy weight of external influences and societal expectations that had been pressing down on me for so long.

I had lived much of my life according to the standards set by others, trying to please people or fit into molds that never quite felt right.

But in that moment of understanding, I realized that nothing, no matter how hard I tried, could alter the future or push back the inevitable.

That knowledge liberated me from the chains I had willingly wrapped around myself, thinking they were necessary for survival.

I came to understand that my life, my journey, was uniquely mine, and its purpose was not to fulfill someone else's vision but to live it according to my own choices, desires, and dreams. It was a turning point that shifted my entire perspective on life and its meaning.

This realization was not just an intellectual understanding, but a deep emotional liberation that resonated throughout every part of me.

For the first time, I recognized that I was not bound to the expectations of others, not tied to any future outcome, and certainly not obligated to follow a path that wasn't truly mine.

In this newfound awareness, I embraced the freedom to live authentically.

No longer did I feel compelled to mold myself into a shape that fit someone else's idea of who I should be.

My decisions, my actions, and my dreams became entirely my own, freed from the constraints of societal pressures or the fear of judgment.

I was no longer concerned with fitting into a box or worrying about the opinions of those around me.

The invisible chains that had once held me back, those unspoken rules and assumptions about how I should think, feel, or act, lost their grip on me. I was free to live as I was, not as others expected me to be.

Over the years, countless people had tried to shape me according to their own ways of thinking, their own belief systems.

They never truly understood me or the essence of who I was.

They didn't see the deeper truth that I was trying to live, and their attempts to mold me into something I wasn't only deepened the disconnect between us.

But in that moment of clarity, I knew that their inability to see me for who I truly was didn't diminish my worth or my purpose.

I trusted that one day, they too would reach a similar understanding, the same profound realization that I had come to.

And when they did, they would finally understand the very essence of freedom, the power to live authentically without fear or compromise.

This was the core of the Creation Energy teachings: to live in alignment with your truest self, to honor the uniqueness of your existence, and to embrace the freedom that comes with that.

In accepting this truth, I also came to a deeper understanding of the singular nature of my existence.

This personality, this essence of who I am right now, exists only once in the vastness of time and space.

There will never be another version of me, another opportunity to live this life in this form. That truth hit me hard, it reminded me of the preciousness of this moment, of this incarnation.

There would be no repetition, no second chance to experience life as I was experiencing it.

And with that realization came a profound sense of responsibility, not to others, but to myself.

To deny my authentic self in favor of societal approval would be to waste this one, extraordinary opportunity to live fully and truthfully.

I chose not to squander it.

Instead, I decided to honor my fleeting existence by embracing its full potential, by stepping into my power and living in alignment with the truest version of myself.

I understood that to live authentically was not just a right, but a privilege.

This embrace of freedom brought with it a deep sense of peace.

I felt liberated in a way I had never felt before.

The burdens of conformity, judgment, and fear lifted, and in their place, a sense of calm and clarity emerged.

I had a renewed sense of purpose.

Life, once complicated by the need to meet others' expectations, now felt like a blank canvas, one that was mine to fill as I chose.

Each day became an opportunity to express myself fully, to create the life I wanted without hesitation or apology.

I realized that the most genuine way to honor this singular life was to live it unapologetically, as a reflection of my truest self.

There was no longer any need to hide, to pretend, or to conform.

I could stand proudly in my truth, knowing that the only judgment that mattered was the one I placed upon myself.

Through this journey of self-realization, I became not just a free human being, but a creator of my own destiny.

I understood that the power to shape my life was within me all along.

By embracing my authentic self and stepping away from the pressures of societal expectations, I had unlocked a limitless potential for growth, happiness, and fulfillment.

Life was no longer something that happened to me, it was something I actively shaped.

I had finally become the master of my own fate, living with the clarity, purpose, and freedom that only come when one is willing to live authentically.

NO ONE

No one has the authority to dictate how another human being should live, think, or act.

Every individual is endowed with the right to make their own choices, follow their own path, and determine what is best for themselves.

Attempting to impose control over someone else's decisions is not only an infringement on their autonomy but also an exercise in futility.

Genuine change and transformation cannot be forced from the outside, they must arise from within.

The most effective way to inspire meaningful change in others is not through coercion or force but by leading through example.

When you embody the principles and values you believe in, you naturally become a source of influence and inspiration.

People are more likely to reflect on their own choices and perspectives when they witness someone else living authentically.

The power of personal transformation radiates outward, creating a ripple effect that can impact those around you.

Change that is inspired rather than imposed is more likely to be meaningful and lasting.

It is essential to recognize that every person is at a different stage in their personal growth and development.

No two individuals share the exact same journey, as each life is shaped by unique experiences, perspectives, and challenges.

Some may be ready for change, while others need more time to reflect and evolve.

This diversity in personal evolution demands patience, understanding, and compassion.

It is not our role to rush or force anyone to think or act differently.

Instead, we should foster an environment of openness and acceptance, where people feel safe to explore new ideas at their own pace.

Forcing change often results in resistance.

When people feel pressured or judged, they are more likely to cling to their existing beliefs and behaviors, even if those beliefs no longer serve them.

True transformation happens when individuals feel respected and supported, not criticized or coerced.

Acceptance and empathy create a foundation of trust, which in turn opens the door for meaningful discussions and personal revelations.

This is why I never attack others for their beliefs. Instead of condemning or dismissing perspectives that differ from my own, I choose to engage in thoughtful dialogue.

Questioning ideas is not about imposing my own views, but about encouraging deeper reflection and understanding.

Change is not instantaneous.

It is a gradual process that unfolds over time.

Expecting immediate results can lead to frustration and disappointment.

However, embracing the natural progression of personal and societal transformation allows for more sustainable and profound growth.

The key to meaningful change lies in patience and consistency.

Individual growth serves as the foundation for broader societal evolution, as the lessons and improvements we cultivate within ourselves inevitably extend to our communities.

Above all, respecting the free will of others is paramount.

Every individual deserves the freedom to make their own choices, even if those choices differ from our own.

Honoring this principle fosters an atmosphere of peace, understanding, and cooperation.

It is through mutual respect that we build authentic relationships, where everyone feels valued and heard.

More than just a moral ideal, this respect for autonomy and diversity is essential to creating a more compassionate, balanced, and unified world.

WHEN I DIE

When I die, I do not want my passing to be mourned with sorrow and regret, but rather to be celebrated as the conclusion of a life that was fully embraced, shaped by my own choices, passions, and desires.

My time here will have been my own, lived on my own terms, filled with experiences that enriched my soul.

I want my departure to be a moment of gratitude for the love I shared and the joy I found, rather than a source of pain for those I leave behind.

I hope my friends and family can take comfort in the knowledge that my love for them was deep, unwavering, and freely given.

Every conversation, every shared laughter, every quiet moment of understanding was an expression of that love.

My greatest wish is that, when they think of me, they do not feel loss but instead remember the warmth of our time together.

I want my presence to linger not as a shadow of grief but as a light that continues to bring smiles, comfort, and inspiration.

Love, in its truest form, does not end with death. It is not bound by the limitations of a single lifetime, nor does it fade with the passing of time.

I know the connections we forge in this existence transcend the physical and weave themselves into the very fabric of our being.

My love for those I cherish is not confined to this body or this moment in time, it carries forward, beyond this life, into whatever lies ahead.

Should we meet again in another existence, in another form, I am certain that the love we shared will persist.

Though the faces may change and the circumstances may be different, there will be something familiar, a feeling, a recognition, a spark that reminds us of our eternal connection.

In some way, in some place, we will find one another once more, drawn together by the invisible threads of love that bind us beyond time.

I do not see death as something to be feared or lamented.

To me, it is a natural transformation, no different from the changes we experience throughout life.

Just as a child grows into an adult, shedding one stage to embrace another, death is merely the next step in our journey.

It is not an end but a continuation, a doorway to whatever comes next.

We do not grieve the passing of childhood, for it is a necessary part of growth, why, then, should we grieve the transition that is death?

What truly deserves our sorrow is not the inevitability of death but the tragedy of a life unlived.

A life spent in fear, devoid of love and joy, is the only real loss.

If anything, my departure should serve as a reminder to those I leave behind: to embrace life in all its beauty, to love without hesitation, to seek meaning and fulfillment in every moment.

So when my time comes, do not weep for me.

Do not let grief overshadow the memories of laughter, adventure, and love that we shared.

Instead, let my passing be a gentle nudge, a whisper from beyond, encouraging you to cherish every second of your existence.

Celebrate the bonds that make life worth living, and know that love, true, boundless love, never dies.

WE ARE UNIVERSES

We are not merely individuals navigating a fleeting existence, we are universes unto ourselves, vast, infinite, and brimming with the potential to create, transform, and shape reality.

Within each of us lies the power to birth entire worlds, to forge experiences so rich and profound that they become indistinguishable from the fabric of reality itself.

Our minds, vast and boundless, construct dimensions of thought and imagination that extend far beyond the limitations of the physical world.

Through our dreams, we access realms where the impossible becomes tangible, where we are both the architects and the inhabitants of entire universes of our own making.

These dreamscapes are not mere illusions but expressions of our deepest selves, fragments of the limitless creativity and wisdom that reside within.

In these moments of boundless exploration, we are reminded that the universe does not simply exist outside of us, it is also within us, woven into the very essence of who we are.

But our ability to create extends far beyond the world of dreams.

Every thought we think, every emotion we cultivate, and every action we take shapes the reality we experience. We are not passive spectators in this life.

We are its architects, crafting experiences, relationships, and legacies with every choice we make.

The stories we tell ourselves, the beliefs we hold, and the perspectives we nurture are the building blocks of our own unique universe.

What we choose to create is entirely in our hands.

Our emotions, thoughts, and intentions ripple outward, influencing not only our own lives but also the lives of those around us.

When we choose love, we invite warmth, connection, and joy to flourish within us and in the world we touch.

When we choose fear, anger, or hatred, we construct barriers that divide us from the beauty of existence.

Every decision we make is an act of creation, shaping the energy that defines our experience and, ultimately, the collective experience of all.

To see ourselves as universes is to awaken to the immense power and responsibility we hold.

Just as galaxies expand and stars are born, so too do we have the ability to evolve, to grow, and to illuminate the world with the light of our own becoming.

When we cultivate compassion, wisdom, and love, we bring forth realities filled with harmony and meaning.

When we embrace the depth of our own existence, we unlock the potential to transcend limitations and craft a life that reflects the infinite possibilities within us.

We are not confined by circumstance, nor are we bound by the past.

At any moment, we can choose to reshape our narrative, to redefine the boundaries of our reality, and to step into the fullness of our creative power.

Just as the universe is ever-expanding, so too are we, endless in our capacity for transformation, connection, and creation.

The inner worlds we carry are limitless, and through the choices we make, we shape not only our own existence but also the collective consciousness of humanity.

When we recognize ourselves as the creators of our reality, we step into the vastness of our own being, embracing the responsibility and the beauty of shaping a universe that reflects the love, wisdom, and boundless potential that exists within us all.

FORGIVENESS

Many people mistakenly believe that forgiveness is an act performed for the benefit of others, a kindness we extend to those who have wronged us.

However, in truth, forgiveness is an act of self-liberation, a deeply personal decision made for our own emotional well-being.

When we forgive, we release ourselves from the burden of anger, resentment, and pain that, if left unchecked, can fester within us and weigh heavily on our hearts and minds.

Forgiveness is not about excusing or condoning the harmful actions of another.

It does not mean that what happened was acceptable or that we must welcome the offender back into our lives.

Instead, it is about refusing to allow past pain to dictate our present and future happiness.

Holding onto resentment does not punish the person who wronged us, it only prolongs our own suffering.

By choosing to forgive, we take back control of our emotions and free ourselves from the shackles of bitterness.

At its core, forgiveness is about self-healing.

It is a conscious decision to move forward rather than remain stuck in a cycle of negativity.

This process does not always happen instantly.

It can take time to work through feelings of betrayal, hurt, or anger.

But in choosing to forgive, we open the door to emotional freedom, allowing ourselves to embrace peace rather than dwelling in suffering.

An apology, on the other hand, serves a different purpose.

Unlike forgiveness, which is an internal decision, an apology is an external action, a way of acknowledging harm and taking responsibility for our words or deeds.

A sincere apology is not just a formality but an offering, a way to express genuine remorse and validate the emotions of the person we have hurt.

Apologies have the power to mend relationships, heal wounds, and restore trust.

When we apologize with sincerity, we create an opportunity for the other person to process their pain and, if they choose, to forgive.

An apology does not demand forgiveness, nor does it guarantee reconciliation, but it does lay the foundation for understanding.

It is a way of saying, "I see your pain, and I acknowledge my role in causing it." This recognition alone can be incredibly powerful.

Although forgiveness and apologies are often intertwined, they serve distinct functions.

Forgiveness is an internal act of letting go, undertaken for the sake of our own emotional well-being.

An apology, by contrast, is an outward gesture, given in the hope of helping someone else find relief from their pain.

One does not necessarily depend on the other, we can forgive without receiving an apology, and we can apologize without being forgiven.

However, when forgiveness and apology come together, they create a profound cycle of healing.

When someone sincerely apologizes, and the other person chooses to forgive, both individuals are given the opportunity to heal and move forward with a renewed sense of understanding and peace.

This cycle fosters growth, allowing people to learn from past mistakes and strengthen their relationships.

To embrace both forgiveness and apology is to cultivate compassion, both for ourselves and for others.

These acts require vulnerability, courage, and strength, but their rewards are immeasurable.

By letting go of resentment and taking responsibility for our actions, we create space for emotional freedom, inner peace, and deeper connections.

In doing so, we free ourselves from the weight of past conflicts and open our hearts to a life filled with greater harmony and understanding.

TIME

The future is not an abstract concept waiting to unfold, it is continuously shaped by the actions we take in the present.

Every choice, every decision, and every moment of effort contributes to the path ahead, influencing outcomes in ways both seen and unseen.

Because of this, the present is the most powerful moment we will ever have.

It serves as the bridge between what has been and what is yet to come, allowing us to actively participate in the unfolding of time rather than merely being carried along by it.

Each moment presents an opportunity to decide the course of our lives.

Even seemingly small choices ripple outward, affecting not only our personal journey but also the world around us.

The present is the only point in time where we possess true agency, where we can take action, make changes, and set in motion events that will shape the future.

In this way, time is not something that simply happens to us, it is something we continuously create.

If one were to travel into the past, their actions in that time would still be happening in their present.

The traveler would not perceive themselves as altering history, because from their perspective, they are merely living in the moment available to them, making choices as naturally as they would in any other present reality.

These actions, however, seamlessly integrate into the timeline, becoming part of what has already transpired.

What seems like an intervention from the outside is, in truth, simply another moment within the flow of time, reinforcing the idea that the past, present, and future are intrinsically linked.

This interconnectedness highlights a fundamental truth: the present and future are direct consequences of the past.

Every moment we experience now is built upon the decisions, actions, and circumstances that came before it.

Likewise, the future will be the result of what we do today.

Time is not a series of isolated events but an ongoing, interwoven chain where each link influences the next.

Nothing exists in complete isolation, every cause has an effect, and every action sets something in motion.

By recognizing this, we begin to see time not as a rigid structure of past, present, and future, but as a fluid and evolving continuum.

The past informs the present, the present shapes the future, and the future, in turn, will one day become the past.

This cyclical nature of time suggests that every decision carries weight, no matter when it occurs.

It is not about one moment being more significant than another, rather, all moments are equally vital in the grand design of existence.

When we fully grasp this concept, we realize the profound responsibility that comes with our choices.

If we wish to create a better future, it starts with conscious, intentional action in the present.

If we seek to learn from the past, we must integrate its lessons into the choices we make now.

Whether we desire progress, healing, or transformation, the key lies in how we engage with the present moment.

In essence, time is not something happening to us, it is something we actively participate in shaping.

Every action taken today lays the foundation for what comes next.

The seeds of tomorrow's reality are planted in the soil of today's decisions.

By embracing this understanding, we step into our role as architects of the future, ensuring that the time ahead reflects the wisdom, purpose, and intention we bring to the present.

OPPOSITES

They say opposites attract, but in reality, this notion is more of a romanticized myth than a reflection of how relationships actually function.

While the idea has been widely accepted and perpetuated through movies, books, and popular culture, it often oversimplifies the deep and intricate nature of human connections.

People hold onto this belief, thinking that stark differences naturally create balance, but this assumption overlooks the essential elements that truly foster harmony and lasting bonds.

The belief that contrasting personalities or opposing qualities strengthen relationships suggests that conflict and friction are necessary ingredients for connection.

However, in most cases, fundamental differences in values, priorities, and lifestyles lead to more challenges than compatibility.

Clashing perspectives and opposing mindsets can create unnecessary misunderstandings, requiring constant effort to bridge gaps that may never truly be reconciled.

In reality, relationships flourish not because of opposing forces, but because of shared experiences, values, and perspectives.

It is not the attraction of opposites that brings people together, but rather the recognition of similarities that creates a sense of belonging.

When two individuals share a foundation of common interests, mutual values, and aligned goals, their connection becomes effortless and fulfilling.

Understanding flows naturally, communication is smoother, and there is a sense of being truly seen and understood.

This principle of "same attracts same" is evident in all areas of life. Friendships often form between people who share similar interests, worldviews, and ways of approaching life.

Romantic relationships tend to thrive when both partners have compatible lifestyles, shared visions for the future, and mutual ways of expressing love and affection.

Even professional collaborations are more successful when individuals operate from a similar mindset, valuing the same work ethic, creativity, or ambition.

The strongest relationships are those built on a solid foundation of mutual respect, trust, and emotional resonance.

While minor differences can add variety and excitement, fundamental similarities provide the stability necessary for long-term success.

People naturally gravitate toward those who reflect aspects of themselves, whether it's shared ambitions, passions, or ways of seeing the world.

This resonance is what makes relationships feel effortless and enriching rather than draining and difficult.

The notion that "same attracts same" extends beyond just personal relationships, it also applies to the energy we put into the world.

Like attracts like in terms of mindset and emotional state.

Positive, motivated individuals tend to surround themselves with others who uplift and inspire them, whereas negativity often breeds more negativity.

Recognizing this dynamic allows us to be more intentional about the kind of people we choose to engage with and the environments we immerse ourselves in.

By shifting our understanding of attraction and compatibility, we can move beyond superficial notions of opposites attracting and instead focus on cultivating relationships that are built on authenticity and mutual appreciation.

Acknowledging that similarities, rather than differences, are what sustain meaningful connections helps us navigate relationships with greater clarity and purpose.

Ultimately, the key to deep and lasting connections lies in shared understanding and common ground.

When people are aligned in their values, communication styles, and life goals, relationships become sources of joy, support, and fulfillment.

By embracing this truth, we empower ourselves to seek out and nurture relationships that genuinely enrich our lives, rather than struggling to force connections based on an outdated and misguided cliché.

BILLY MEIER UFO PICTURES

Personally, I have no particular fascination with UFOs themselves, nor do I see them as the most significant aspect of what is unfolding on Earth.

Many who study Billy Meier's teachings feel the same way.

These spacecraft, while undeniably impressive, are simply advanced intergalactic vehicles, technological evidence of extraterrestrial civilizations that exist beyond our world.

Their presence is not the main story but merely a fragment of a far greater and more profound reality.

For those newly awakening to the inevitability of intelligent life beyond Earth, images of these crafts often serve as a crucial entry point.

They act as a catalyst for deeper questions, prompting individuals to reconsider their perception of reality and the limitations of human knowledge.

Such images have the power to disrupt long-held assumptions, forcing people to expand their worldview and entertain the possibility that humanity is not alone in the vastness of space.

However, these images are only the beginning, a surface-level glimpse into something far greater.

They should not be mistaken for the ultimate revelation but rather as an invitation to explore beyond conventional understanding.

The true significance lies not in the UFOs themselves, but in what they represent: the existence of higher knowledge, more advanced civilizations, and a path forward for humanity that extends far beyond the limits of our current thinking.

Billy Meier's teachings go far beyond the UFO phenomenon.

They are not about chasing lights in the sky but about grasping the deeper truths of existence.

They offer an understanding of our place in the Universe, our responsibilities as conscious beings, and the immense potential we hold within us for personal and collective transformation.

These teachings challenge us to think independently, to reject blind faith and superstition, and to embrace logic, self-responsibility, and universal wisdom.

The journey of this understanding is not confined to the present, it is the beginning of a planetary movement that will expand across generations.

We are laying the foundation for a new era of enlightenment, planting seeds of awareness that will one day grow into an entirely new way of thinking.

These seeds, once cultivated, will flourish into towering trees of wisdom, providing guidance and clarity for those who come after us.

The future of humanity depends on the choices we make today, the knowledge we embrace, the misconceptions we abandon, and the courage we summon to challenge outdated beliefs.

Yet, the road to this higher state of consciousness is not an easy one.

It demands fearlessness, intellectual honesty, and the willingness to question societal norms that have kept humanity in a state of ignorance and stagnation.

To move forward, Earth humans must break free from the shackles of indoctrination and learn to think for themselves, without being controlled by religious dogma, political deception, or cultural conformity.

Independent thought is the key to progress, and only through self-responsibility can humanity break free from the cycles of destruction that have plagued our history.

Billy Meier, the Prophet of the New Age, the Aquarian Age, has provided the knowledge necessary for this transformation.

His teachings illuminate a path forward, guiding those who seek truth toward a future rooted in logic, wisdom, and universal understanding.

He does not ask for blind belief but instead encourages people to critically examine their reality, to search for truth through reason and personal experience.

In embracing these principles, humanity has the opportunity to rise above its limitations, to evolve beyond the primitive mindsets that have kept it divided and in turmoil.

This is not just about recognizing the existence of extraterrestrial life, it is about understanding ourselves, our place in the cosmos, and the infinite possibilities that lie ahead.

The future is in our hands, and it is through knowledge, responsibility, and self-determination that we will shape a new world, one built not on illusion and ignorance, but on truth and enlightenment.

NEGLECT NOT

Take care of your body, for it is the vessel through which you experience life on Earth.

It is your means of perceiving, learning, and growing, and it serves as the physical foundation that allows you to fulfill your purpose.

Treat it with respect, nourish it with proper food, keep it strong through movement, and honor it by maintaining its well-being.

Your body is not merely a possession, it is a sacred instrument that enables you to walk your path in this lifetime.

However, do not become so fixated on the body that you lose sight of what truly matters.

The body is temporary, a fleeting structure that will one day return to dust, but your Creation Energy, your true essence, endures beyond time.

It is this eternal part of you that connects to the infinite fabric of existence, spanning across lifetimes and dimensions.

While the body allows you to interact with the material world, it is your spirit that carries the knowledge and wisdom gained through every incarnation.

The true meaning of life is evolution, the continuous journey of growth, wisdom, and understanding.

Every experience, whether joyful or painful, serves as a stepping stone toward higher awareness.

Life on Earth is but one chapter in an eternal process of becoming, a brief moment in a much greater cosmic journey.

Through countless incarnations, you will take on many different forms, each offering unique lessons designed to expand your consciousness and refine your spirit.

Eventually, as you progress through the vast cycles of evolution, the need for a physical body will diminish.

You will reach a state where the material form is no longer required, and your existence will transcend into higher planes of being.

The limitations of flesh and bone will fall away, allowing for an existence based purely on thought, energy, and the profound interconnectedness with the Creation itself.

This is the natural course of spiritual evolution, an endless journey toward greater understanding, harmony, and unity with all that exists.

Never lose sight of your true essence.

At your core, you are not merely a human being confined to a single lifetime, you are Creation Energy, a Spirit form, an eternal fragment of the infinite Creation.

This realization is the key to understanding your purpose and aligning yourself with the universal laws that govern existence.

The more you recognize and cultivate this awareness, the more in tune you become with the grand unfolding of life and evolution.

Though the physical world is fleeting, your connection to the eternal is unbreakable.

Do not allow yourself to be trapped by the illusions of the material realm, where superficial desires and distractions can lead you away from the path of growth.

Instead, seek wisdom, knowledge, and understanding. Look beyond the temporary and strive for that which is everlasting.

Your spirit's journey is infinite, and every lifetime is an opportunity to progress further along the path of enlightenment.

To live fully, you must maintain balance, caring for both the temporary and the eternal.

Nurture your body so that it may serve you well, but do not forget that it is only a vessel.

The true work of life happens within, in the evolution of your consciousness and the expansion of your understanding.

Each experience, each challenge, and each moment of insight contributes to your eternal journey, shaping you into a being of greater wisdom and harmony.

Your journey is sacred, and every step brings you closer to realizing your unity with Creation.

Walk this path with awareness, gratitude, and a deep respect for the infinite potential that resides within you.

In doing so, you will not only fulfill your purpose in this lifetime but also contribute to the greater unfolding of the Universe itself.

NO EARTH HUMAN

No Earth human, apart from Billy, has the ability to physically interact with the highly advanced extraterrestrial beings known as the Plejaren.

These beings operate on an extraordinarily high level of consciousness, existing within refined and sensitive vibrational frequencies that Earth humans simply cannot withstand.

Their advanced state of being is a result of millennia of spiritual and technological evolution, elevating them far beyond the limitations of terrestrial existence.

Among the Plejaren, some have even attained the Ishwish, or "God" level, a designation that signifies immense wisdom, spiritual enlightenment, and an energy state vastly superior to that of any Earth human.

The presence of such advanced beings in direct contact with lower vibrational entities, such as those on Earth, poses a significant risk to both parties.

For the Plejaren, this interaction can be not only disruptive but even life-threatening due to the extreme energetic incompatibility.

Billy remains the sole Earth human capable of maintaining safe and direct physical contact with the Plejaren.

His vibrational frequency, unlike that of any other human, aligns harmoniously with theirs, allowing for sustained interaction without adverse consequences.

This rare and exceptional compatibility is not a coincidence but a result of deep spiritual evolution spanning multiple incarnations.

His unique role as a bridge between Earth and the Plejaren civilization underscores the profound differences in consciousness levels between humanity and these advanced beings.

The dangers of vibrational incompatibility were demonstrated in a striking incident involving Semjase, one of the Plejaren, at the FIGU Center.

During an encounter with an Earth human who wished to meet her, the energy disparity was so severe that it nearly resulted in her death.

This event serves as a powerful reminder of the extreme risks involved when beings from vastly different evolutionary states attempt direct interaction.

The Plejaren, fully aware of this danger, must therefore avoid physical contact with Earth humans, with Billy remaining the only exception.

This fundamental truth also dispels a deeply ingrained misconception: the belief that "God" communicates directly with human beings.

Many people claim to receive divine messages, hearing voices they interpret as guidance from a higher power.

In reality, these experiences are products of their own subconscious minds, internalized thoughts, or psychological constructs shaped by religious conditioning.

The concept of divine communication is a projection of human longing for external guidance rather than an actual interaction with an advanced being.

If a true Ishwish, an entity of immense wisdom and power, were ever to approach an Earth human in physical form, the vibrational disparity would be catastrophic.

The overwhelming energy shift would result in the advanced being's death, demonstrating the insurmountable divide between the realms of evolved cosmic existence and the current state of Earth humanity.

This truth further emphasizes the importance of inner spiritual growth rather than external worship or reliance on supposed divine intervention.

Humanity, in its present stage of development, remains spiritually and consciously immature, often seeking higher truths through distorted beliefs rather than genuine self-discovery.

The Plejaren, through their interactions with Billy, emphasize the necessity of personal evolution, encouraging humans to cultivate wisdom, self-responsibility, and a deeper understanding of the true nature of existence.

Their teachings offer a path to higher knowledge, but it is up to individuals to take the necessary steps toward enlightenment.

For now, direct interaction with the Plejaren remains impossible for the rest of Earth humanity.

However, through the wisdom imparted by Billy, people have the opportunity to elevate their consciousness, align with the universal laws of Creation, and gradually move toward a future where such interactions may one day be possible.

Until then, the focus must remain on self-improvement, logical reasoning, and the pursuit of true knowledge, rather than clinging to misconceptions rooted in misunderstanding and wishful thinking.

IN EVERY INTERACTION

In every interaction, there lies a lesson waiting to be discovered, a hidden gem of wisdom that can shape the way we perceive the world.

Some lessons are obvious, arriving in grand, unmistakable moments of clarity, while others are subtle, woven into the fabric of daily life, waiting patiently to be noticed.

I see these lessons everywhere I look, and when I do, they bring a quiet smile to my face.

Each discovery, no matter how small, enriches my understanding and deepens my appreciation for existence.

To me, this is the true essence of beauty, not something superficial or fleeting, but the ability to learn and grow from every moment, no matter how ordinary or insignificant it may seem.

Over time, I've trained myself to see beauty even in what others might call ugly.

A cracked sidewalk, an aging face, a stormy sky, each carries a story, a lesson, a reason to pause and reflect.

This perspective has allowed me to live with a profound sense of peace and gratitude, unshaken by the chaos that often engulfs the world around me.

I've arrived at a place of genuine contentment, where I no longer measure life by external standards but by the quiet joy of simply being.

It is not material wealth, societal status, or the pursuit of recognition that brings me happiness.

Rather, it is the ability to find meaning in the ordinary, to see the good in everything, and to embrace each moment as an opportunity for growth.

I wish everyone could experience this sense of freedom, this lightness of being that comes from detaching from expectations and immersing oneself in the present.

By conventional standards, I am a poor man.

I do not own extravagant possessions, nor do I occupy a position of great importance in society.

I clean houses for a living, a job often dismissed as menial or unremarkable.

Yet within this simplicity, I have discovered a profound truth: I live freely.

My work does not chain me to a rigid schedule or demand that I sacrifice my autonomy for financial gain.

I dictate my own time, move at my own pace, and decide how I engage with the world. This, to me, is a treasure beyond measure.

There is a misconception that freedom is tied to wealth, that only those with financial abundance can live life on their own terms.

But I have found that true freedom comes not from what you own, but from how you choose to live.

It is not the accumulation of possessions that grants independence, but the ability to control your own time, to act with purpose, and to exist without the burden of societal expectations dictating your every move.

For me, the greatest luxury is the ability to wake up each morning knowing that my time belongs to me.

I do not chase after fleeting goals set by others, nor do I measure my worth by external validation.

Instead, I embrace the simple joys of existence, walking in the fresh air, engaging in meaningful conversations, and taking pleasure in the work I do, no matter how humble it may seem in the eyes of others.

This life, though simple, is rich in ways that money cannot buy.

It is filled with moments of genuine connection, quiet understanding, and deep appreciation for the things that truly matter.

While the world rushes by in pursuit of more, more money, more status, more approval, I find fulfillment in less.

Less attachment, less stress, less expectation.

The truest form of freedom lies in living authentically, in being true to oneself without bending to the pressures of societal norms.

It is about embracing life as it is, rather than constantly seeking something else.

This freedom is my greatest treasure, and it is something I hope everyone can find in their own way, not through the pursuit of wealth or power, but through the realization that happiness lies in simplicity, contentment, and the ability to see beauty in all things.

IN THE BEGINNING

In the beginning, Creation, the Universal Consciousness, manifested an extraordinary diversity of life, a tapestry woven with a vast array of beings, each unique in form and expression.

Among this stunning variety were 343 distinct skin colors, each represented by the equation 7x7x7, a symbolic reflection of the boundless creativity that lies at the heart of existence.

This inherent diversity was not a coincidence, nor an afterthought, but rather a deliberate expression of the unity within Creation itself, a unity that thrives in multiplicity, where differences are not just tolerated but celebrated as essential elements of the grand design.

From the very start, these original hues formed the foundation of a spectrum that would continue to grow and evolve over time.

Through the mixing of races, cultures, and histories, this original palette has expanded, creating an even broader spectrum of colors and shades.

Each new combination represents the beauty of human diversity, illustrating that our differences are not barriers but rather reflections of the infinite creative potential that exists within us all.

This ever-growing diversity is a testament to the richness of human experience and the complexity of the interconnected web of life we all share.

However, despite the beauty and richness of this diversity, racism has emerged as a destructive force.

It arises from ignorance, a deep misunderstanding and lack of appreciation for the unity that binds us all together.

Racism is born of fear, the fear of the unknown, the fear of difference, and the fear of what is perceived as "other."

This fear is often perpetuated by societal conditioning, a system of beliefs that devalues certain groups while elevating others, creating division and sowing distrust.

In this way, racism is not an innate or natural response, but rather a learned behavior, passed down through generations, often rooted in the ignorance of those who fail to see the broader truth.

At its core, racism stands in stark contrast to the natural diversity intended by Creation.

It negates the fundamental truth that our differences are not obstacles but rather strengths that enrich the human experience.

Each skin color, culture, and tradition is an expression of the endless variety within Creation, and it is through embracing these differences that we come to understand our shared humanity.

The diversity we see in the world is not something to fear but something to cherish, a source of strength, wisdom, and beauty that makes us all richer.

Combating racism begins with the recognition that we all share a common origin.

We are all children of Creation, linked by the same universal consciousness, regardless of the color of our skin or the place we call home.

This shared origin is a powerful antidote to the ignorance that breeds prejudice.

By spreading the truth about our shared humanity, we can begin to dismantle the barriers of racism that have been built up over centuries.

Knowledge is a powerful tool in this fight, and the more we learn about one another, the more we can understand the deep connections that bind us.

As we foster understanding and acceptance, we create a foundation for peace and harmony to flourish.

The process of enlightenment is gradual, but every step we take toward increasing awareness, whether through conversations, education, or personal reflection, brings us closer to a world free from the poison of racism.

Each effort, no matter how small, contributes to this greater mission, and when these efforts are combined, they have the power to change the world.

As we share these truths with others, we invite them to join in the journey toward greater understanding, love, and acceptance.

This is the path to unity, and it is one that we must walk together.

Salome, the message of peace and harmony, serves as a constant reminder of our ultimate goal: to live in unity and mutual respect.

It calls us to rise above the divisions that separate us, to embrace each other as we are, and to work toward a world where love and acceptance are the guiding principles.

By continuing to spread this message, we can inspire others to follow suit, creating a ripple effect that will carry us forward.

The truth of our shared humanity is undeniable, and it is through this understanding that humanity can progress toward greater wisdom, enlightenment, and unity.

Let us commit to this mission, knowing that each act of kindness, each moment of understanding, and each expression of love brings us one step closer to a world that truly reflects the divine unity of Creation.

NO LONGER

I no longer find myself questioning my choices or my reactions.

The uncertainty that once clouded my mind has been replaced with an unwavering trust in my ability to act with clarity and inner strength.

I have come to realize that I will always respond in the right way, guided by a deeper wisdom that transcends any doubt.

This confidence has not arisen out of thin air.

Rather, it is the product of the transformative teachings I've embraced, especially those from Billy and the profound wisdom within the Creation Energy Teachings.

These teachings have opened my eyes to a broader understanding of life, revealing my true purpose and aligning me with the deeper truths of existence.

They have given me a firm foundation, a source of stability that keeps me grounded, even when life's challenges arise.

Through these teachings, I've learned that the true measure of a person's journey is not just in their actions but in understanding where they are coming from.

Every individual has their own unique set of experiences, perspectives, and struggles, and it is only by taking the time to recognize these that we can begin to truly connect with one another.

My focus has shifted from judgment to empathy, and I now find myself deeply interested in hearing others' stories, appreciating the complexities of their lives.

This understanding allows me to offer respect and love more freely, without the interference of preconceived notions.

I recognize that each person's journey is valid and that by acknowledging this, I can build more authentic, meaningful connections.

This shift in focus has enriched my relationships, turning them into bonds founded on mutual understanding and deep respect.

In addition to cultivating empathy, I've learned to embrace joy and laughter as an essential part of my life.

Even in moments of seriousness, I allow myself to find humor and lightness.

Laughter, when it arises naturally, serves as a reminder of the shared humanity we all possess.

It is easy to forget that beneath our surface differences, we all experience the same range of emotions, joy, sorrow, love, and pain.

By allowing ourselves to laugh and embrace these moments of joy, we create spaces for connection, even in the most unlikely places.

Humor becomes a bridge that unites us, dissolving the barriers of judgment and fostering a sense of community.

This balance between seriousness and laughter reminds me that we do not have to take ourselves too seriously, even as we face life's challenges.

Laughter serves as a reminder of the lightness of being, which makes navigating life's complexity more bearable.

At the heart of this transformation is my commitment to understanding others, to seeing them for who they truly are.

By embracing this practice, I cultivate patience, knowing that everyone is on their own journey and that their pace may differ from mine.

This patience becomes the foundation for harmony in my relationships, allowing them to grow in a space of mutual respect and trust.

It encourages openness, dialogue, and understanding, and fosters a deeper sense of unity among those around me.

Rather than viewing the world through a lens of judgment or superiority, I have come to see it through a lens of compassion, knowing that every individual is deserving of respect and care.

In the grander scheme of life, this approach serves as a blueprint for living with intention and purpose.

By committing to understanding, empathy, and patience, I am creating a life that is aligned with the values of compassion, respect, and unity.

These principles are the bedrock of a more peaceful existence, not just for myself but for those I interact with.

Every act of kindness, every attempt to understand, and every moment of laughter contributes to building a more connected world.

In embracing these values, I find myself not only living more harmoniously with others but also nurturing my own sense of fulfillment and peace.

It is through this commitment to others that I ultimately find a deeper connection to my own self, reinforcing the beautiful, interconnected dance of humanity.

RECOGNIZING

Recognizing that this life as Waid is my only life infuses every moment with a sense of urgency and purpose, inspiring me to live fully and authentically.

The awareness that this singular lifetime is all I have drives me to embrace each day with intention, ensuring that I remain true to myself, my values, and the purpose that I feel deep within.

I no longer let time slip by unnoticed or live in a way that is disconnected from my true essence.

I approach each moment with sincerity, with the understanding that this life, unique and fleeting, is not something to take for granted.

It serves as a constant reminder that now is the only time I can truly live, and in embracing this, I cultivate a deeper appreciation for every experience, no matter how big or small.

The understanding that my actions in this lifetime ripple outward, affecting not just my present reality but also the future, has brought a new depth to my decisions.

I am more aware of the profound impact each choice can have, not only on the world around me but on the trajectory of my own journey as a being of Creation Energy.

This awareness has become a cornerstone of how I live, guiding me to think deeply before acting.

The concept of cause and effect is no longer an abstract idea but a guiding principle in every area of my life.

It encourages me to take a pause, to reflect, and to choose consciously, knowing that every decision creates an outcome that shapes the future, both mine and the larger collective.

This deeper understanding has infused my life with clarity, giving me a sense of responsibility I hadn't fully embraced before.

Life is no longer a series of disconnected events or a random sequence of happenings.

Instead, it feels like a beautiful, intricate tapestry being woven moment by moment by my thoughts, actions, and choices.

There is purpose in everything, and each choice, whether seemingly insignificant or monumental, adds to the larger picture.

It reminds me that I am not a passive observer of my life but an active participant in its creation.

Each step, each breath, is part of a greater whole, part of the unfolding story of my journey, which is a reflection of the choices I make and the energy I put into the world.

With this understanding, life has become a path of growth, a continuous process of self-reflection, learning, and evolution.

It is no longer about simply existing but about actively shaping who I am, what I contribute, and how I relate to the world.

This journey, fueled by intention, is filled with opportunities for development, for deepening my understanding of myself, and for expanding my capacity to love and connect with others.

Every experience I embrace, whether it be a challenge, a joy, or a simple moment of reflection, becomes a stepping stone toward the realization of my fullest potential.

As I continue to walk this path, life has revealed itself to me as the most beautiful expression of love.

I see love in every corner of my existence, in every relationship I nurture and every connection I make.

Love is not just a feeling but a force that binds the universe together, and I am now more attuned to its presence.

From the interactions I have with those around me to the quiet moments spent in solitude, I recognize love in all its many forms: love for others, love for myself, love for life itself.

This perspective transforms my existence from a mere sequence of days into a celebration, a celebration of connection, purpose, and profound gratitude for the gift of life. I no longer take anything for granted.

Instead, I find myself deeply thankful for each moment, each lesson, and each connection, knowing that all of it is woven together in a grand tapestry of love and light.

In this way, the purpose of my life is clear: to embrace each moment with authenticity and intention, to choose wisely and thoughtfully, and to live as an expression of love.

It is through this love that I can connect with others, contribute to the world, and continue evolving into the person I am meant to be.

Every step I take on this journey is imbued with the beauty of life itself, and it is this beauty, this eternal dance of growth, love, and connection, that I seek to honor and celebrate every single day.

ALTERING THE DNA

It is time for humanity to confront the pervasive influence of negative thoughts and the profound impact they have on our behavior, shaping the course of our actions and influencing the way we interact with the world.

Negative thought patterns are not just fleeting mental occurrences.

They are powerful forces that, when left unchecked, can deeply affect the course of an individual's life and society as a whole.

When individuals claim that they are being commanded by entities like God or the devil to commit heinous acts, they are, in truth, acknowledging the reality of these destructive forces that influence them.

These external influences are not imaginary or insignificant but represent real, tangible energies that permeate human consciousness, directing thoughts and actions toward darkness, violence, and despair.

The tragic result of these negative energies is seen in the rise of serial killers, perpetrators of barbaric crimes, and the general degradation of humanity into what some may call "Barbarians."

This is not a reflection of the inherent evil within humanity but rather a consequence of external, destructive forces taking hold of the minds and hearts of individuals.

It is a disturbing reality that these tendencies toward violence, cruelty, and dehumanization have become deeply embedded in the human DNA, passed down across generations, influencing our behavior in ways we may not even consciously realize.

From the moment of birth, we are all susceptible to these influences, which shape the way we think, act, and relate to others.

These deeply ingrained behaviors are not easily overcome, they require conscious effort and awareness to address and transform.

To protect oneself from these negative influences requires more than just intellectual understanding, it demands an active, conscious effort to recognize these destructive forces, understand their origins, and take deliberate steps to neutralize them.

This is not a passive process, nor is it a task that can be tackled by merely thinking positively or suppressing dark thoughts.

It requires a deep engagement with the mind, body, and spirit, acknowledging the presence of these forces within and making a concerted effort to resist their pull.

It involves healing the wounds within humanity that have allowed these negative energies to fester and thrive.

Only by addressing the root causes of these negative influences can we begin to build a foundation for transformative change, both on a personal level and within society as a whole.

This transformation, while deeply challenging, is essential for creating a more harmonious and enlightened existence, where humanity can rise above its basest instincts and unlock its true potential.

True and lasting transformation demands that we address the genetic roots of humanity's susceptibility to negativity, rather than merely treating the symptoms.

The cycle of violence, fear, and hatred cannot be broken simply by attempting to suppress negative emotions or thoughts, it requires a fundamental shift in the way humanity operates on a genetic level.

By altering the very DNA that makes humans vulnerable to these harmful influences, it is possible to neutralize their impact entirely, rendering them powerless to control our behavior.

This change is not a mere wishful thinking or a dream of a utopian future.

It is a realistic goal that can be achieved through conscious effort, knowledge, and understanding.

By changing the genetic makeup that predisposes us to negative influences, humanity can break free from cycles of violence, barbarism, and suffering, and instead move toward a future of peace, wisdom, and understanding.

The key to this transformation lies in the Creation Energy Teachings, which offer a pathway to altering human DNA and undoing the genetic manipulations imposed on humanity in ancient times.

This knowledge, passed down through generations, provides the tools needed to break free from the destructive influences that have plagued humanity for millennia.

At the heart of Billy Meier's mission is the guidance of humanity toward reclaiming its original, unaltered state, the state in which humanity was designed to live in harmony with itself and the universe, free from the negative influences that have shaped our history.

The teachings of the Creation Energy offer the means to unlock this potential, to heal the wounds of the past, and to guide humanity toward a future of peace and understanding, where the destructive forces that have plagued us are no longer in control.

By embracing these teachings and applying them in our lives, we can begin the process of healing not just our minds but our very genetic makeup, ultimately allowing humanity to rise above its destructive tendencies and achieve its highest potential.

This journey is not an easy one, but it is one that offers hope and possibility for the future, a future where humanity can live in peace, wisdom, and unity, free from the dark forces that have held us back for so long.

Through conscious action and understanding, we can break the cycle of negativity and begin to create a new reality for ourselves and for future generations.

UNDERSTANDING

Understanding is not a destination but a never-ending journey that perpetually expands, growing with every step you take.

The more you understand, the more capable you become of comprehending even deeper truths, unlocking new layers of knowledge and wisdom.

This process is not linear but cyclical, it spirals inward and outward, feeding itself and creating a continuous unfolding of insight and awareness.

With each revelation, your perception of existence becomes more refined, broadening your view of life and the universe.

As you gain greater understanding, it transforms how you interact with the world, shaping your thoughts, actions, and relationships in profound ways.

The deeper you go, the more you realize how vast the journey truly is, and that each truth discovered leads to even greater mysteries waiting to be explored.

The teachings of Creation Energy offer an endless well of knowledge, a boundless source of wisdom that invites you to dive deeper with each passing day.

These teachings are not mere lessons to be learned and then set aside.

Rather, they are living principles that complement and enhance life itself, offering guidance and illumination on how to align more closely with the essence of creation.

They provide insights that allow you to see beyond the surface of reality, helping you to perceive the interconnectedness of all things and the infinite possibilities that lie within the universe.

As you delve into these teachings, you will find that they are not just intellectual concepts but profound truths that resonate with your very being, awakening a deeper sense of purpose and connection to all that exists.

In your studies, you may come to realize that life and the universe are not separate entities, but rather reflections of one another.

This profound understanding shifts your perspective on the nature of reality, showing you that everything in existence, from the smallest particle to the vast expanse of the cosmos, is a mirror of your own inner state.

As above, so below, as within, so without.

This realization deepens your connection to everything around you, blurring the lines between yourself and the world.

You begin to see that your being is not isolated but intricately woven into the fabric of the universe.

The boundaries between you and the cosmos dissolve, and you come to understand that your existence is a part of something much greater, something infinite and boundless.

The more you explore these teachings, the more you uncover that everything, every thought, every action, every event, is a reflection of the divine energy that flows through all things.

As you continue your journey, each discovery within these teachings reveals another layer of this profound truth.

Every new piece of knowledge you uncover peels back another veil, offering you a glimpse of the interconnected web of existence.

With each insight, you grow closer to understanding the ultimate reality, and yet, the deeper you go, the more you realize that there is always more to learn, more to explore, and more to experience.

This journey is not about reaching an endpoint but about constantly expanding your awareness and understanding, about continually pushing the boundaries of what you know and who you are.

You begin to see that understanding is a lifelong process, one that never truly ends but continuously evolves and deepens over time.

Eventually, there will come a moment, a profound shift in consciousness, when you experience a deep clarity that shakes your understanding to its very core.

It is a moment that forever changes the way you perceive yourself and the universe.

You will be struck by the realization that the universe is not just something that exists around you, separate and external, but that it is also within you.

This transformative understanding reveals the truth that you are not a passive observer of the cosmos but an active participant in the grand unfolding of creation.

You are not merely a being who lives in the universe, but you are the universe itself, experiencing and expressing its vastness through your own existence.

This moment of clarity transcends any previous understanding, and you will see that everything, your thoughts, your actions, your very essence, is connected to the vast, boundless energy of Creation.

This awareness will forever alter how you view yourself and your place in the cosmos, as you come to understand that you are both a reflection of the universe and an integral part of its continuous evolution.

You will begin to see yourself not as an individual isolated from the world, but as an expression of the eternal, infinite essence that flows through all things.

This understanding will transform your life in ways that words cannot fully capture, leading you into a deeper state of harmony, peace, and unity with all that exists.

OPEN TABS

Many people unknowingly carry around mental burdens, much like leaving multiple open tabs in a web browser, each one slowly draining their energy and focus.

These "tabs" often represent unresolved thoughts, worries, or distractions that consume mental space without adding any true value to our lives.

We tend to keep these mental tabs open, thinking we need to address them or that they are important, when in reality, they only add noise to our inner world.

These concerns may not even be our own, they might be borrowed from others or created by the media and outside influences.

By learning to close these mental tabs, we free ourselves from unnecessary stress and the weight of irrelevant concerns.

This act of closure creates mental space for clarity, peace, and purpose in our daily lives, allowing us to focus on what truly matters and connect with our inner selves.

Too often, we become tangled up in matters that don't directly involve or affect us, causing unnecessary distraction and mental clutter.

We might feel compelled to carry the emotional burdens of others, thinking that by doing so, we are being compassionate or helpful.

However, it is important to recognize that everyone has the right to live their lives as they see fit, and their choices, beliefs, and actions are not ours to control, judge, or fix.

While it's natural to feel empathy and compassion for others, their experiences and struggles are theirs alone to carry, not ours to shoulder.

We can observe, learn, and offer support, but we don't need to take on their burdens unnecessarily.

This doesn't mean we should turn a blind eye to the world's injustices or tragedies.

On the contrary, it's crucial to speak up against atrocities, hatred, discrimination, and violence, such as the ongoing tragedies in Palestine and Ukraine.

Silence in the face of injustice only perpetuates the suffering.

However, there's a delicate balance to maintain.

While it's essential to take action and lend our voices to causes of justice, we must also guard against becoming so consumed by these issues that we lose our sense of self.

Becoming overwhelmed by the world's problems can strip away our personal peace and scnsc of purpose.

We can contribute meaningfully without letting the weight of every global issue take over our lives.

Life itself is inherently simple, but we often complicate it with unnecessary worries, judgments, and mental clutter.

We overthink, worry about things we can't control, or judge ourselves and others too harshly.

We get caught up in cycles of mental noise, allowing distractions and external pressures to shape our thoughts.

However, if we take a step back, simplify our mental processes, and focus on what truly matters, we can align ourselves more closely with the natural flow of life.

By quieting the mental chatter and letting go of thoughts that don't serve our greater purpose, we make room for inner peace and clarity.

This space allows us to nurture compassion, foster meaningful connections, and grow in a way that is both intentional and fulfilling.

When we direct our energy toward growth, self-improvement, and kindness, we begin to rediscover the beauty of living with purpose.

The simplicity of life becomes more apparent, and we realize that happiness does not come from external circumstances, but from within.

By cultivating a mindset of simplicity and intention, we re-engage with the joy of living authentically and purposefully, embracing each moment for what it is, without the burden of unnecessary mental clutter.

This process of decluttering our minds allows us to reconnect with the present and live more fully, finding peace not in the absence of challenges, but in our ability to navigate them with clarity and grace.

BELIEVE

For many years, I have made a conscious decision to refrain from using the word "believe" to express my thoughts or feelings.

In fact, I have completely eliminated it from my vocabulary.

The word "believe" carries with it an inherent uncertainty, and I no longer wish to operate from a space that contains even the faintest shadow of doubt.

Belief, at its core, is a state of uncertainty, and when someone says they "believe" in something, they are acknowledging that there is a possibility they might be wrong.

This acceptance of doubt inherently limits our ability to experience clarity and truth.

It's an acknowledgment that something is not fully known, and yet the person chooses to accept it regardless, often without question.

To me, this reliance on belief is restrictive, it prevents us from tapping into the more profound and certain aspects of our consciousness.

The subconscious mind, which holds the key to deeper understanding, operates from a space of absolute clarity and certainty.

It does not function based on the concept of belief, instead, it is anchored in knowing.

The subconscious understands truth in its purest form, and it is free from the fog of doubt that belief inevitably creates.

Belief is a veil that clouds the mind and blocks our connection to the inner wisdom that can guide us toward greater understanding and self-awareness.

In many ways, the act of believing is a form of avoidance. It's a way of dealing with uncertainty without seeking the truth that lies beneath it.

If one does not know something, it is far more powerful and honest to admit, "I don't know." There is no shame in acknowledging that we lack knowledge on a particular subject.

In fact, this admission opens the door to learning and growth, whereas belief simply closes it off, keeping us trapped in a loop of uncertain assumptions.

Unfortunately, most people on Earth live in a state of persistent doubt because they are caught in the trap of belief.

They go through life constructing their understanding of the world around them based on what they "believe" to be true, and not what they know to be true.

This is a precarious foundation upon which to build a life because beliefs are by nature unstable.

They fluctuate, evolve, and shift with circumstances, often leading individuals into confusion and frustration.

Humanity is currently living in an era dominated by belief. But this age is drawing to a close, and the time has come for change.

We are standing at a crossroads, where we can either continue to cling to outdated thinking and the comfort of belief or choose to embrace the pursuit of genuine knowledge.

The shift from belief to knowing is not merely a mental exercise. It is a fundamental evolution of the human consciousness.

Belief may offer a temporary sense of comfort, but it no longer serves the progress of individuals or society as a whole.

We must let go of the shackles of belief and open ourselves to the transformative power of true understanding.

It is only through this shift that we will be able to break free from the limitations that have long held us back from reaching our full potential.

This is not just a call for personal growth but for collective evolution.

Humanity, as a whole, is being asked to move beyond belief and into the realm of knowledge.

This is a call to embrace clarity, to recognize the importance of truth, and to approach the world with an open mind that is willing to learn, grow, and adapt.

The time has come to shed the rigid, outdated structures of belief that have dominated our thinking for so long.

We must enter an era of enlightenment, one in which clarity and truth guide our actions, our decisions, and our path forward.

Only by doing so can we tap into the infinite potential that lies dormant within us all.

The age of belief is over, now is the time for humanity to awaken to the power of knowledge and understanding.

THANK YOU

I want to take a moment to express my heartfelt gratitude to all of you who have shown the courage to share the truth on your own platforms.

It takes a great deal of bravery to stand up and speak out, particularly in a world where so much of the narrative is controlled and manipulated by powerful forces.

Your willingness to speak the truth and share your knowledge is a profound act of personal freedom, authenticity, and integrity.

You are paving the way for more people to follow, creating spaces where honest conversations can thrive and deeper understanding can be nurtured.

The courage to be truthful and unapologetically yourself is a powerful signal that we are moving away from a world of conformity and toward one of individuality and expression.

It's inspiring to witness this shift, where more and more people are stepping into their own power, finding their voices, and contributing their unique perspectives.

Each time one of us shares a piece of truth, we not only enlighten others but also make the world a bit more transparent, helping to break down the walls that have kept so many from seeing things as they truly are.

Throughout the years, I've crossed paths with many individuals who attempted to mold my thoughts to align with their own.

Whether through societal pressures, personal expectations, or the influence of those who thought they knew better, they did not realize that I had already cultivated a sense of independence, a mental freedom that allowed me to remain unshaken by outside influence.

I had learned to stand strong in my own truth, to think critically, and to reject ideas that didn't resonate with my authentic self.

This internal strength, this sovereignty of thought, has allowed me to live authentically, and I am grateful for the clarity that has come from embracing that power.

Now, what I find most exciting is witnessing this same transformation happening in others.

More and more, I see people shedding the constraints placed upon them by society, refusing to conform to outdated standards and expectations.

They are learning to embrace their individuality, to share their insights without fear of judgment or reprisal.

This growing movement of truth-telling and self-expression is a beautiful and inspiring shift in human consciousness, one that promises to create a more honest, open, and connected world.

It's a revolution of thought, a shift toward authenticity, and a powerful reminder of the strength that lies in simply being true to oneself.

As we continue on this path, it's essential that we support one another and nurture this growing movement.

Let's encourage each other to stay brave, to remain true to our inner calling, and to be open in our communication.

By doing so, we not only uplift ourselves but also contribute to the creation of a community where truth is honored, freedom is cherished, and every voice, no matter how small, has the power to inspire change.

When we share our unique perspectives, we are part of a greater collective effort to create a world that celebrates authenticity, where everyone is empowered to speak their truth without fear or hesitation.

Together, we are building a foundation for a future that values honesty, freedom, and the beauty of diversity in thought.

THE FEAR OF DEATH

If the fear of death and the fear of judgment from an all-knowing deity did not dominate the minds of human beings, they would live far more freely, presenting themselves as they truly are.

The constant anxiety over what happens after death, and the worries of divine retribution or eternal damnation, keep people in a perpetual state of self-censorship.

This fear prevents individuals from expressing their true selves, forcing them into roles and behaviors that conform to societal expectations and religious doctrines.

Without these fears haunting every decision and action, humanity could embrace authenticity, no longer bound by the illusion of divine punishment or the concept of moral debts to be repaid in some afterlife.

A great portion of human behavior is dictated by concern over how others perceive them, whether through the lens of religion, societal pressure, or familial expectations.

People often act in ways that are contrary to their true nature in order to gain approval, avoid judgment, or secure their place within social structures.

However, when viewed from a broader perspective, the opinions of others are ultimately insignificant.

It is not the judgments of others that should shape our actions, but the deep understanding and acceptance of ourselves.

The real power, the true freedom, comes when we realize that the only opinion that truly matters is our own.

This self-empowerment allows us to live life without the need for external validation, breaking free from the constant cycle of approval-seeking behavior.

The notion of an omniscient being watching over every thought and action serves as a massive barrier to self-expression and the pursuit of authenticity.

It's as if humanity is constantly under surveillance, constantly afraid of being judged, of making mistakes that could lead to eternal consequences.

This fear stifles creativity, individuality, and personal growth.

But imagine a world where that surveillance is removed, where people no longer feared punishment for their actions, and where they could live fully in the moment, embracing who they truly are without worry.

Without the threat of divine retribution, humanity could begin to access a deeper connection to their true nature and their desires, creating a world where self-expression and authenticity are the norm rather than the exception.

The constructs of God, hell, and heaven, so often presented as absolute truths, are not universal realities, they are beliefs passed down through generations, narratives created to provide structure to a society but also to maintain control.

These ideas are deeply ingrained in cultural and religious teachings, and while they serve a purpose in organizing communities, they also function as tools for control.

Through the promise of eternal rewards and the threat of eternal punishment, they manipulate behavior and dictate what is considered acceptable.

These concepts have been perpetuated for centuries, but they are ultimately not objective truths.

They are products of human imagination, shaped by the stories told over time rather than any intrinsic knowledge about the nature of existence.

These beliefs, while deeply rooted in human history, are not universal truths, but rather constructs that bind people to a way of thinking.

They create a framework built on fear, guilt, and control, preventing individuals from exploring their own thoughts and feelings.

People become so entrenched in these narratives that they cease to question them, fearing that challenging these beliefs might mean losing their moral compass or facing eternal consequences.

Yet, by questioning these beliefs, by confronting the ideas of sin, judgment, and divine surveillance, individuals can reclaim their autonomy.

They can begin to define their lives based on their own values and experiences rather than on a system of punishment and reward designed to maintain control.

When humanity lets go of the fears associated with divine judgment, the guilt instilled by religious dogma, and the belief in a controlling force that monitors every action, it opens itself to a new realm of possibility.

In this newfound freedom, individuals can create their own meaning, live their own truths, and embrace their authentic selves.

Without the restrictions of dogma, humanity can move closer to understanding its true nature and can begin to live harmoniously with its surroundings.

It is through this liberation, by recognizing the self-imposed nature of these limitations, that people can truly find their peace, their purpose, and their connection to the vast, unbounded essence of life.

By shedding these old fears, we create space for growth, exploration, and a deeper understanding of what it means to truly live.

EVERYONE

Everyone you encounter in life, from the stranger on the street to your closest friends, is truly a version of yourself.

Each person you meet is a mirror reflecting your own consciousness, thoughts, and experiences.

This is a manifestation of the universal truth that all is one, each individual, regardless of how different they may seem, shares a profound interconnectedness with you.

The boundaries we perceive between ourselves and others are illusions, arising from limited perspectives, and these divisions often mask the deeper truth of our shared existence.

This realization can radically shift how we see and interact with the world.

It encourages us to embrace every encounter as a reflection of our own inner world, and through this lens, we begin to recognize that every person is playing their part in the grand tapestry of life, just as we are.

When you notice something in someone that you dislike, it's not a time for judgment but an opportunity for profound self-reflection.

Our reactions to others are often more about us than about them.

The traits that irk or trigger us may point to parts of ourselves that we have yet to understand or accept.

In these moments, rather than casting judgment, we can pause and ask ourselves: Why does this behavior bother me?

What is it about this person or situation that stirs something within me?

Is there an unresolved part of myself that I need to acknowledge or heal?

Through such self-inquiry, the interactions that we often label as negative become powerful opportunities for growth and transformation.

When we view the world through this lens of reflection, every encounter becomes a teaching moment, a chance to deepen our understanding of ourselves and the world around us.

In this shared reality of interconnectedness, we are all simultaneously students and teachers. No matter where we are in life, we are always learning from others, and in turn, others are learning from us.

The lessons we impart may be overt, such as through teaching or sharing knowledge, but they can also be subtle, like through our actions, our energy, or even our silence. Each person you meet, even for the briefest of moments, has something to teach you.

They may offer a perspective or insight that shifts your own worldview, or they may hold a mirror up to your unconscious biases and assumptions.

In the same way, you teach those around you, sometimes without even realizing it.

Every interaction, whether it's a meaningful conversation or a passing glance, serves as an opportunity for both giving and receiving wisdom.

This reciprocal process of learning and teaching is how we all grow, evolve, and expand our understanding of the world.

One of the most liberating realizations in life is that no one is inherently above or below another. In the interconnected web of existence, we are all truly equal, regardless of our role, status, or identity.

Hierarchies that are based on external achievements or societal labels are illusions, temporary structures that have no bearing on our true worth.

In the grand scheme of the universe, we are all equal expressions of the same energy, and when we come to understand this, the judgments and comparisons that often fuel our conflicts lose their power.

The idea that some people are more deserving of respect or admiration than others is a construct that keeps us in a state of separation, limiting our ability to connect and empathize with those around us.

Once we see through this illusion and recognize the inherent equality of all beings, we can engage with the world from a place of love, acceptance, and understanding.

This understanding of equality and interconnectedness played a pivotal role in shaping my perspective during my time as a high school math teacher in New York.

I entered the profession with the hope that I could make a difference in my students' lives, not only by teaching them math but by encouraging them to think critically and see the world in new ways.

However, as I spent more time in the classroom, I began to feel a disconnect between the hierarchical structure of the education system and the values I held dear.

Specifically, I became uncomfortable with the traditional titles used to address teachers, namely, being called "Mister."

While this might seem like a small issue, to me, it represented a deeper problem.

These titles reinforced a separation between teacher and student, positioning the teacher as an authority figure who was inherently different from or superior to the students.

In truth, I didn't see myself as above my students in any way.

I viewed them not only as learners but as teachers in their own right, each with their own insights and perspectives that could enrich my understanding of the world.

By addressing me with a formal title, it created a barrier between us, one that I felt hindered the authentic connection I hoped to cultivate in the classroom.

In my mind, this artificial hierarchy was unnecessary and counterproductive.

I wanted my students to see themselves as equal partners in the learning process, where their contributions were valued just as much as mine.

However, the administration couldn't understand my perspective.

To them, maintaining the traditional structure of authority was a non-negotiable aspect of the educational system.

They believed that teachers needed to be set apart from students, that titles like "Mister" were essential to maintaining order and respect.

But I could not reconcile myself to this view.

I could not in good conscience perpetuate a system that contradicted the very values I was trying to teach, values of equality, mutual respect, and authenticity.

So, I made the decision to resign.

It wasn't a decision I took lightly, but it was one that felt necessary for my own integrity.

I could not continue to be part of a system that I felt was fundamentally misaligned with my beliefs. To me, authenticity and integrity are non-negotiable.

If I had stayed, I would have been compromising my own values, and that is something I have never been willing to do.

Walking away was not an act of rebellion, but an act of self-honor.

It was about choosing to live in alignment with my truth, no matter how uncomfortable or unconventional that might seem.

The larger lesson here, and one that I have come to deeply understand over the years, is the importance of always being true to yourself, even when others may not understand or agree with your choices.

It's easy to be swayed by the opinions of others, to seek validation or approval from external sources.

But when you live authentically, you empower not only yourself but those around you as well.

Your example can inspire others to step into their own truth, to break free from societal expectations, and to live more fully and freely.

When you live authentically, you become a beacon of light, guiding others toward their own authentic selves.

In this way, we are all connected, constantly influencing one another in both visible and invisible ways.

Our actions, our choices, and our energy create ripples that reverberate throughout the world, shaping the collective consciousness and helping to elevate all of humanity.

The truth is, we are all learning from one another, constantly teaching and being taught, and through this process, we create a more connected, compassionate, and authentic world.

WHAT TRULY MATTERS

What truly matters in life, the cornerstone upon which all happiness and fulfillment rests, is how you see yourself.

How you perceive your own worth, your values, and your purpose defines the quality of your existence.

It is not the approval or disapproval of others that should guide you, nor is it their expectations that should determine your path.

When you realize that your self-perception holds the key to your peace and joy, everything else falls into place.

The judgments and opinions of others, though pervasive in society, become irrelevant.

Once you come to this understanding, you free yourself from the shackles of external validation.

You reclaim the power to live life on your terms, liberated from the weight of trying to meet others' expectations.

It's your journey to navigate, and how you view yourself sets the tone for everything that follows.

Life is yours to live, and it is meant to be lived authentically, fully embracing your own truths.

This is your one and only life, there are no do-overs or rewinds.

The choices you make today form the life you will live tomorrow.

You have within you the ability to craft your journey according to your passions, dreams, and values.

As long as your actions do not bring harm to others, you have every right to live according to what feels true for you.

You are the creator of your reality.

Every choice, every step you take, should reflect who you are at the core, not who others want you to be.

Each moment presents an opportunity to align your actions with your truest desires and most authentic self.

Living authentically does not mean living a perfect life, but it does mean living a life that is true to who you really are, not a life built on someone else's version of you.

Authenticity requires courage, and it is a path that can feel daunting at times, but it is by far the most rewarding path you can take.

To be true to yourself is not only a gift you give to yourself but to the world around you.

Your authenticity has the power to inspire others to do the same, creating ripples of genuine self-expression that transform communities.

When you embrace who you are, even when it means standing out or stepping away from the norm, you are honoring the uniqueness that resides within you.

Society may pressure you to conform, to shrink yourself to fit within certain boundaries, but your authenticity thrives when you let go of these external pressures and embrace your individuality.

If your heart calls you to be bold, to speak loudly, to dare greatly, don't hesitate to heed that call.

Too often, people hold back from expressing their true selves out of fear, fear of judgment, fear of rejection, fear of not fitting in.

But those fears are rooted in an illusion, because true belonging comes when you allow yourself to be unapologetically yourself.

When you step into your truth and live boldly, you not only open doors for yourself but for others as well.

You give the world the gift of your true self, and in doing so, you create space for others to do the same.

The greatest gift you can give to yourself and to the world is to live unapologetically.

To honor your unique voice, your passions, your quirks, and your dreams is a powerful act of self-love.

Life is not about fitting into molds or seeking external approval, it is about being who you are meant to be, without compromise.

The world does not need another version of someone else, it needs the full expression of you.

In the end, life is about embracing and living fully in your own truth.

The approval of others is fleeting and temporary, but the approval you give yourself, the acceptance and love you offer your own soul, is eternal.

It is the foundation on which everything else can stand.

Be brave enough to live boldly, to embrace your truth, and to show up as your authentic self, even when it's difficult or uncomfortable.

Know that your value does not come from the opinions or judgments of others, but from your own deep understanding of who you are and what you stand for.

Life is not about conforming to societal standards or seeking validation from others, it is about being true to yourself and living with confidence, pride, and joy in who you are.

Every moment you live authentically, you add more light to the world, and in turn, you shine brighter yourself.

The world is waiting for you to step into the fullness of your truth. Don't hold back.

IN THIS LIFE

In this life, I am deeply grateful to have found my true purpose.

It feels as if every experience, every challenge, and every lesson I have encountered has led me to this moment of clarity, where I can say with certainty that I have discovered what I am meant to do.

I feel a profound, almost unshakable calling within me to share everything I know, everything I've learned, and everything I've experienced with humanity.

This is why I have written these books, to offer my perspective and my knowledge to others in the hopes that it will resonate with them, challenge them, or spark something within them.

My desire is not to impose my truth on anyone but to share it openly, knowing that it may be a catalyst for growth, change, or new ways of thinking.

While my intentions have always been peaceful and rooted in a deep desire for connection and understanding, I understand that my approach can sometimes be misinterpreted.

There have been moments when others have perceived my sharing of ideas as arrogant or presumptuous.

I want to make it clear that my goal is never to attack, criticize, or belittle others.

Rather, it is simply to offer my perspective, just one of many possible perspectives, inviting dialogue, encouraging thought, and creating space for a deeper understanding.

My aim is to foster conversation and curiosity, not to dictate what others should think or believe.

To me, true freedom means the ability to express one's views openly and without restriction.

It means having the courage to share ideas, to question the status quo, and to challenge deeply held beliefs in a way that promotes growth and enlightenment.

I live by the understanding that "who are we to judge?", a reminder to myself and others that each person has their own unique journey and perspective, and it is through respecting those differences that we come to know each other more fully.

I genuinely welcome differing opinions, as I see them not as threats but as opportunities for mutual learning.

It is in the sharing of ideas, the respectful exchange of differing views, that true understanding and growth become possible.

When we allow ourselves to engage with differing perspectives without fear or defensiveness, we open the door to deeper connections and greater wisdom.

What I struggle with, however, is when others try to tell me how I should be, how I should think, or how I should live my life.

I find this deeply insulting and, to be honest, quite harmful.

It feels as though my autonomy and individuality are being disregarded, as if my voice and my perspective are somehow invalid.

This behavior undermines the very essence of personal freedom, which I hold sacred.

No one has the right to dictate another person's path or limit their expression.

The freedom to be oneself, to think for oneself, and to act in alignment with one's own truth is the bedrock upon which all true freedom rests.

As a free human being, I hold my autonomy and individuality in the highest regard.

These are not things I take lightly or allow others to trample on.

Each person has the right to walk their own path, to express themselves authentically, and to live their life in a way that feels true to who they are.

My purpose, in part, is to remain authentic in all that I do.

I am committed to staying true to myself, even if that means standing apart from the crowd or challenging conventional norms.

In doing so, I hope to inspire others to embrace their own uniqueness, to honor their own truth, and to trust in the power of their own voice.

By staying true to who I am and continuing to share my knowledge with the world, I hope to create a space where different perspectives are not only welcomed but celebrated.

It is through this exchange of ideas, through the respectful sharing of knowledge and experience, that true freedom of thought can thrive.

When we allow ourselves to be open to new perspectives, to hear each other without judgment or fear, we create a world where ideas can evolve, where growth is limitless, and where the fullness of human potential can be realized.

In the end, my goal is simple: to contribute to a world where freedom of thought is cherished, where authenticity is honored, and where individuals can live according to their own principles without fear of judgment or repression.

I hope to inspire others to find the courage to do the same, to live authentically, to share openly, and to create a world where all voices, all perspectives, and all individuals are respected.

This is my purpose, and it is one that I will continue to pursue with love, humility, and unwavering commitment.

SPEAKING NEGATIVELY

Refraining from speaking negatively about others in their absence is a practice that stems from a deep sense of respect and integrity.

It is an approach grounded in the understanding that how we treat others, even when they are not around to hear it, speaks volumes about who we are as individuals.

When we opt to criticize or demean someone who isn't present to defend themselves, we not only diminish that person's reputation but also damage the trust others place in us.

This creates unnecessary discord, fostering an environment where suspicion, animosity, and resentment can grow unchecked.

Instead of contributing to meaningful conversations, we open the door to negativity that can spiral and poison the atmosphere in which we live and work.

This behavior often reflects a lack of empathy, fairness, and an unwillingness to see things from another person's perspective.

It casts a shadow over our own credibility and tarnishes how we are perceived by others.

Furthermore, it breeds an unhealthy culture where gossip and petty remarks thrive, rather than one that nurtures healthy dialogue, understanding, and support.

When we speak ill of others behind their backs, we reveal much more about ourselves than we do about the person being criticized.

It often signals deep-seated insecurity, bitterness, or a longing for validation by pointing out the flaws of others.

In doing so, we fail to recognize that true strength lies not in tearing others down, but in lifting ourselves up.

We neglect the important task of self-reflection and growth, choosing instead to distract ourselves with the imperfections of those around us.

Focusing on the shortcomings of others also diverts our attention away from our own opportunities for self-improvement.

Rather than using our energy to enhance our own character, we waste it on undermining others, ultimately weakening the very connections we should be nurturing.

In essence, we exchange the potential for building bridges and fostering understanding for the destructive act of eroding relationships and compromising our own integrity.

On the other hand, when we choose to speak with kindness and consideration, even in the absence of others, we demonstrate emotional maturity and inner strength.

This choice reflects our commitment to fairness and decency, which in turn builds trust and respect in the relationships we hold dear.

By taking the high road, we set a powerful example of how to engage with others in a positive, constructive way, even when challenges arise.

Such an approach fosters an environment where healthy dialogue and open communication can flourish.

It encourages individuals to express differing opinions, but in a manner that is respectful and solution-oriented, rather than driven by hostility or judgment.

Upholding these principles not only strengthens our relationships but also cultivates a positive atmosphere where everyone is encouraged to be their best selves.

Indeed, the way we speak about others, whether they are present or not, reveals much about the values we hold dear and the person we strive to become.

It is a reflection of our inner character and our commitment to living a life of integrity.

Choosing to avoid negative talk does not mean we ignore the need for honest critique or feedback.

Rather, it is about approaching these conversations with sincerity, kindness, and a genuine desire to improve, both in ourselves and in the way we relate to others.

By making the choice to use our words thoughtfully, we not only enhance our own character but also nurture the connections we share with those around us.

In doing so, we leave behind a legacy of respect, compassion, and honor that will resonate far beyond our words.

FELLOW HUMAN BEINGS

I have come to view my fellow human beings as reflections of myself, each one a different version at varying stages of evolution.

This perspective has profoundly altered the way I interact with others, not from a place of pity or judgment, but from a place of deeper empathy and understanding.

I no longer see people as separate or distant from me, but as fellow travelers on a shared journey, each walking their own unique path, shaped by their individual experiences, struggles, and growth.

This shift in perspective has opened my heart in ways I could never have imagined, enabling me to approach others with a sense of connectedness rather than separation.

Understanding that we are all navigating life in our own ways, each step informed by our unique histories and challenges, has allowed me to relate to others with greater compassion.

Instead of approaching others with a sense of superiority or criticism, I now understand that we are all evolving, each at our own pace, and each facing trials and triumphs that are part of our growth process.

This recognition is a deeply humbling one, as it reminds me that, despite our differences, we are all united in the pursuit of becoming the best versions of ourselves.

At the core of this understanding is the awareness of the oneness of creation.

We are not isolated beings, separate from one another, but rather minute, interconnected particles of a vast, intricate whole.

This realization has made me see that our lives, while unique, are deeply intertwined with one another.

The boundaries we perceive between ourselves and others are largely illusions, and the essence of all life is connected by unseen threads that bind us together in ways that go far beyond our individual experiences.

Recognizing this shared essence has humbled me, opening my eyes to the deeper unity that exists beneath the surface of our everyday lives.

It is a humbling awareness that has enriched my sense of gratitude for the ways in which we are all connected, both to one another and to the larger fabric of existence.

When we truly come to see and accept this unity in all things, loving one another becomes the most natural response.

Love no longer feels like a task or a responsibility.

Instead, it flows effortlessly, arising from the fundamental recognition that we are, in essence, the same.

In recognizing the self within others, we see not only their humanity but our own reflected in their eyes.

It is a realization that transcends any notion of otherness or separation.

Love becomes a natural expression of this oneness, a free-flowing energy that transcends the need for justification or reason.

It is simply a truth that emerges when we acknowledge the interconnectedness of all life.

For me, this realization has been nothing short of transformative.

The more I see the oneness of creation and recognize myself in others, the more I understand that love is not just a possibility, it is the easiest, most natural, and most powerful way to live.

This shift in perspective has changed the way I approach my relationships, allowing me to embrace others with open arms and a full heart, free from judgment or fear.

It has reshaped the way I engage with the world, helping me to see every interaction as an opportunity to express love, kindness, and understanding.

This understanding of oneness has deepened my sense of what it means to coexist.

It has taught me that true coexistence is not about tolerance or acceptance from a distance, but about fully recognizing and embracing the humanity in others as part of the same greater whole.

It has transformed my view of the world and the people in it, teaching me that love is not something that needs to be earned or given under obligation, but a natural and inevitable expression of our shared essence.

When we see ourselves in one another, loving each other becomes as effortless as breathing, and the world around us is transformed by the simple, profound power of connection.

KNOWLEDGE

Knowledge is an incredibly powerful and transformative tool that provides individuals with the ability to deeply understand the world around them.

It allows people to navigate life's complexities with greater ease and wisdom, giving them the capacity to make informed and thoughtful decisions.

Armed with knowledge, individuals can recognize opportunities, avoid pitfalls, and address challenges head-on, often in ways that lead to significant improvements in their lives.

This process of acquiring knowledge equips people with a sense of empowerment, as it enables them to feel more in control of their circumstances, decisions, and futures.

Whether solving immediate problems or planning for long-term success, knowledge is an essential instrument that not only enhances individual potential but also contributes to the overall progress of society.

Beyond its tangible benefits in terms of practical application, knowledge holds a unique and intrinsic value that is not limited to utility alone.

It is a source of immense joy and fulfillment, offering a depth of satisfaction that cannot be reduced to mere functional use.

The act of learning, of pursuing understanding, often stirs a deep sense of curiosity and wonder in individuals.

This curiosity sparks a desire to explore new ideas, to ask questions, and to delve into unfamiliar territories of thought.

Whether through academic study, personal exploration, or engaging with the experiences of others, the pursuit of knowledge brings a richness to life that is deeply rewarding.

These moments of discovery, whether small or grand, offer a sense of inspiration, lighting up the mind and soul in ways that are uniquely tied to the journey of learning.

As we expand our minds, we not only increase our comprehension of the world but also enrich our emotional and intellectual lives, elevating our spirits in ways that transcend mere intellectual gain.

In addition to its personal benefits, knowledge holds the profound capacity to foster connection and empathy between individuals.

The more we understand about the diverse cultures, histories, values, and perspectives that shape the world, the more we develop an appreciation for the richness and diversity of human experience.

Knowledge allows us to step outside of our own limited viewpoints and consider the world through the eyes of others, opening the door to deeper empathy and mutual respect.

This broader perspective cultivates a sense of solidarity, breaking down barriers and helping to build bridges between people of different backgrounds.

In this way, the joy that knowledge provides is not confined to the individual, but extends outward, influencing our relationships and interactions in positive and profound ways.

By embracing the full scope of human experience through knowledge, we foster a sense of unity and harmony, strengthening the fabric of society and creating a more interconnected, compassionate world.

However, knowledge is not simply a tool for empowerment and joy, it also carries with it a set of responsibilities.

The more we know, the more we are required to act thoughtfully and ethically, considering the implications of our understanding.

While knowledge can be a source of inspiration, it can also present uncomfortable truths, forcing us to confront difficult realities about ourselves, others, and the world.

These truths can be challenging, requiring us to adjust our beliefs, rethink our actions, or even make difficult decisions.

But it is precisely in grappling with these complexities that the true power of knowledge is revealed.

Embracing the fullness of knowledge, its complexities, contradictions, and sometimes harsh truths, allows us to grow in ways that are both humbling and enlightening.

It teaches us that knowledge is not just about accumulating facts or acquiring information, but about learning to navigate the nuances of life with integrity, humility, and a sense of responsibility toward others.

When we approach knowledge with this sense of balance, it becomes a force for positive change.

By using knowledge not only to enrich our own lives but to contribute meaningfully to the well-being of others, we harness its full potential.

In doing so, we create a better world, one where progress is driven by understanding, compassion, and a shared commitment to learning.

In this way, knowledge becomes a timeless source of strength and joy, one that empowers us individually and collectively, while also fostering the deeper connections and insights that make life truly meaningful.

It is through this balance of personal growth and societal contribution that the transformative power of knowledge is fully realized, making it a cornerstone of both individual fulfillment and collective progress.

KARMA

Karma, as commonly understood, does not exist.

The belief in karma is an extension of the same human desire that fuels the belief in an existence of Heaven or Hell: the innate need for revenge and the pursuit of cosmic justice.

People who believe in karma are often hoping that those who commit wrongs will eventually face punishment, mirroring the way many believe in Heaven and Hell as mechanisms for rewarding the virtuous and punishing the wicked.

At its core, karma, like the concepts of Heaven and Hell, reflects a human yearning for order and fairness in the universe, a longing to see those who have caused harm meet their consequences in a way that satisfies our sense of justice.

But this belief in karmic retribution, like the belief in eternal damnation or eternal reward, stems from a desire to impose moral judgment on life's events, rather than accepting that life operates in a different way altogether.

This mindset also perpetuates outdated and often cruel practices, such as the death penalty, which is rooted in the conviction that wrongdoers must suffer for their misdeeds in a manner that is equal to their offense.

This desire for punishment and retribution is deeply ingrained in certain cultural and religious ideologies, which often reinforce the belief that the universe operates on a principle of moral balancing, where actions must be met with equal consequences.

The idea that people must pay for their actions through suffering or that justice must manifest through punitive measures reflects not just a fear of divine wrath but a broader, more human desire to feel that there is a form of cosmic order, one that rewards virtue and punishes vice in a manner that matches the severity of one's deeds.

However, this view fails to acknowledge a deeper and more profound truth about the nature of the universe.

Creation, or what some might call the Universal Consciousness, does not operate according to the principles of vengeance or punishment.

The cosmos is entirely neutral, free from any agenda of retribution or moral judgment.

The universe does not impose justice by retaliating against wrongdoing or rewarding virtuous acts with a corresponding benefit.

This is not the way that Creation functions, nor is it how the natural world operates.

Creation's essence is impartial and indifferent to human notions of right and wrong. It does not measure actions on a moral scale and deliver consequences accordingly.

In this neutral, expansive system, there is no such thing as karma, no invisible hand guiding wrongdoers to suffer for their transgressions or good people to be rewarded for their virtuous actions.

There is no inherent moral framework in the fabric of existence that dictates that life will always operate in a cause-and-effect structure based on justice.

To truly live in harmony with the laws of Creation, we must let go of any attachment to vengeance or retribution.

These human desires for payback distort our understanding of how life works and trap us in cycles of anger and frustration.

When we expect the universe to deliver justice through punishment or reward, we remain locked in the illusion that life's difficulties are met with an equal and opposite reaction.

In truth, life unfolds through the natural law of causality, cause and effect, not through a moral framework of punishment and reward.

This means that life's events are not governed by any divine balance of right and wrong, but rather by the interweaving of causes and consequences that play out according to the laws of nature.

One of the most difficult realities to accept within this framework is that bad things can happen to good people, and good things can happen to bad people.

This can be deeply disheartening, as it challenges our natural desire for fairness and for justice to be served in the way we think it should be.

It can be difficult to understand why innocent people might suffer, while those who commit harm seem to go unpunished.

Many innocent individuals are locked behind bars, while those responsible for crimes walk free, and there are countless instances where the natural world or human society does not appear to align with our sense of justice.

But such events are not signs of karma at work. They are simply the natural unfolding of causes and their effects.

Life, in its complexity, does not always follow a moral framework but instead operates according to the simple, impartial law of cause and effect.

In the grand scheme, the universe does not concern itself with dispensing moral rewards or punishments, it simply moves forward, with actions creating consequences that unfold in their own time and way, regardless of human ideas about what is "fair" or "just."

In embracing this view, we let go of the burden of expecting cosmic retribution or cosmic reward, and instead accept that life unfolds according to its own natural laws.

The belief in karma, like other beliefs in moral judgment and cosmic fairness, can limit our understanding of the world and keep us trapped in cycles of resentment, fear, and frustration.

When we shift our perspective to recognize that the universe operates in a way that is neutral and impartial, we can free ourselves from the expectations of karma and embrace life for what it truly is, an ongoing dance of cause and effect, without the need for retribution or moral judgment.

This understanding allows us to live with greater peace, compassion, and acceptance, rather than clinging to the idea that the universe owes us or anyone else something in return for their actions.

THE EMPIRE WILL FALL

The world stands on the precipice of an extraordinary transformation.

The Empire we have known, built on power, dominance, and systems that have long controlled the global order, is teetering on the edge of collapse.

The structures that many thought would endure for generations are crumbling from within, signaling the end of an era that was once considered unshakable, and that seemed destined to persist indefinitely.

This collapse may create unease and uncertainty for many, as change often brings fear and discomfort.

However, there is no need for regret or sorrow over what is being lost.

While it may feel like a significant part of our history is slipping away, this shift is not something to fear, it is a necessary step forward.

The Empire's fall is not the end of hope, it is the beginning of something far greater.

In its dissolution, a new chapter will unfold, one full of boundless potential and opportunity.

The end of the Empire marks the dawn of a new era, one in which the long-standing conflicts and inequalities that have plagued human society for centuries can be addressed and ultimately healed.

With the collapse of outdated systems, we are presented with the chance to forge a future that prioritizes peace, justice, and equality for all.

The ashes of this old world, which may seem bleak and disorienting in the moment, will give rise to new beginnings.

From these ashes, the seeds of global peace and cooperation will begin to sprout, growing slowly but surely across the globe like a much-needed balm for wounds that have been open for far too long.

This is the beginning of a healing process, a transformation that, though born of struggle and hardship, carries the promise of a more harmonious and interconnected world.

The change we are witnessing is not just the fall of an Empire, but a shared sacrifice.

It is a moment where humanity as a whole is called to rise above individual desires and contribute to a greater purpose.

In the face of adversity, we may feel overwhelmed or exhausted, as the challenges ahead seem daunting and at times insurmountable.

Yet, we must remember that each of us is playing a part in something larger than ourselves.

We are not merely spectators in this grand transition.

We are active participants in the shaping of the future.

This is our time to take on the burden of change, to endure the hardships that come with the end of a world that was built on division and control.

Every setback, every difficulty, is a step forward for humanity as a collective.

We are not simply moving backward with the collapse of this old system, we are moving toward unity, healing, and a future that is built on compassion rather than conflict.

These events unfolding before us are not simply random occurrences.

They are lessons that carry profound meaning and purpose.

They are guiding us toward a deeper understanding of who we are as a species and what we can become.

We are being given the opportunity to recognize the interconnectedness of all life on Earth, to see that the suffering of one is the suffering of all, and that the joys of one are the joys of the entire human family.

In this pivotal moment, we are being called to grow beyond our own narrow, individual ambitions and to look at the bigger picture, to consider the well-being of the human race as a whole, rather than just ourselves.

The fall of the Empire is not a loss. It is an invitation to rise above our divisions and work together toward a shared future of peace and prosperity.

Now is the time for humanity to truly understand what it means to live for one another.

This is a moment in history when we can choose to be more than just individuals fighting for our own interests.

We have the chance to become a unified global community, where our shared struggles, our shared sacrifices, are the stepping stones to a better world.

As the old systems of control, greed, and inequality fall away, they make space for a new world to be born, one where kindness, empathy, and mutual respect are the cornerstones of society.

The challenges we face and the hardships we endure are not in vain.

They are laying the foundation for a society where we treat one another with dignity and care.

In this moment of upheaval and uncertainty, we can take solace in the knowledge that what is unfolding, though challenging, is ultimately leading us to a future in which we can heal together.

The transition may be difficult, but it is necessary, and it is filled with the promise of a better tomorrow. We are on the cusp of a profound shift, one that may reshape everything we know about ourselves and the world we share.

And though the road ahead may be long, it is a road we walk together, with the hope that the future we create will be one in which every person has the opportunity to thrive in peace, harmony, and mutual understanding.

Through this collective effort, we can create a world that not only survives the fall of an empire, but emerges stronger, more compassionate, and more united than ever before.

WORRIES

It is a rare occurrence for individuals on Earth to experience a life free from the constant weight of worries and concerns clouding their minds.

The majority of people find themselves burdened by a never-ending stream of thoughts, each one vying for their attention and disrupting their inner peace.

These worries often come in the form of replays of past conversations, where regrets over unspoken feelings and unexpressed thoughts plague the mind, leaving the individual to ruminate over what could have been.

Alternatively, the mind is consumed by immediate, pressing concerns, whether it's the uncertainty of securing enough money to cover rent, purchasing food, or the looming anxiety surrounding the next fix or the next step in an addictive cycle.

For some, there's even the added weight of carrying the burden of lies, attempting to juggle multiple falsehoods and remember past deceptions in order to maintain their carefully constructed façades.

The human mind is endlessly bombarded by a multitude of problems, each one competing for space and attention.

When a person attempts to address these issues without first cultivating a sense of inner peace, they only add to the chaos.

The more they struggle to find answers amidst the turmoil, the more the confusion deepens.

The brain, already overloaded with stress and worry, becomes tangled in itself, amplifying every problem until they seem insurmountable.

This creates a vicious cycle, where the desire to solve one problem leads to greater mental unrest and the overwhelming sensation that things are spiraling out of control.

Without inner peace, clarity becomes elusive, and the problems that arise appear far more complex and difficult to resolve.

However, the moment inner peace is achieved, the entire landscape of the mind shifts.

Problems that once felt overwhelming and all-consuming begin to appear manageable, as if the solutions were always there, quietly waiting to be discovered.

In a state of calm, the individual experiences an intuitive clarity, as if the clutter of anxious thoughts has been cleared away.

This mental stillness creates a fertile ground for insight, allowing the person to see solutions that previously seemed hidden behind layers of stress and distraction.

With a clear mind, decisions are made with greater ease, and the path forward is illuminated in a way that was impossible to perceive when consumed by worry.

The true power of the human mind lies in this very inner peace.

It is within this calm, quiet space that the individual finds not only the clarity to solve problems but also the emotional stability to endure the challenges that life inevitably presents.

When a person is at peace with themselves, they can face life's obstacles with a resilience that cannot be shaken by external circumstances.

In this tranquil state, they discover the strength to move forward with confidence, knowing that solutions will arise and that they are equipped to handle whatever comes their way.

Inner peace is not simply the absence of worry, it is the foundation from which true empowerment emerges.

It is the gateway to emotional well-being, where the mind operates at its highest capacity.

In this space, decisions are not driven by fear, anxiety, or confusion, but by clarity, wisdom, and a deep connection to one's own inner strength.

The ability to navigate life's ups and downs with grace and stability is a direct result of cultivating inner peace.

When a person learns to maintain this state of calm amidst the turbulence of life, they unlock the true potential within themselves, an unshakable sense of purpose and the resilience to face any challenge that may arise.

True inner peace transforms not just the individual, but their entire experience of the world.

It enables them to move through life with a sense of ease and equanimity, unaffected by the constant noise of external distractions or the chaotic storms of the mind.

When inner peace becomes a consistent presence in one's life, the person begins to navigate the world with a newfound sense of grace, making decisions that reflect their highest values and aspirations.

In this way, inner peace is not just a personal benefit, it is a source of power that ripples outward, affecting relationships, work, and the way one interacts with the world as a whole.

It is the secret to a life lived with purpose, clarity, and resilience, where challenges are seen as opportunities for growth and solutions are found in the stillness of the mind.

It is through the cultivation of inner peace that we unlock our true potential, both as individuals and as members of the collective human experience.

When the mind is free from the constant barrage of worries and distractions, it becomes a powerful tool for creating the life we desire, responding to challenges with wisdom and confidence, and facing each day with the unwavering belief that, no matter what obstacles arise, we have the strength within us to overcome them.

DISTRACTIONS OF MATERIALISM

A time will inevitably come when humanity, as a whole, will come to fully recognize the profound beauty and the unparalleled freedom that comes from living a simple life.

In an era where distractions seem to consume every waking moment, there will be a collective shift toward detaching from the pressures of materialism and excess.

People will gradually realize that the pursuit of possessions, status, and wealth is not the answer to their longing for fulfillment and contentment.

As they begin to release their attachment to these external markers of success, they will open themselves to a deeper appreciation for the peace, serenity, and lasting satisfaction that simplicity offers.

This shift in consciousness will not only transform individual lives but will ripple out, creating a more compassionate, mindful, and conscious society that values presence over possession.

When this shift occurs, individuals will begin to embrace a more meaningful, purposeful existence, one that is centered around authentic connection, both with others and with the self.

In this new way of being, the noise of the outside world will begin to fade, leaving space for inner peace and clarity to take root.

With this newfound stillness, people will find that life itself becomes more vivid, more vibrant, and more aligned with what truly matters.

The frantic search for external validation will be replaced by an inner knowing that peace and fulfillment are found in the simplest of things, connection, love, and a life lived in harmony with nature.

Many people, however, have yet to realize that the true purpose of life is not to accumulate, to build empires, or to attain endless desires.

Instead, the purpose is to lighten the load, to shed the heavy weight of worldly concerns and ego-driven desires.

These attachments weigh down the spirit, keeping us from fully experiencing the present moment and from connecting with our true selves.

The more we release these attachments, whether they be to material possessions, achievements, or the validation of others, the closer we get to a state of being that is in alignment with our true essence.

Life is not about what we hold onto.

It is about what we can let go of in order to make room for the things that truly nourish our souls.

For me, this practice of letting go has become a way of life.

If I find something I like, I give it away.

This act of releasing material possessions or even emotional attachments has been part of my routine for years, and each time I do it, I feel lighter.

It's as if a weight has been lifted, not just physically but energetically as well. Life becomes less about accumulation and more about liberation.

The process of freeing ourselves from the things that hold us back, be they physical, emotional, or spiritual, creates the space needed for growth, evolution, and greater understanding.

At a higher level of existence, particularly at the level of the High Council, which represents the final stop in the material realms, we approach a state of being where we become almost transparent.

Our existence becomes so pure, so refined, that we are no longer defined by the material world around us.

We transcend the need for possessions, titles, and accolades, as our true essence shines through.

At this level, we are in the process of returning to the Universal Consciousness, the light from which we all originated.

It is this light that represents the ultimate truth and purity of our being, the state to which we are all meant to return once we have shed the layers of illusion created by the material world.

This light is not something external to us.

It is within us, a part of who we have always been.

It is our true nature, untainted by ego or desire, and it represents the perfect harmony and balance that we all strive to reconnect with.

As we evolve, both individually and collectively, we gradually realign ourselves with this higher consciousness.

This process of return is not one of struggle, but of remembrance.

It is the gradual unfolding of our true nature, the shedding of all the layers that have obscured our vision of who we really are.

With each step on this journey, we become more attuned to the essence of the light that resides within us, and we move closer to the ultimate truth.

The ancient saying "as above, so below" reflects the deep and inherent connection between the spiritual and the physical realms.

What occurs in the higher planes of existence is mirrored in our earthly lives.

The struggles, lessons, and transformations that we experience in the material world are reflections of the spiritual growth and evolution that is happening simultaneously in the higher planes.

By understanding this profound connection, we begin to see that the path to enlightenment is not just about transcending the physical world, but about living in alignment with universal truths in both our inner and outer worlds.

The two realms are not separate, they are one and the same, intricately interconnected and interdependent.

This planet, in all its beauty and complexity, is not something separate from us. It is a reflection of our inner selves.

The way we treat the Earth, the way we live in harmony or disharmony with it, mirrors the state of our own consciousness.

As we move toward greater inner peace, understanding, and connection, the world around us will begin to reflect these changes.

In turn, by cultivating peace and simplicity within ourselves, we can help bring about the kind of world we wish to live in, a world where love, kindness, and spiritual awakening guide our every action.

This is the journey of evolution: not to escape the world, but to heal it by first healing ourselves.

As we evolve, we move closer to the light, closer to our true selves, and closer to the universal consciousness that unites all life.

SIZE MATTERS NOT

The question of whether size truly matters has been a topic of debate for centuries, with opinions ranging widely.

Yet, the answer is fundamentally straightforward: it does not.

True pleasure, in all its forms, is not governed by physical measurements or the external appearance of something.

Rather, it is shaped by the internal experience and perception of the individual.

What brings fulfillment in life and intimacy is not a particular size or feature, but how one connects with and responds to their experience.

Pleasure, therefore, becomes something deeply personal, subjective, and unique to every individual.

Consider, for example, the wide range of experiences that humans find fulfilling.

A serial killer may derive satisfaction from taking lives, while a masochist might find pleasure in experiencing pain, humiliation, or suffering, whether psychologically or physically.

On the other hand, a sadist may take pleasure from inflicting pain or distress on others.

These extreme cases may seem disconnected from ordinary experiences of pleasure, but they underscore a critical point: pleasure is not a product of physical attributes alone.

It is rooted in the mind, the emotional and psychological landscape of the individual.

It is the way a person perceives and processes the world around them that shapes their experience of fulfillment.

When we move beyond physical traits, the power of human connection becomes overwhelmingly clear.

The true source of satisfaction and joy in life is not found in the superficial features or physical measurements that society often elevates.

Instead, it resides in the way two people communicate, understand each other, and meet one another's needs on a deeper, emotional level.

Emotional intimacy, trust, and mutual respect foster an environment in which pleasure thrives, much more so than any external factor such as appearance or physical size.

However, societal perceptions and cultural influences often magnify the importance of size, creating unrealistic and damaging expectations.

These standards are reinforced by media portrayals, which frequently depict exaggerated ideals of what intimacy should look like, further deepening insecurities and misconceptions.

Individuals are led to believe that certain physical traits are essential for satisfaction, even though this simply isn't true.

What truly matters is not adhering to the ideals set forth by others but rather focusing on what feels right, authentic, and fulfilling on a personal level.

When people choose to prioritize connection, mutual understanding, and communication over comparison or societal norms, they discover that pleasure is far more nuanced, profound, and complex than mere physical attributes.

Moreover, the human body and mind are highly adaptable, capable of finding fulfillment and joy in an array of circumstances.

Pleasure is not a fixed, rigid experience that only happens under specific conditions, rather, it is a dynamic, evolving interplay of emotions, attraction, and desire. It can manifest in countless forms and is not confined to a set formula.

The more one shifts their focus from the physical realm to the emotional and psychological dimensions of connection, the more profound and enriching their experiences become.

When individuals learn to cultivate emotional intimacy, prioritize mutual understanding, and value trust above external appearances, they unlock a deeper, more satisfying and meaningful connection.

Truly, the belief that size matters is a misconception that is rooted more in external pressures, societal expectations, and misconceptions than in reality.

True pleasure and satisfaction arise from within, through confidence, emotional connection, and mutual understanding.

When people shift their focus from superficial concerns to the deeper emotional and psychological aspects of intimacy, they unlock the potential for an authentic and fulfilling experience that transcends physical measurements altogether.

By embracing these deeper aspects, individuals can discover a richer, more meaningful form of pleasure that is not bound by arbitrary standards or ideals.

LIFE

Life is a truly remarkable journey, brimming with an infinite array of possibilities, challenges, and experiences that continually shape our existence.

Each day, we are presented with opportunities to grow, to explore, and to push the boundaries of what we thought was possible.

Life unfolds as a beautiful blend of highs and lows, triumphs and setbacks, each moment contributing to the rich and complex story that we each uniquely create.

From the grand milestones of achievement to the quiet, intimate moments of reflection, it is the diversity of experiences that makes life so profoundly meaningful.

The world offers a spectrum of emotions that we navigate on our journey, ranging from the exuberant laughter shared with loved ones to the peaceful solitude found in quiet moments of introspection.

It is within this vast emotional landscape that we discover our true sense of self, as we learn to embrace joy, sadness, hope, fear, and everything in between.

Life's beauty often emerges in the simplest of moments, the warmth of the sun gently kissing your skin, the soothing comfort of a familiar voice calling your name, or the feel of a soft breeze on your face as you walk through nature.

These moments, though small and seemingly insignificant, have the power to bring the greatest sense of joy, fulfillment, and connection, reminding us of the beauty found in the present.

What makes life so incredibly captivating is its unpredictability.

It is this very unpredictability that calls us to embrace change, to welcome uncertainty, and to find strength in the unknown.

Life does not follow a clear, fixed path.

Rather, it constantly shifts, presenting us with new opportunities, challenges, and surprises.

It is within this ever-changing flow that we are invited to discover who we truly are, to evolve, and to transform.

We are called to step into the unknown, to have faith in ourselves, and to trust that the journey will unfold as it is meant to.

Every twist and turn adds depth and richness to our journey, teaching us valuable lessons along the way.

At the heart of life lies the quest for purpose and connection.

It is a search for meaning that drives us to explore the world around us, to connect with others, and to find our place in the grand scheme of things.

This search challenges us to grow beyond the limits we once placed on ourselves, to stretch and expand into new realms of possibility, and to discover our true potential.

Through our relationships with others, our passions, and the dreams we pursue, we weave a tapestry of experiences that shape who we are and who we are becoming.

Each connection we make, each moment of growth, becomes a thread in the intricate design of our lives.

Life constantly reminds us of the importance of appreciating the present.

We are often so focused on what comes next that we forget to find gratitude in the ordinary moments that fill our days.

It is in these moments, in the laughter of a friend, the taste of a favorite meal, the feeling of accomplishment after a day's work, that we find meaning and joy.

The extraordinary is often found within the ordinary, and it is in our ability to slow down, to pause, and to fully experience the present that we discover the true essence of life.

This appreciation for the now helps us to stay grounded, to remain mindful, and to find peace amid the chaos of daily existence.

Living a meaningful life is a delicate balance between holding on and letting go, striving and surrendering.

We must learn when to push forward and when to allow things to unfold naturally, trusting that the universe will guide us in the right direction.

This balance is essential for living with intention and authenticity, for it is only when we are aligned with our true selves that we can fully embrace the potential of life.

We must dare to live with purpose, to act with integrity, and to follow our hearts as we navigate the twists and turns of our journey.

Every breath we take offers us the chance to create, to love, and to leave a lasting imprint on the world.

In every moment, we have the opportunity to shape our story, to impact the lives of others, and to make a difference in the world around us.

Life is a gift, and it is up to us to make the most of it, whether by sharing our passions, building meaningful relationships, or contributing to something greater than ourselves.

It is the choices we make, the connections we forge, and the love we give that define the legacy we leave behind.

Life is a journey of self-discovery, growth, and connection, and in every step, we are invited to embrace the beauty and wonder of the adventure.

TRUTH

Truth is like a refreshing drink of water when you're parched, a source of clarity and relief when doubt clouds your mind and confusion reigns.

Just as the body yearns for water to quench its thirst and restore balance, the mind seeks truth to ground itself in reality, providing a sense of understanding and direction.

Truth has a way of calming the inner storm, offering an anchor when everything around us feels uncertain or chaotic.

It revitalizes us, not just physically but intellectually and emotionally, helping us make sense of the world and our place within it.

It cuts through the noise, cutting away at the layers of misconception and misunderstanding that cloud our judgment.

Much like a nourishing drink of water, truth replenishes us from within, allowing us to approach life with a renewed sense of purpose and insight.

It is not just a revelation but a fundamental need that we all share, a need to know what is real, what is honest, and what truly serves our growth.

Just as water sustains the body, truth nourishes the mind and soul, allowing us to move forward in life with greater clarity.

It opens doors to new perspectives, broadening our understanding and helping us make informed decisions.

It is not a luxury but a necessity in a world filled with distractions, half-truths, and conflicting opinions.

The pursuit of truth is an ongoing journey, one that demands attention, dedication, and an open heart.

In moments of uncertainty or struggle, truth is a guiding light that leads us toward deeper understanding and self-awareness.

It is often not easy to confront, as it can be uncomfortable or challenging, shaking our beliefs and forcing us to face things we may not want to acknowledge.

Yet, it is in this very discomfort that truth has the power to transform us.

It forces us to look beyond our biases, to challenge assumptions, and to confront our fears.

And in doing so, it opens up a path to growth, wisdom, and greater authenticity.

My thirst for truth remains unquenchable, a constant and driving force that propels me forward in my quest to uncover what is real and authentic in this world.

This unrelenting pursuit is not always smooth or straightforward.

In fact, it often brings discomfort and struggle.

The search for truth can be like a journey through uncharted waters, full of uncertainty, hidden depths, and unexpected revelations.

But despite the challenges, this pursuit remains vital because it is in this process of discovery that we grow and evolve.

Truth is not always convenient or easy to diges.

It may not fit neatly into our preconceived notions or desires.

Sometimes, the truth is hard to bear, but it is precisely this raw honesty that makes it so powerful.

It strips away the layers of illusion and pretense, revealing the core of what is real.

While it may not always be what we want to hear, it is always what we need to hear, and it serves a greater purpose, one of integrity and authenticity.

When truth presents itself, it is important to remember that it is not meant to harm but to enlighten.

Even when the truth feels uncomfortable or difficult to accept, it is still a gift, a moment of clarity that helps us see things as they truly are.

It can be tempting to turn away from truth, to reject it because it disrupts our sense of comfort or challenges our ego.

But to do so is to deny ourselves the opportunity for growth and transformation.

Truth demands courage, it calls on us to look beyond our own desires, to let go of illusions, and to face the world with open eyes.

In embracing truth, we allow ourselves to shed the weight of falsehoods and assumptions, making room for a deeper, more authentic connection with ourselves and others.

It is through truth that we begin to live in alignment with our true selves, shedding the layers of pretense that separate us from who we are meant to be.

Basking in the presence of truth is a rare and precious privilege.

In a world that is often clouded by misinformation, deception, and confusion, the light of truth shines brightly as a beacon, guiding us toward a more honest and meaningful existence.

Standing in this light brings a profound sense of clarity, stripping away the distractions and illusions that obscure our vision.

It frees us from the chains of false beliefs, allowing us to see the world and ourselves more clearly.

Truth offers us the courage to live authentically, to speak our minds, and to act with integrity.

It is a force that empowers us to align our actions with our values, to be true to ourselves even when the world pressures us to conform.

In its presence, we find not only understanding but the strength to embrace our purpose and live with intention.

Truth is not just a concept, it is a living, breathing force that shapes our lives and guides us toward a more fulfilling and authentic path.

Truth is a beacon that leads us toward a more meaningful existence.

It is the foundation upon which we build our lives, and it is through truth that we find the courage to live boldly, to love deeply, and to embrace our true selves.

Truth offers us the freedom to be honest with ourselves and others, to let go of the facades that keep us separated from our authentic nature.

It invites us to step into the light, to shed the shadows of doubt and fear, and to live fully in the presence of what is real.

When we choose truth, we choose freedom, clarity, and authenticity, and in doing so, we open the door to a life that is rich with meaning, purpose, and connection.

WITHIN

Truly, real life is lived within, not in the external world or the things we accumulate, but in the depths of our inner being.

The essence of our existence is shaped by our thoughts, emotions, and our sense of self, this inner realm is where the true experience of life unfolds.

While the external world constantly bombards us with distractions, pressures, and challenges, it is within our inner world that we find the meaning, purpose, and fulfillment we seek.

How we perceive and respond to life is determined not by the outer circumstances, but by the state of our mind and heart.

It is through nurturing our inner selves that we are able to truly live, finding a sense of peace and alignment that reflects in everything we do.

The way we experience and interact with the external world is a direct mirror of what is happening inside of us.

If we harbor chaos, fear, or unresolved emotions within, these feelings will manifest in our actions, thoughts, and relationships.

For example, when we are angry or anxious inside, it colors our interactions with others, often causing friction or misunderstanding.

Conversely, when our inner world is in a state of balance, clarity, and peace, it radiates outward, influencing how we engage with the world around us.

Our internal state becomes the lens through which we see everything, affecting how we handle life's challenges, relate to others, and even how we view ourselves.

The outer world may be unpredictable, but it is the condition of our inner being that determines how we perceive and respond to it.

In the face of external turmoil, the power of inner peace becomes even more evident.

A person who has cultivated a deep sense of calm and stability within can face the storms of life with resilience and grace.

When the world seems chaotic, this inner peace acts as an anchor, keeping them grounded and centered amidst the confusion.

It becomes a shield, protecting them from being overwhelmed by the ups and downs of life.

No matter what happens outside, if the foundation of peace is strong within, it provides the clarity and strength needed to move through life without being consumed by stress, anxiety, or fear.

In this way, true peace is not about controlling the external environment, but about mastering the internal world, creating a sense of harmony that withstands the shifting tides of circumstance.

A fulfilling and meaningful life is not built on the acquisition of wealth, success, or material things, it begins with the cultivation of a peaceful inner life.

By prioritizing self-awareness, mindfulness, and emotional balance, we create an internal foundation that can weather any storm.

Our ability to navigate the ups and downs of life with resilience depends on how well we nurture our inner selves.

The world outside will always be in flux, filled with uncertainty and challenge, but when we establish a sense of peace within, we find that we can meet life's challenges with strength and grace.

This internal peace provides the clarity we need to make wise decisions, maintain healthy relationships, and approach our goals with purpose and confidence.

The more we invest in our inner world, the more we are able to live a life that is grounded in meaning and fulfillment.

Life's external challenges may never fully disappear, but when we are rooted in our inner peace, we become less affected by the turbulence of the outside world.

We develop the ability to focus on what truly matters and to let go of distractions that no longer serve us. In the end, it is the condition of our inner life that determines the quality of our existence.

The more we cultivate a peaceful, centered, and balanced inner world, the more we are able to live authentically and joyfully, regardless of external circumstances.

True contentment comes from within, and it is this inner peace that forms the foundation for lasting fulfillment, resilience, and a life lived with purpose.

True fulfillment is not found in the pursuit of external achievements, but in the nurturing of our inner world.

It is in our thoughts, emotions, and sense of self that we find the ultimate source of peace and joy.

The more we tend to this inner life, the more we can create a meaningful and fulfilling existence that transcends the limitations of the material world.

As we cultivate greater awareness, balance, and emotional health, we develop the resilience to face life's inevitable challenges with strength and grace.

In the end, the inner journey is the most important one, for it is through this path that we find true contentment and lasting fulfillment.

TRUE POSSESSIONS

In life, the only true possessions we can truly claim are wisdom and knowledge.

These intangible assets are uniquely ours, forged by the sum of our experiences, the lessons we've learned, and the reflections we've made upon them.

Unlike material possessions, which are susceptible to loss, theft, or destruction, wisdom and knowledge are impervious to such fates.

They become ingrained in our being, evolving over time and becoming the solid foundation upon which our sense of identity rests.

They are the compass by which we navigate the world, influencing our decisions, actions, and interactions with others.

In this sense, wisdom and knowledge are not only enduring, they transcend time, circumstance, and even the very course of our lives.

While material wealth, property, status, or possessions may come and go, wisdom and knowledge endure.

These physical things may feel permanent in the moment, but in the grand scheme of life, they are fleeting.

The material things we acquire are but temporary acquisitions, transient at best.

Our wealth may grow, our homes may expand, and our status may rise, but in the end, these possessions are nothing more than borrowed gifts, lent to us for a brief moment in the great span of time.

A century, or even a few decades, is often all we have with these material possessions before they, too, fade away.

Whether they are passed on to others or deteriorate into oblivion, they remain just as impermanent as the passage of time itself.

This realization of impermanence is a powerful reminder.

It brings clarity to the fact that clinging too tightly to material wealth and the trappings of status is ultimately futile.

No matter how much we accumulate, we cannot escape the eventuality that we will leave everything behind.

In fact, the more we accumulate, the more we become bound to these fleeting things, which only increases the potential for suffering when they slip from our grasp.

This awareness, however, can free us from the heavy burden of unnecessary attachment and desire for things that cannot offer lasting fulfillment.

It invites us to shift our focus from the material to the timeless, from the fleeting to the eternal.

When we begin to understand that material wealth and possessions are not what define us, we can begin to focus on the qualities that truly matter, those qualities that are lasting and invaluable.

Wisdom and knowledge are not only enriching in and of themselves, but they also offer the ability to shape our lives in ways that truly matter.

They allow us to confront life's challenges with confidence, to build meaningful relationships grounded in understanding and empathy, and to leave a lasting positive impact on the world around us.

With wisdom, we have the power to shape not only our own lives but also the lives of others, to lift up those around us and contribute to a greater good.

Knowledge empowers us to take on life's obstacles with clarity, to make decisions that are rooted in truth, and to live with purpose.

Investing in our inner growth, our wisdom and our knowledge, becomes, then, far more rewarding than accumulating material wealth.

While external possessions may bring temporary satisfaction, they never provide the deep sense of fulfillment that comes from understanding oneself and the world.

Wisdom and knowledge are treasures that cannot be stolen, lost, or destroyed.

They cannot fade with time, nor be reduced by age or circumstance.

They become part of us, growing and developing as we continue our journeys through life.

This inner growth not only nourishes our souls but also serves as the beacon that guides us toward greater meaning and fulfillment.

Life, at its core, is not a journey of ownership but one of learning and growth.

Understanding that the material world is transient allows us to relinquish the unnecessary attachment that often leads to suffering.

By embracing wisdom and knowledge, we align ourselves with what is truly important, with that which transcends the passing trends and fleeting desires of the material world.

In this way, we cultivate a deeper sense of contentment and peace, because we know that these are the things no one can take away.

When we prioritize the intangible treasures of wisdom and knowledge, we find that we live more fully, more authentically, and with a greater sense of purpose.

In the end, these are the only things that we can truly call our own, our legacy, our guideposts, and our source of lasting fulfillment.

LIKE A FAUCET

Belief is a subtle but potent force, much like a faucet that is only semi-open.

The water may trickle out slowly, yet over time, the steady stream has the power to fill a basin.

In the same way, belief, even when expressed in a small, quiet manner, can influence reality in profound ways.

It does not demand an overwhelming flood of conviction to create change.

Instead, it requires only a consistent, persistent flow to alter the course of events.

Whether it's a deeply held personal belief or a collective conviction shared by an entire society, the effect is cumulative.

Tiny drips of faith, confidence, or ideology accumulate over time, building momentum until they become powerful enough to transform not just individuals, but entire civilizations.

This process is slow and almost imperceptible at first, yet its impact is undeniable.

Just as water slowly fills a basin from a leaking faucet, so too does belief gradually seep into the fabric of our existence, shaping destinies and transforming lives.

A single person who harbors a quiet but unwavering belief in their own potential can, over time, achieve extraordinary things.

The accumulation of their faith and self-confidence will carve out opportunities, opening doors where once there seemed to be none.

These seemingly small acts of belief gradually build a foundation upon which greater achievements can stand.

The power of belief doesn't lie in immediate success, but in its steady persistence.

The same principle applies to societies.

When entire civilizations or groups of people share a belief, whether it's a spiritual conviction, a philosophical idea, or a scientific theory, that belief, over time, manifests in reality.

It may begin with only a handful of individuals, but as they persist, the movement grows.

The collective faith in that idea gains strength, and what started as a small spark becomes a powerful current of change.

The most significant advancements in human history often started with a few brave souls, their belief acting as the first drops of water that eventually filled a river.

These early believers created the conditions for breakthroughs that later changed the course of humanity.

Whether it was the belief in human rights, the idea of equality, or the pursuit of knowledge itself, these initial seeds of belief grew into forces that shaped the world.

However, belief is not only about the personal or societal impact it creates.

There is also a deeper, more mysterious element at work, an unseen force that responds to belief.

The universe, in its vast complexity, seems to react to our faith, subtly shaping circumstances to align with the energy we project.

Belief acts as a magnet for opportunity, guiding the subconscious mind toward choices that can bring one closer to their desired outcome.

Whether through chance encounters, serendipitous events, or a seemingly inexplicable alignment of circumstances, belief has a way of drawing favorable conditions into our lives.

This connection between belief and outcome is not fully understood, yet the results are clear.

Even the smallest acts of faith, a moment of trust, the courage to hold onto hope, or the ability to imagine a different future, can set in motion a chain of events that ripples outward, affecting things far beyond what one might initially perceive.

Yet, despite belief's profound power, we are entering an era in which the reliance on faith alone is no longer enough.

The age of belief is coming to an end, and humanity must now evolve beyond this dependency.

Earth's people must transition from reliance on belief to the pursuit of knowledge.

For while belief has served as a catalyst for many changes throughout history, it has its limitations.

Belief, in all its power, can only take us so far.

It may ignite the spark of transformation, but without the foundation of knowledge, it will ultimately leave us without the tools to fully realize our potential.

Knowledge, on the other hand, is a far more potent force.

It opens the door to boundless possibilities.

Unlike belief, which often relies on faith alone, knowledge is grounded in understanding, in truth, and in the constant pursuit of discovery.

As humanity stands on the precipice of monumental change, it is time to move beyond blind belief and begin to seek knowledge.

We are entering a new chapter in our evolution, one that requires not just faith, but inquiry, exploration, and understanding.

It is no longer enough to merely believe in something, we must question, explore, and seek to know.

Knowledge is the key that will unlock the doors to our true potential, enabling us to reshape the world in ways that belief alone could never achieve.

It is through knowledge that we can fully awaken, elevate our consciousness, and fully realize the scope of our existence.

The shift from belief to knowledge will be the catalyst for the great transformation that awaits us, opening the floodgates of possibility and creating a future shaped by clarity, insight, and wisdom.

Only through knowledge can we transcend the limitations of belief and step into a new era of enlightenment and understanding.

TRUE PEACE

I've observed that many individuals on Earth pride themselves on their strong sense of morality, believing that they hold a clear understanding of right and wrong.

However, when faced with real-life situations that put their values to the test, they often fall short of their own ideals.

It's one thing to claim moral integrity in abstract terms, but it's an entirely different challenge to maintain it when confronted with difficult choices or pressures.

This stark contrast between theory and practice reveals a troubling truth: for many people, morality is not as solid and unyielding as they believe it to be.

Instead, it appears more like an ideal, something to aspire to but not necessarily something they live by consistently.

This inconsistency between one's claimed morality and their actions when tested suggests that morality, for most, is more about how it sounds or what they think it should be than about truly internalizing it as a guiding principle.

The true test of a person's morality often comes when the stakes are high, when the right decision requires sacrifice, discomfort, or the courage to challenge the status quo. In those moments, we see the gap between belief and action.

People may say they value fairness, compassion, or justice, but when circumstances demand those qualities, the reality can be much more complicated.

This is the point at which moral integrity is truly revealed, and sadly, many falter.

To me, morality should be an intensely personal matter, something that is shaped by each individual's experiences, perspectives, and understanding of the world.

What one person considers virtuous or right may not resonate the same way with another, and yet both viewpoints should be acknowledged and respected.

The diversity of human thought and belief is too vast to be condensed into a single, rigid set of moral standards that everyone must adhere to.

The notion of forcing a singular moral code onto all people disregards the richness of human experience and the complexity of cultural and individual identity.

What is morally acceptable to one society may be unacceptable to another, and these differences should not be the source of division but rather a reflection of our shared humanity.

Instead of imposing a universal definition of right and wrong, society should focus on fostering an environment where individuals are free to define their own moral beliefs while still maintaining mutual respect for the beliefs of others.

True progress lies in creating a world where every person is free to live according to their own moral compass, without fear of judgment, ridicule, or external pressure, as long as their actions do not cause harm to others or exploit those who are vulnerable, especially minors.

Suppressing individuality in the name of a so-called universal morality only leads to division, resentment, and unnecessary conflict.

People should be allowed to follow their own ethical paths without the burden of conforming to the beliefs and values of others.

For humanity to move forward and create a truly peaceful society, we must reach a point where every individual feels free to express themselves authentically without the fear of being condemned for their personal values.

Genuine freedom is about respecting others' autonomy and moral choices, as long as those choices do not infringe on the rights and well-being of others.

This is the foundation of a society built on trust, compassion, and acceptance.

As long as people continue to impose their beliefs on others, rather than embracing and respecting the diversity of perspectives that exist, peace will remain an elusive goal.

The tensions that arise from these impositions breed conflict, distrust, and division, preventing humanity from achieving lasting harmony.

Real peace, then, is not about uniformity or conformity to a single set of values.

Lasting peace can only emerge when we learn to understand and respect the differences that make each person unique.

It is when we allow for these differences to coexist, while also ensuring that basic ethical principles, such as not causing harm to others and respecting individual freedoms, are upheld, that we can truly create a world where peace is possible.

Until we achieve this level of acceptance and respect for individual differences, the dream of global harmony will remain out of reach.

True progress comes not from uniformity of belief but from a collective commitment to mutual respect, tolerance, and understanding.

Only then will we begin to build a future where peace, in its truest sense, can flourish.

SUICIDE

Life is a journey, one filled with challenges that, at times, may seem insurmountable.

But every obstacle, every setback we encounter, is not a hindrance but rather an opportunity to evolve, to become a better version of ourselves.

The path was never meant to be easy, if it were, there would be no lessons to learn, no strength to gain.

The struggles we face are not arbitrary, they are precisely the experiences we need to shape us into stronger, wiser individuals.

Each hardship serves as a stepping stone, each setback as a lesson in resilience.

Though life can be difficult, even in the most trying of circumstances, there is always meaning to be found.

It is through the struggles that we discover our inner strength, our capacity for growth.

The darkness that we sometimes feel envelops us does not define us.

Rather, it is the very thing that leads us to uncover the light within.

Even in moments of sorrow, beauty is present, and within that beauty, there is love.

The love we find, not in the perfection of life, but in our ability to endure, to rise from the ashes of our despair and emerge stronger.

Every challenge, no matter how small or large, holds the potential for transformation.

Suicide, in contrast, is not a solution.

It is not a way out, nor is it an escape.

It is an act of surrender, a way of avoiding the very experiences that are meant to help us grow, to teach us what we are truly capable of.

When we reach the point of despair, it may seem as though there is no other option, but we must remember that those feelings are fleeting, and the potential for change lies in facing the difficult moments rather than fleeing from them.

Difficult times are overwhelming, yes, but they are never impossible to overcome.

Life will never give us anything we cannot handle, because, in truth, we are the creators of the challenges we face.

The obstacles in our path are reflections of our inner struggles, pushing us to confront what we are capable of overcoming.

The challenges we face in life are not meant to break us, they are designed to reveal the strength that often lies dormant within.

It is through the confrontation of our struggles, the willingness to endure and persevere despite the pain, that we unlock the potential we never knew we had.

Running from our challenges may seem like an escape, but it only delays the inevitable. Facing our fears, our pain, and our weaknesses head-on is the only way forward.

Growth is never easy, and it is often painful, but the rewards of this journey, self-awareness, strength, resilience, are worth every step.

The act of enduring, of choosing to keep going even when it feels impossible, is what leads to transformation.

I know this truth personally.

I have walked through the darkness myself.

There were times in my life when I saw no other way out, when the weight of everything seemed unbearable.

I attempted to take my own life three times, convinced that escape was the only answer.

But each time I failed.

And today, I am grateful for those failures, for it is through them that I found the strength to survive, to rebuild, and to emerge as the person I am today.

What I once thought of as unbearable suffering became the catalyst for my growth.

The struggles I so desperately wanted to escape from ultimately ended up teaching me the most valuable lessons of my life.

They showed me my resilience, my capacity to love myself again, and the profound meaning that can be found even in the darkest of times.

From those experiences, I have learned that life will never give us challenges that we are incapable of handling.

We create our challenges, and within us lies the strength to face them.

The courage to overcome hardship has always been within us, even if we don't always see it.

In the moments of doubt and pain, it can be hard to believe in that strength, but it is there, ready to be tapped into.

We are not powerless. We are not defeated.

We may stumble, we may fall, but we are not broken.

No matter how hard life gets, there is always a way forward, and that way is paved with the strength we summon when we refuse to give up.

We are not merely surviving, we are creating, evolving, and becoming more than we ever thought possible.

Through every trial, we have the chance to shape our own destiny, to transform ourselves and our lives in ways we never imagined.

Every step forward, no matter how small, is a step toward the person we are meant to be.

We are not defined by our struggles, but by our ability to rise above them. Every challenge is a chance for growth, and every hardship is an opportunity to discover just how strong we truly are.

In the end, life's challenges are not what break us, they are the forces that mold us into who we are meant to become.

And in that process of becoming, we find purpose, strength, and an unwavering belief that no matter what comes our way, we have the power to endure and transform.

NIGGA

To me, every person, regardless of race or background, should have the freedom to speak their minds openly.

This includes the freedom to use words like "Nigga, " a term that, for many, carries deeply personal significance, shaped by individual and cultural perspectives.

The issue lies not in the word itself, but in how we choose to interact with it, and the power we give it.

Many people, of all races, fall into the habit of avoiding uncomfortable conversations or suppressing certain topics, thinking that by ignoring them, they will simply disappear.

However, life does not work this way. Ignoring a problem does not make it go away, it only allows it to fester and grow beneath the surface, often leading to deeper misunderstandings and divisions later on.

Problems need to be confronted directly and honestly, no matter how difficult it may seem in the moment.

Only through honest confrontation can we begin to find solutions and foster growth.

People, regardless of their background, should be free to express themselves in a way that feels true to them.

When individuals are allowed to speak openly, they experience a sense of release, of authenticity that brings them closer to their true selves.

In the act of speaking our truth, we often find that the weight of unspoken thoughts and emotions lifts.

Open and honest communication allows for understanding to flourish, breaking down walls and building bridges between people.

It is through this kind of dialogue that genuine connections are formed, and real relationships are built, ones rooted in mutual respect and peace.

On the other hand, suppressing or censoring thoughts and emotions only deepens the divide, creating tension and bitterness that can lead to further conflict.

A society that encourages and celebrates free expression is one where growth, both personal and collective, is possible.

When people are free to speak their minds without fear of judgment or repression, they become empowered to tackle issues head-on, and the potential for healing and reconciliation becomes greater.

As a black man, I personally do not feel burdened by the word "Nigga." To me, it holds no power unless I allow it to.

No word has the inherent ability to control your emotions or sense of self unless you allow it to influence you.

Our power lies in how we choose to respond to the world around us.

The words others use, or the opinions they express, do not define who we are unless we choose to give them that power.

What truly matters is how we define ourselves and how we choose to live with integrity and self-awareness.

External circumstances may impact us, but they do not determine our worth or disrupt our inner peace.

It is our internal strength, our ability to remain steadfast in our convictions and values, that allows us to navigate the world with resilience and grace.

True freedom is found not in being unaffected by the external world, but in the ability to remain unaffected in the face of external challenges.

With this mindset, life becomes much easier to navigate.

When we are firmly rooted in our sense of self, we are no longer easily swayed by the judgments or opinions of others.

We are free to stand in our truth, expressing ourselves authentically without fear or resentment.

It is this inner strength that fosters a society where open, meaningful, and respectful interactions can take place.

When we are free to express ourselves without the burden of judgment or fear, we create a world where understanding and respect take precedence over division and conflict.

In this world, we no longer need to walk on eggshells or suppress difficult conversations.

Instead, we can engage with each other honestly, knowing that our worth and identity come from within, and that we are all capable of growth, understanding, and healing.

Through open communication and mutual respect, we can build a society where everyone is free to speak their truth, and where differences are celebrated rather than feared.

DIFFERENT VIEWS

Human beings have an inherent tendency to seek out others who share similar views, beliefs, and values.

This inclination, deeply ingrained in our social nature, serves to provide a sense of comfort, safety, and belonging.

When we are surrounded by people who think like we do, we feel validated, supported, and reassured in our thoughts and decisions.

These shared understandings create a communal bond, reinforcing the way we see the world and our place within it.

It's in these environments that we find affirmation, as we know we are not alone in our perspectives.

This sense of belonging plays a vital role in shaping our identity, our sense of purpose, and our overall well-being.

Having a community that reflects our own values can bolster our confidence and self-esteem.

However, this natural inclination toward homogeneity can sometimes have unintended consequences.

When surrounded only by like-minded individuals, there is a tendency for an echo chamber to form.

In such spaces, differing opinions are rarely encountered, and those that are often go unexamined or dismissed outright.

Over time, the reinforcement of identical viewpoints creates a narrow lens through which individuals see the world.

This isolation from opposing viewpoints can make it increasingly difficult for individuals to engage in meaningful discussions or adapt their thinking.

A rigid mindset takes root, one that becomes resistant to change, innovation, or the introduction of new ideas.

The comfort of familiarity slowly transforms into intellectual stagnation, as the individual becomes less inclined to challenge their beliefs or critically evaluate alternative perspectives.

Without exposure to diverse viewpoints, one risks becoming trapped in a bubble of self-reinforcement, where growth and personal development are stunted.

On the other hand, engaging with people who hold differing views offers an invaluable opportunity for intellectual growth and critical thinking.

When individuals step outside of their comfort zones and confront opinions that challenge their own, they are forced to critically examine their beliefs.

These conversations, though often uncomfortable, push us to refine our arguments, question assumptions, and clarify our positions.

This process of intellectual discomfort is, in fact, where true growth happens.

Engaging with differing perspectives encourages individuals to stretch their thinking, recognize blind spots, and develop a more nuanced understanding of complex issues.

Such discussions foster intellectual humility, as we come to realize that no one person holds the absolute truth.

The more we engage with different viewpoints, the more we refine our ability to reason, argue effectively, and see the broader picture.

Additionally, exposure to diverse viewpoints encourages tolerance and empathy.

By understanding the experiences and thought processes of others, we can appreciate the variety of human perspectives that shape how people approach life, politics, and morality.

The more we engage with those who think differently, the more we understand their experiences and reasons for holding their views.

This understanding helps to bridge the gap between us and others, fostering respect and cooperation despite our differences.

Through these exchanges, we can cultivate a culture of tolerance, one where diversity is seen as a strength rather than a threat.

We also come to recognize the limitations of our own perspectives, realizing that our experiences, values, and beliefs are just one of many ways to see the world.

Truly, while it is only natural to seek familiarity and camaraderie within social circles, embracing diversity in thought is not only crucial for personal growth but also for societal progress.

Societies that encourage open dialogue and exposure to a wide range of ideas are better equipped to innovate, solve problems, and adapt to change.

Without the constant infusion of new perspectives and the challenge of intellectual engagement, societies risk stagnation, unable to move forward or address the complexities of the modern world.

By embracing diversity in thought, we create a space where individuals and communities can evolve, learn, and contribute meaningfully to the progress of humanity as a whole.

Through this commitment to openness, we allow for the flourishing of ideas, the bridging of divides, and the creation of more inclusive, dynamic societies.

The true strength of a community lies not in its uniformity, but in its ability to celebrate and learn from its differences.

INTERNAL SHIFT

The world we experience every day is not just a random collection of events and circumstances.

Instead, it is a direct reflection of all of us, our collective actions, choices, and beliefs.

It is a product of the sum of each individual's thoughts, feelings, and behaviors, continuously shaping and reshaping the reality we live in.

Every act of kindness, every moment of anger, every decision made, whether big or small, ripples through the collective human experience, influencing the course of history, society, and our day-to-day lives.

It's a vast web, where every individual plays a crucial role, and where no one is immune to the impact of others.

No single group, race, or person can be held solely responsible for the state of the world, because each of us contributes, consciously or unconsciously, to the larger picture.

When we point fingers at others or place blame on certain individuals or groups, we miss the deeper, more profound truth.

We ignore the fact that the state of the world, both good and bad, is a manifestation of what exists within us.

The global challenges we face are not just the result of bad policies or corrupt leaders, nor are they caused by a single ideology or political party.

Rather, they stem from the collective mindset of humanity, the fears, desires, and imbalances that exist inside each of us. If we look around, we see that the chaos we witness externally is often a reflection of the internal turmoil experienced by individuals.

The fear, resentment, and division we feel within ourselves play out on the global stage, manifesting as conflict, violence, and unrest. Societies are built upon the individual experiences, emotions, and values of their members.

When negativity, division, and unrest dominate, they become embedded within the very fabric of our cultures, economies, and institutions.

The result is a world that mirrors these same qualities, unsettling, fractured, and dissonant.

However, true and lasting transformation cannot come simply from external changes alone.

The solution to the challenges we face as a global community does not lie solely in altering systems, policies, or structures.

It must begin with a deep internal shift in the collective human consciousness.

If we want to see a world free from violence, hatred, and fear, we must first cultivate those qualities within ourselves.

Inner peace is the foundation for global peace, without it, no amount of external effort will truly lead to harmony.

The world outside is a reflection of the inner world of its people, and until we address the conflicts within ourselves, our inner fears, doubts, and divisions, we cannot hope to create a peaceful, just, and balanced society.

This is why I always urge people to protect their inner peace, by any means necessary.

We must guard our thoughts, our emotions, and our hearts, because they are the building blocks of the world we experience.

The path to a better world, one that is truly harmonious, begins with mastering our own minds and emotions.

It starts with self-awareness, self-regulation, and an unwavering commitment to personal growth.

of us holds within us the power to shape the reality we live in, not just for ourselves, but for the collective.

Every individual has the potential to contribute positively to the world by cultivating inner peace, compassion, and understanding.

cannot simply sit back and complain about the state of the world, hoping that someone else will make a difference.

Instead, we must actively take part in creating change, beginning with our own lives and minds.

If we want to see kindness, unity, and justice in the world, we must first embody those qualities ourselves.

The world is shaped by the sum of all our actions, and each of us is a vital piece in the greater puzzle of existence.

Our individual choices and behaviors, no matter how small they may seem, ripple out and influence others, creating a chain reaction of transformation.

If we believe we are powerless, that our actions do not matter, we will remain stuck in the cycles of despair and frustration that seem to dominate the world.

However, if we recognize our own strength and potential, we realize that nothing can prevent us from contributing to a better future.

Each of us has the ability to become the change we wish to see, to inspire others through our actions, and to create a reality rooted in peace, understanding, and respect.

By awakening to our power and taking responsibility for our own inner state, we can collectively build a world that reflects the highest ideals of human nature.

The future we desire is within our grasp, and it begins with each of us, every thought, every choice, every action matters.

Together, we can shape a reality that is truly reflective of the peace, love, and harmony we seek.

THE RICHEST MAN

No human being can ever claim to be the richest person on Earth, for true ownership is a concept that, when examined deeply, proves to be impossible.

The Earth, in all its vastness and wonder, does not belong to anyone.

It is not a possession to be held, controlled, or manipulated to serve personal desires.

It is a creation of Creation itself, an intricate and beautiful expression of the universe, continuously evolving and transforming with each passing moment.

No matter how much wealth or power one amasses, it does not equate to true dominion over the forces that govern all existence.

The Earth and all that it encompasses were never meant to be controlled by humans, rather, they exist as part of the ever-unfolding process of life, beyond the constraints of human ownership.

Wealth, power, and material success are, at best, temporary illusions, offering only a brief sense of satisfaction before they fade away.

These fleeting achievements cannot grant any lasting mastery over the deeper forces of the universe.

The laws of Creation, the fundamental principles that shape existence, operate beyond the reach of human influence.

No mortal can ever regulate or control the natural order that determines the course of life.

While it is true that people may accumulate riches, influence, or authority, they remain, in the grand scheme of things, utterly subject to the powerful forces far greater than themselves.

The belief that one can conquer or master Creation is a falsehood, a self-deception.

Creation, by its very nature, operates independently of human desires, ambitions, or designs.

It is not bound to the whims of those who seek to control or dominate it.

In light of this, worrying about material wealth or attempting to control such things is a futile endeavor.

Anxiety and fear surrounding money, success, and power only serve to entrap individuals in illusions, distracting them from the true nature of existence.

The pursuit of material success, when it becomes an obsession, blinds people to the deeper, more meaningful aspects of life.

Instead of being consumed by these concerns, individuals must come to understand the transient nature of worldly success.

The fleeting nature of these pursuits makes them ultimately unworthy of our full attention.

It is not through the accumulation of wealth or the desire for control that true fulfillment is found.

True wisdom lies in accepting that everything in life follows its course, regardless of human interference.

The natural world, with all its complexity, does not bend to human will.

It flows in harmony with its own inherent rhythm, which cannot be rushed, altered, or dominated.

Yet, it is equally misguided to adopt a stance of complete passivity.

While it is true that no one can control Creation, this does not mean one should stand idly by, waiting for things to unfold on their own.

To be passive is to relinquish one's power and potential, leading only to stagnation and a life of unfulfilled potential.

Fear of acting, in the belief that one cannot change or influence the world, only serves to prevent growth and progress.

The wise understand that action is not about trying to control or dominate the course of existence, but about actively participating in the flow of life.

In embracing life's natural order, we are called not to fight against it, but to move with it, fully engaged and present in every moment.

True courage is not in the attempt to alter or dominate Creation, but in the willingness to align oneself with it, to work in partnership with the forces that shape existence.

To live with courage and purpose is to acknowledge that we are not passive observers of life, but active participants in its unfolding.

It is the ability to embrace the journey, to take action with purpose, not in defiance of life's flow, but in harmony with it.

By doing so, we contribute to the greater whole, creating meaning and impact in a way that reflects the wisdom of understanding our place in the universe.

The role of human beings is not to command the world around them, but to engage with it, to contribute to its evolution and to learn from it.

Only when we understand this balance between action and surrender, between engagement and acceptance, do we truly participate in the grand flow of life.

This is where true wisdom and fulfillment reside, not in the futile attempt to control, but in the embrace of life as it is, and the courage to live in alignment with its natural, ever-changing course.

HEAVEN

True heaven, the ultimate state of peace and contentment, is found within the human being, not in the external world, nor in the fleeting validation of others.

It is an internal state of being, deeply rooted in self-awareness, inner peace, and fulfillment.

This inner heaven is not something that can be bestowed upon us by external circumstances, nor can it be handed to us through the approval of others.

It is not dependent on the passing praise or recognition from the outside world.

True peace, the kind that nourishes the soul, is something that emanates from within, growing stronger with each step toward self-understanding and self-acceptance.

When one realizes this, they begin to see that happiness is not a product of the world outside, but something that arises from deep within themselves, a wellspring of fulfillment that remains steady regardless of external conditions.

As long as an individual remains dependent on the validation and approval of others, they will forever be caught in an endless cycle of neediness, constantly seeking external confirmation to feel worthy or fulfilled.

They look to the opinions of others, the societal standards and expectations, and the attainment of material success as the markers of their happiness and self-worth.

In doing so, they inadvertently place their well-being in the hands of things beyond their control, leaving them vulnerable to the whims and judgments of the world around them.

This dependence on the unpredictable nature of external validation creates a sense of instability and unrest. Since these factors are constantly changing, they can never provide lasting peace.

The result is a continual pursuit of something elusive, as the true essence of peace remains just out of reach, always dependent on forces that are beyond one's control.

True peace and lasting fulfillment cannot be found in this way.

They are found by turning inward, by learning to trust oneself, to be at peace with who we are, and to accept ourselves as we are.

This is where true strength and serenity lie, in the ability to cultivate self-acceptance and inner stability, regardless of the turbulence that may swirl around us.

When a person begins to rely on their own values, their own sense of purpose, and their inner wisdom, they can begin to free themselves from the heavy burden of seeking approval from outside sources.

They recognize that no matter how others may perceive them, they are enough just as they are.

This inner foundation is unshakable, it cannot be torn down by the changing tides of the world or the judgment of others.

It is solid and enduring, allowing one to face life with confidence, clarity, and poise, knowing that their worth is not contingent upon the approval of others or the attainment of external markers of success.

True peace, therefore, is not a destination that can be reached through external achievements or the pursuit of approval.

It is a personal journey, one that begins within the depths of the soul.

It is something that cannot be handed to us by others nor taken away by circumstances.

Peace must be nurtured and cultivated from within, through a commitment to self-reflection, personal growth, and emotional balance.

It is the process of creating a life where the inner self is in harmony with one's true nature.

This journey requires a deep commitment to understanding who we are, embracing our uniqueness, and accepting ourselves fully without needing others to affirm our worth.

As we learn to trust ourselves and our intuition, we create a space where peace can thrive.

We are no longer swayed by the changing winds of external approval, instead, we stand firm in our own truth, free from the distractions and pressures of the outside world.

By embracing this understanding, we can free ourselves from the noise and chaos of the world around us.

The distractions of seeking external validation, the endless chase for approval and success, all fall away as we realize that true peace lies not outside of us, but within.

It is a peace that arises when we align with our authentic self, living from a place of self-awareness, acceptance, and balance.

When we embrace the truth that happiness and peace are born from within, we begin to live a life of greater purpose and harmony.

We no longer need the validation of others to feel complete, for we have already found completeness within ourselves.

In this way, we can live a life that is not dictated by the external world, but one that is shaped by our inner truths and the peace that flows from within.

The journey of inner peace is the path to true freedom, freedom from the tyranny of others' opinions, freedom from the shackles of materialism, and freedom to live fully as our true selves.

LIVE AND LET LIVE

When we allow others to speak freely without judgment, we are not merely showing tolerance, but affirming one of the most fundamental principles of human dignity: that every individual has the right to their own opinions and perspectives.

This act of open-mindedness is crucial, as it creates a space where all individuals can voice their thoughts, share their beliefs, and express their experiences without fear of rejection or hostility.

It is only when we accept that others are entitled to their own viewpoints, whether we agree with them or not, that we pave the way for true, meaningful communication.

The more we practice this openness, the more we build an environment that encourages the free flow of ideas, creating a foundation where everyone feels heard and valued, regardless of how different their opinions may be from our own.

By nurturing this kind of open space, we create an atmosphere where dialogue can thrive and where mutual respect becomes the cornerstone of all interactions.

In this environment, the act of respecting differing viewpoints is not just a passive tolerance, it is a conscious choice to foster understanding and coexistence.

True peace and harmony arise when we are able to see that another person's knowledge, or ignorance, is not something that directly affects us or threatens our beliefs.

Their perspective, whether well-informed or misguided, is theirs to carry, and it does not have the power to define us or dictate the course of our lives.

It is when we internalize this truth, acknowledging that others are entitled to their beliefs as we are to ours, that we are freed from the overwhelming need to correct, control, or be affected by every opinion we encounter.

This ability to detach from the weight of others' thoughts gives us the freedom to continue our own journey of growth and self-expression without constantly feeling the need to engage in every debate or argument.

Living by the principle of "live and let live" is one of the most effective ways to achieve lasting peace.

This principle does not ask us to accept or adopt every perspective or belief, nor does it require us to agree with every opinion that comes our way.

Instead, it calls upon us to respect the fundamental right of each individual to think as they choose.

This kind of respect does not mean we remain silent in the face of harm or injustice, but rather that we acknowledge the value of differing perspectives and allow others the space to grow in their own time, just as we grow in ours.

When we embrace this mindset, it becomes much easier to avoid unnecessary conflict and to foster an environment where meaningful discussions can take place.

These discussions, even when they involve opposing viewpoints, can be productive and enlightening, because they are grounded in mutual respect and understanding.

Moreover, the freedom we extend to others, the freedom to hold their own beliefs, make their own decisions, and live their lives according to their own values, is the same freedom we create for ourselves.

By upholding the principles of open dialogue and mutual respect, we not only empower others to live authentically but also secure the space for ourselves to do the same.

In this way, we are not sacrificing our personal beliefs or integrity, but instead ensuring that the diversity of thought in the world enriches us all.

As we create an atmosphere of respect and free expression, we are laying the groundwork for a society where differences no longer lead to division, but rather to a deeper understanding of one another's experiences, backgrounds, and beliefs.

It is through this deep understanding, fueled by empathy and open communication, that we can create a true sense of unity among people, even in the face of profound differences.

This is the path to peace that does not require uniformity but thrives in the richness of diversity, the recognition that we are all interconnected in our shared humanity.

It is through embracing this understanding that we build the foundation for a world where peace is not just an ideal, but a tangible reality.

TRUMP

At first glance, I find Trump to be an immensely frustrating figure.

His presence, both in the media and in the political sphere, feels overwhelming and at times unbearable.

He appears to be completely self-absorbed, almost entirely focused on his own interests, while showing little regard for the lives and opinions of others.

His ego is vast, and his decisions often seem motivated by nothing more than a desire for personal gain or validation.

What's particularly striking is his arrogance, a conviction in his own superiority that is coupled with a lack of intellectual depth.

This is a man who frequently showcases an alarming disregard for facts, truth, and the consequences of his actions.

Despite this, there is something undeniably compelling about him.

His self-assurance is unshakable, and this raw confidence often manifests as an almost magnetic energy.

Trump exudes a sense of power that is difficult to ignore, an aura that demands attention.

This power, though flawed in its origin and execution, gives him an extraordinary level of influence, not just in America, but across the globe.

He's a figure that can both inspire passionate loyalty and generate intense opposition.

His ability to control narratives, dominate public discourse, and wield political influence is remarkable.

His sheer audacity, though repulsive to many, commands a level of attention and focus that few others can ever hope to achieve.

This unique form of power, which stems largely from his unshakable belief in his own abilities, allows him to affect change in ways that seem both radical and impossible.

One of the most striking elements of his leadership is his willingness to disregard conventional wisdom and challenge long-standing norms, especially those related to America's global dominance.

His actions, often viewed as reckless or even dangerous, have the potential to undermine the very foundation of American power and influence.

This, in itself, is an unsettling thought.

For someone like Trump, whose policies often seem erratic and self-serving, to have the power to potentially dismantle a centuries-old hegemonic system is both unnerving and awe-inspiring.

On the surface, this all seems chaotic.

His leadership style is far from traditional.

Instead of measured diplomacy and calculated decision-making,

Trump thrives in environments of chaos, making decisions that creates more problems than they solve.

His approach to foreign policy, particularly in the Middle East, has resulted in considerable upheaval.

His tendency to provoke conflicts, often through provocative rhetoric or rash policy moves, generates instability rather than fostering resolution.

These are not isolated instances, the consequences of his actions ripple across the globe, and often in unpredictable ways.

There is no denying the turbulence that follows his every move.

Yet, despite the constant volatility and upheaval, I have come to see that, in a broader sense, his actions may serve to break down a system that has been in place for far too long.

While the disruption he causes is seen as a negative by many, it also has the potential to undermine the deeply entrenched hegemonic structures that have governed the world for decades.

America's dominance on the global stage, though once considered a force for stability and progress, has also been the source of many injustices, conflicts, and imbalances.

Trump's leadership, though erratic, may be serving to disrupt this unbalanced system in ways that no one else could.

He is pushing against the status quo, breaking down the empire of influence that has kept global power structures in a stranglehold.

Of course, this process is far from smooth, and the chaos that results from his actions cannot be ignored.

The volatility he introduces into the system is palpable, and many have suffered as a result of his policies.

Yet, in the midst of the instability, I can see that there is a certain kind of shift taking place, one that may ultimately lead to a more equitable reordering of global power.

As destabilizing as his actions may seem, they are forcing conversations and shifts in perspectives that could have long-term, positive implications.

While I cannot deny my personal distaste for him, I have come to recognize that Trump is playing a role in shaping the future, albeit in a way that is uncomfortable and difficult to accept at times.

His actions are not without harm, but they are also not without purpose.

Whether by accident or design, he is challenging the power structures that have defined the global order for generations.

This type of disruption, though messy and often damaging, could be the catalyst for a new era of global relations, one in which the status quo is no longer accepted without question.

Perhaps, in the long run, his impact will be viewed as a necessary turning point in history, one that reshapes the future of nations and global cooperation in ways we can hardly imagine now.

While his style may not be one of diplomacy or caution, it is undeniably reshaping the world, and that, in itself, holds tremendous power.

SELF-DISCOVERY

Self-discovery is one of the most powerful and essential processes of personal growth, yet it requires dedication, effort, and a willingness to question everything.

Never simply take the words of another person as absolute truth without taking the time to investigate for yourself.

When you blindly accept what others say, without critical thought or independent verification, you risk falling into the traps of misunderstanding, manipulation, and deception.

The reality is that truth cannot be passively absorbed from others, it must be actively sought out, questioned, and understood on your own terms.

Blind belief in others' statements, however convincing they may sound, is a shortcut to ignorance.

While it is easier to accept the words of those we trust or admire, such unquestioning faith can create an illusion of knowledge, leaving us vulnerable to misinformation.

True wisdom is not achieved by simply adopting the perspectives of others without scrutiny, it comes from doing the hard work of forming our own opinions based on personal research, observation, and critical thinking.

The search for truth is an individual journey, and only when you take the time to examine the facts independently can you form an opinion that is genuinely informed and objective.

If you fail to seek the truth on your own, your understanding will inevitably be shaped by the biases, preferences, and influences of others.

This leads to a distorted version of reality, one that is based on personal attachments or ideologies rather than factual, unbiased information.

Beliefs built on assumptions, half-truths, or incomplete understandings can easily become false convictions that feel accurate because they align with preconceived notions.

But this kind of belief lacks true substance and understanding. Without verification, what you think you know could very well be a misconception that has been unknowingly reinforced by others or by your own biases.

True objectivity, then, requires much more than just hearing or reading information, it demands that you question everything.

Don't accept statements at face value, especially those that confirm your existing beliefs.

Ask yourself: How do I know this is true?

What evidence supports this claim?

Is there another perspective that challenges what I am being told?

By constantly questioning and critically evaluating the information you encounter, you ensure that your understanding of the world remains grounded in reality, not in assumptions or unfounded beliefs.

What I share with you in this moment is only true when you decide it is true for yourself.

I offer my perspective as a guide, a catalyst for your thinking, not as a truth to be blindly adopted.

I cannot force truth upon you, you must arrive at it on your own, through your own investigation and introspection.

My words are simply the starting point, but the real value lies in your ability to analyze them, reflect on them, and, ultimately, determine their authenticity through your own reasoning and experiences.

This is why it is crucial to approach knowledge with an open but questioning mind.

When you read or hear something, do not simply accept it because it comes from an authoritative source or because it fits into your existing worldview.

Allow yourself to question, to wonder, to seek answers.

True understanding and clarity come from challenging what you are told and forming your own conclusions, based on evidence and thoughtful reflection.

Trusting your intuition and reasoning can often guide you toward truth in a way that simply accepting others' opinions never will.

Therefore, as you navigate the world and seek knowledge, always approach it with a healthy skepticism and a genuine desire for understanding.

Do not let external influences, whether they are from other people, institutions, or societal norms, dictate how you see the world.

True comprehension of reality, and the ability to discern what is true, comes only through personal investigation and self-discovery.

This journey may not always be easy, but it is the only way to uncover the truth and to live a life rooted in true knowledge, not illusion.

AT PEACE

I am at peace, so deeply and profoundly at peace that the very fabric of existence seems to hum with harmony.

Everywhere I turn, in every corner of life, there is beauty, not because the world is without suffering, but because I no longer seek to resist what is.

My heart beats in quiet rhythm with the universe, and my mind rests in a place untouched by fear.

Chaos may rise like a storm on the horizon, and sorrow may weave its threads into the tapestry of life, but I remain steady.

I witness the struggles of the world not with detachment, but with understanding.

I do not deny pain, nor do I shy away from the reality of hardship, yet neither do I allow them to shape my essence.

They are but waves upon an endless ocean, fleeting and ever-changing, while I remain the stillness beneath.

This peace I carry is not a fragile thing, not something that crumbles under pressure or fades in the face of adversity.

It does not depend on the world's stillness or the absence of conflict.

It is not a fragile glass that shatters upon impact, but a light that burns unwaveringly, no matter the winds that seek to extinguish it.

Even amid suffering, I find meaning.

Even where disorder seems to reign, I perceive an intricate order at play.

Life is not a chaotic mess, nor is it a series of random misfortunes, it is a masterpiece, a grand symphony composed of both gentle melodies and thunderous crescendos.

I see now that every note, even those filled with sorrow, is part of something greater, something vast and incomprehensible yet deeply purposeful.

I do not seek to control what is beyond my grasp, nor do I hold tightly to things meant to pass. I release, I surrender, and in doing so, I find freedom.

I do not resist the tides of existence, for I understand that resistance only brings suffering.

Instead, I allow life to move through me, knowing that nothing truly belongs to me, except for this peace within.

This peace is not an escape, not a retreat from the world's troubles, but a way of seeing, a way of being.

It is a quiet strength that allows me to stand firm where others might falter.

It does not mean I am untouched by the world, it means I can move through it with grace.

Because I have cultivated stillness within, my outer world reflects that serenity. Where once I saw obstacles, I now see opportunities for growth.

Where once I felt separation, I now sense unity.

Situations that once frustrated me now teach me patience.

People who once seemed distant now appear as reflections of myself, fellow travelers on this journey of existence.

The burdens that once weighed me down no longer cling to me, for I have learned to let go, to trust in the flow of life.

I walk forward with open hands, with an open heart, knowing that true peace is not found in a perfect world, but in the way I choose to move through it.

This peace is not given by the world, and so it cannot be taken away.

It is mine, forever, within me.

EXTERNAL TURMOIL

The world outside may be filled with noise and chaos, but it does not have to define your reality.

The constant distractions, conflicts, and uncertainties of the external world can only affect you if you allow them to.

It is easy to be swept up in the turbulence of current events, social pressures, and the expectations of others, but none of these things truly determine your inner peace.

You have the ability to remain centered, regardless of what happens around you.

What truly matters is the world within you, the thoughts, emotions, and inner state that shape your experience.

Your mind is your most sacred space, a place where you hold the power to cultivate peace or invite chaos.

If you allow outside influences to control your emotions, your inner world will always be at the mercy of something beyond your control.

But when you take charge of your thoughts and emotions, you free yourself from the grip of external turmoil.

By nurturing inner balance, you ensure that your sense of peace is not dependent on fleeting circumstances.

The madness of society has nothing to do with your personal peace unless you allow it to.

Every day, the world presents new challenges, crises, and distractions, but none of them are inherently yours to carry.

You are not obligated to absorb its anxieties or be swept away by its distractions.

Many people spend their lives reacting to the chaos around them, believing that their well-being is dictated by the state of the world.

But in reality, peace is an internal choice, not something granted or taken away by external events.

By turning your focus inward, you cultivate clarity and resilience, allowing you to move through life with steadiness and purpose.

Your well-being is in your hands, not in the hands of the outside world.

Achieving inner peace is not a passive state but an intentional practice.

It requires self-awareness, discipline, and the ability to let go of negativity.

It means being mindful of what you allow into your mental and emotional space and making conscious choices to protect your peace.

When you develop control over your thoughts and emotions, you create a life that is not dictated by external circumstances.

Peace becomes your foundation, guiding your actions and decisions with wisdom and calm.

You become the master of your own existence, free from the influence of external turmoil.

This power exists within every human being.

It is not an exclusive gift but an inherent potential that can be awakened and strengthened.

Some people go through life believing that peace is something they must chase, always just out of reach.

But in reality, it has always been within them, waiting to be recognized and cultivated.

When you choose inner peace, it transforms not only your own life but also the way you interact with the world.

A peaceful mind fosters compassionate actions, clear decisions, and a deep sense of fulfillment.

In the end, the world inside you is the one that truly shapes your reality.

No matter what storms rage outside, your inner world remains your sanctuary.

NEVER WISE

It is never wise to argue with the police about your rights, no matter how justified you may feel.

When confronted by law enforcement, the safest course of action is to comply with their instructions and move on with your day.

The reality is that arguing or resisting, even in a non-violent way, can quickly escalate a situation into something far more dangerous.

This is especially true in a world where power dynamics heavily favor those in uniform, who are trained to assert authority with force if necessary.

While it may feel unjust to submit to demands that violate your dignity or rights, the consequences of defiance can be severe, often with little recourse for justice.

For people of color, this reality is even more pronounced.

History and modern events alike have repeatedly shown that racial biases within law enforcement increase the likelihood of aggressive or even deadly encounters.

In many cases, compliance does not even guarantee safety, but resistance almost certainly increases the risk.

It is essential to recognize that the legal system is not designed to offer immediate protection in the heat of the moment.

The best chance of survival often lies in de-escalation, avoidance, or making it through the encounter with as little conflict as possible.

No principle is worth dying for in a situation where the odds are so overwhelmingly stacked against you.

Protect your life by any means necessarry.

Beyond systemic bias, there is a deeper, more unsettling truth about Earth humans that must not be ignored.

The people of this planet were genetically modified in ancient times to be killers, engineered for war, conquest, and domination.

This modification is deeply embedded in their nature, shaping not only their societies but also their institutions, including law enforcement.

Those who wield power, especially through armed authority, are often conditioned to respond to perceived threats with lethal force.

The presence of guns, reinforced by a system that grants officers the legal right to use them with impunity, makes every encounter a potential life-or-death situation.

Given these circumstances, survival should always be the priority.

If an interaction with the police turns violent, the only hope for accountability lies in documentation, video evidence that can expose misconduct.

However, even when incidents are recorded, justice is not always served, as history has demonstrated time and time again.

The goal should not be to prove a point in the moment but to live another day.

There are other ways to challenge injustice, but they can only be pursued by those who are still alive to fight.

THE CLASSROOM

Life is a continuous learning experience, much like a vast and ever-evolving classroom where we are both students and teachers.

Every moment, interaction, and challenge presents an opportunity to grow, adapt, and understand the world more deeply.

Just as students in a school encounter different subjects and teachers, we come across diverse experiences and individuals who shape our perspectives and knowledge.

No matter how old we get, the lessons never truly end, for our journey of learning extends beyond a single lifetime.

Life does not unfold randomly but follows a natural course of cause and effect, providing us with experiences that are necessary for our evolution.

Every situation, whether perceived as pleasant or difficult, serves as a teacher, guiding us toward greater awareness and wisdom.

Some lessons come easily, like understanding kindness through a simple act of generosity, while others are difficult, requiring patience, resilience, and even pain.

Failures, disappointments, and hardships are not setbacks but rather necessary teachings that push us toward wisdom and self-improvement.

Just as a student must sometimes fail a test to realize where they need to focus, life's struggles guide us toward deeper self-awareness and better decision-making.

Every challenge, no matter how painful, is an opportunity for growth and transformation.

The cycle of physical life itself spans between 40 and 60 million years, during which the human being continuously reincarnates, evolving through countless experiences and challenges.

Each lifetime serves as another lesson, another opportunity to refine our understanding and elevate our consciousness.

There is no wasted time, no meaningless struggle, everything we experience has a purpose in the grand scheme of existence.

Moreover, life does not always provide direct answers.

Some lessons are subtle, unfolding over time, requiring introspection and experience to fully grasp their meaning.

We might not immediately understand why certain events occur, but with time, reflection, and growth, the lessons become clearer.

The more we expand our awareness, the more we see that there is truly no good or bad, everything simply is.

What we perceive as positive or negative is merely a matter of perspective, shaped by our level of understanding.

What seems like misfortune in one moment may later reveal itself as a necessary step toward a greater realization.

As we evolve, we begin to recognize that events are neither rewards nor punishments but simply the unfolding of natural laws that help us progress.

Every encounter, success, and misstep contributes to our personal development, shaping the people we become.

This evolutionary journey continues until the human being reaches 100% brain quotient, at which point the need for physical reincarnation ceases, and existence transitions into a purely spiritual state.

At this stage, the lessons of material existence are complete, and consciousness moves into a higher form of being, where learning continues on a purely energetic level.

Ultimately, our Creation Energy is eternal, carrying forward the wisdom and knowledge accumulated over countless lifetimes.

While the physical body is temporary, the consciousness continues to develop, forever seeking higher understanding.

Embracing life as a classroom allows us to approach challenges with curiosity rather than fear.

Instead of resisting difficulties, we can see them as necessary steps in our journey of learning and transformation.

No single experience is wasted when viewed through the lens of growth, and the more we remain open to learning, the more meaningful and enriched our existence becomes.

By understanding that all things happen for the sake of evolution, we can cultivate inner peace and acceptance, knowing that we are always in the process of becoming more aware, more knowing, and more aligned with the truth of existence.

Life is not about seeking perfection but about experiencing, learning, and ultimately returning to the source of all knowledge, where we become one with the eternal flow of Creation.

MY PERSPECTIVE

I do not share what I know with the intention of changing people's minds.

Instead, I share my truth to offer my perspective,

allowing others to consider it without feeling pressured to agree.

My knowledge is not formed lightly.

Before I accept something as true, I investigate it thoroughly, analyze its details, and weigh the evidence with an open yet critical mind.

Only when I am certain of its validity do I adopt it as part of my understanding.

My goal is not to impose my conclusions on others but to inspire independent thought, encouraging people to think for themselves rather than blindly accepting information from any source, including me.

Everything I post is the truth only to myself.

No one should ever accept my perspective, or anyone else's, without first doing their own research and critical analysis.

It is essential for each person to explore, question, and verify information for themselves, as truth is not something that should be taken at face value.

If, after a thorough investigation, someone determines that my perspective is incorrect, then so be it.

That is the nature of intellectual inquiry.

We are not meant to agree on everything, and differences in understanding should not be a source of hostility or division.

Instead, these differences should serve as opportunities for meaningful and respectful discussion, where ideas are exchanged freely, and growth can occur on both sides.

We all come from different backgrounds, experiences, and ways of thinking, which naturally leads to different perspectives on various issues.

This diversity of thought should be embraced rather than seen as a threat.

I have never understood why some people feel the need to force others to see things exactly as they do, as if uniformity of thought is the only acceptable way to exist.

The beauty of open dialogue is that it allows people to learn from one another, to see things from angles they might not have considered, and to refine their own understanding.

Even when disagreements arise, they do not have to lead to animosity because there is always room for respectful discourse.

At the core of all discussions and differing perspectives, however, lies one fundamental truth and one objective reality.

No matter how many opinions exist, the truth itself does not change.

Truly, it remains what it is, whether people recognize it or not.

The challenge for each individual is to seek out this truth through their own exploration, reasoning, and experience rather than accepting or rejecting viewpoints blindly.

In a world where misinformation and bias often cloud perception, the responsibility to uncover and understand reality falls on each of us, not by coercion but through genuine curiosity and thoughtful investigation.

WHY WE DON'T REMEMBER PAST LIVES - A DEEPER LOOK

Imagine being born into a life where you once lived in wealth, surrounded by comfort, only to find yourself in the next struggling to make ends meet.

If you carried full awareness of that previous existence, it would be nearly impossible to live your new life properly.

The memories of past experiences, relationships, and hardships would constantly interfere, preventing you from fully engaging in the present.

The human consciousness is designed to focus on one lifetime at a time.

If we retained all memories from our past incarnations, we would be overwhelmed by an endless stream of emotions, experiences, and attachments.

The mind, as it currently exists, is not developed enough to process multiple lifetimes while still evolving within the present one.

However, some individuals, particularly children, may recall fragments of past lives.

This usually happens due to an incomplete restructuring of the new material consciousness, linked to the rapid cycle of rebirth caused by overpopulation.

Yet, as these children grow, such memories naturally fade away, allowing them to focus on their new existence without the weight of their previous selves.

Until we reach a higher spiritual level, like Billy has, we are unable to access our past lives consciously.

Anyone who claims otherwise is either indulging in wishful thinking or deliberately lying.

Spiritual evolution is necessary before one can process and integrate such knowledge without it disrupting their current experience.

Each life is a fresh opportunity for growth, learning, and development, and retaining past-life memories would hinder that process.

Every new incarnation is a clean slate, offering a new personality, new circumstances, and new relationships.

While the essence of who you are, your Creation Energy/spirit remains eternal, the person you become in each life is different.

You step into a new role, a new character, with different challenges and opportunities to evolve further.

This cycle ensures that every life serves its purpose.

It allows us to grow without being burdened by past mistakes or successes.

And in the grand scheme of existence, this forgetting is not a loss, but a necessary aspect of eternal evolution.

Everyone you've ever loved and all the wisdom and knowledge you've gained in past lives remain within you forever.

OTHER'S ACTIONS

Since coming to the understanding that a person's actions are simply a reflection of their inner self, I've learned to stop taking others' behavior personally.

This shift in perspective has been truly transformative.

I no longer internalize what others do or say, recognizing instead that their actions stem from a complex blend of their thoughts, emotions, and internal struggles, all shaped by their individual life experiences.

Each person is, in essence, a product of their own reality, influenced by their past, their fears, and their unspoken needs.

Therefore, when they act in ways that are unkind or irrational, it's not a reflection of me or my worth, it is merely a projection of their inner world.

This realization has empowered me to detach from the negativity of others and avoid carrying emotional burdens that were never mine to bear.

Rather than reacting with frustration or hurt, I've learned to observe situations from a place of understanding, without judgment.

When someone expresses anger or behaves irrationally, I remind myself that their actions come from their own unresolved emotions and struggles, and not from any fault of mine.

I realize that their actions are more about them than about me, and this has brought me a deep sense of peace.

This shift in mindset has helped me cultivate emotional resilience and approach life's challenges with greater clarity.

I no longer feel overwhelmed by the emotional turbulence of others.

Instead of letting their negativity affect me, I approach every situation with a calm, patient, and compassionate mindset.

I can navigate conflicts with a level-headed approach, understanding that often, people's words and actions are more about their own inner turmoil than they are about me.

As a result, I've fostered healthier, more positive relationships.

I'm no longer weighed down by unnecessary stress or resentment, and I've learned to maintain my emotional well-being, no matter what others might be going through.

This profound understanding has allowed me to engage with life and people in a more balanced way, embracing both the good and the difficult moments with an open heart and a clear mind.

In the end, this realization that everyone's behavior is a reflection of their inner world has been an essential part of my personal growth.

It has freed me from the burden of taking things personally and has allowed me to approach others with empathy and kindness.

Through this, I've learned to live more peacefully and authentically, embracing life's challenges with a resilient spirit.

WORRY

I have no worries because I understand that my existence is not confined to the present moment.

I am not bound by the uncertainty that troubles so many, for I see beyond the now.

The future is not an unknown abyss, nor is it a void filled with fear or doubt.

It is simply an extension of my being, a continuation of what already is.

There is no need to be afraid of what lies ahead, for I know that I persist beyond today.

My awareness does not fade with time but expands, stretching forward into the moments yet to come.

This realization liberates me from the anxieties that often weigh heavily upon others, allowing me to walk through life unburdened.

The passage of time does not diminish me, nor does it pose a threat.

Rather, it affirms my presence, reinforcing the truth that I exist beyond the constraints of a single moment.

Time moves forward, and so do I, without fear of ceasing to be.

This understanding provides an unwavering sense of peace, a foundation upon which I stand with certainty.

Because I know that I exist in the future, I am free to embrace the present fully.

There is no reason to dwell on worry, no need to agonize over uncertainties, for I am already secure in my continued existence.

This knowledge grants me the courage to step forward without hesitation, to experience each moment without the weight of doubt.

The absence of worry is not mere optimism but a reflection of a deeper truth.

It stems from the understanding that I am not a fleeting presence, here one moment and gone the next, but a continuous thread woven through time.

My essence does not wane with the ticking of the clock.

Rather, it stretches onward, unbroken and enduring.

With this certainty, I can move freely, unshackled by fear.

I am not lost in the unknown, for I already exist within it.

My journey does not end simply because time moves forward.

It is a journey that persists, flowing naturally from one moment to the next.

And so, I do not worry.

I live.

THE TEACHINGS

In the vast universe of Creation's Energy Teachings, a profound journey awaits those who seek deeper meaning and understanding.

This path is not one of passive observation but of active engagement, requiring a sincere willingness to explore the depths of wisdom and truth.

By embracing its principles with wholehearted trust, individuals open themselves to new possibilities, allowing their perspectives to shift in ways they may never have imagined.

The teachings serve as a guiding force, offering recommendations that, when followed with sincerity, lead to profound personal transformation.

These insights illuminate the interconnectedness of all things, revealing that life is not a series of random events but a tapestry woven with intention and purpose.

As one delves deeper into this wisdom, an inner metamorphosis begins to unfold, reshaping both thought and action.

This transformation is not forced but rather a natural consequence of absorbing the teachings and applying them in daily life.

Gradually, one becomes attuned to the subtle forces at play in the universe, recognizing patterns and synchronicities that once seemed insignificant.

Events begin to align in ways that feel almost predestined, as if an unseen hand is gently guiding the way.

Miracles, once considered rare and extraordinary, become more frequent, not as supernatural occurrences but as the inevitable result of a life lived in harmony with Creation's laws.

These moments serve as reminders that the universe is alive with intelligence and purpose, always responding to the energy we cultivate within ourselves.

Within this realm of infinite possibilities, awe and wonder emerge at every turn, deepening one's appreciation for the beauty and complexity of existence.

The world, once viewed through the limited lens of material concerns, expands into a vast and intricate masterpiece of interconnected forces.

Nature's rhythms become more pronounced, the movements of the stars more meaningful, and the whispers of intuition more profound.

Dreams, once considered mere fantasies, gain substance and direction, as if the barriers between thought and reality begin to dissolve.

With each revelation, a deeper sense of connection to the universe takes hold, filling the heart with gratitude and the mind with boundless curiosity.

This newfound awareness is not fleeting but enduring, shaping one's understanding of self, purpose, and the greater cosmic order.

At its core, the Creation's Teachings cultivate trust, respect, and an unwavering commitment to truth, serving as the foundation for strong and meaningful relationships.

These principles encourage individuals to engage with others in a spirit of understanding and mutual growth, fostering harmony in all interactions.

By aligning with these teachings, one learns the value of patience, compassion, and integrity, recognizing that true strength lies not in dominance but in wisdom and balance.

Through this lens, relationships are no longer viewed as mere social constructs but as sacred connections that reflect the universal laws of giving and receiving.

In embracing this wisdom, one discovers a world where life is not dictated by chaos or blind fate but by conscious choice and spiritual alignment, illuminating the path toward a future filled with purpose, fulfillment, and peace.

CREATION

Since the dawn of time's first breath, Creation has shaped the universe with sacred intention, giving form to the boundless potential of existence.

It is within this grand cosmic design that the first pure spirits emerged, untouched by the confines of mortality, imbued with the essence of divine energy.

These spirits, unburdened by decay or limitation, became the architects of evolution, igniting the eternal dance of growth and transformation.

Through their presence, the fabric of reality was woven, expanding outward in infinite directions, each thread a manifestation of wisdom and purpose.

The ever-evolving nature of Creation is not chaotic but guided, its principles embedded within the very essence of existence, ensuring that all things move in harmony with the sacred order of the cosmos.

These spirits, existing in collectives both conscious and aware, intertwine their energies to form a vast and luminous network of knowledge.

Their unity is not enforced but arises naturally through the profound understanding that all existence is interconnected.

Bound by love, they radiate wisdom, illuminating the path for those who seek deeper truths.

In their brilliance, individuality does not diminish but flourishes, each spirit contributing its unique essence to the greater whole.

Together, they form a symphony of light, guiding the unfolding journey of all that follows.

The wisdom they share is not kept in secrecy but flows freely, an eternal current that nourishes all who are receptive to its truth.

As this divine radiance spreads, it reminds all beings that separation is but an illusion and that at the heart of Creation lies unity, an unbreakable bond that connects all things.

From the depths of their shared wisdom, new life continuously arises, each impulse drawn from the reservoir of knowledge that governs Creation.

Nothing is left to chance, for within the fabric of existence, an inherent order prevails.

Each soul that emerges carries within it a seed of this divine understanding, a spark that yearns to grow and evolve.

As these creation energy embark upon their journey, they encounter challenges, lessons, and experiences designed to refine their awareness.

Knowledge, pure and unwavering, acts as both a compass and a guide, ensuring that every being, in its own time, comes to recognize its place within the grand orchestration of the universe.

It is within this unfolding process that purpose is revealed, allowing each soul to contribute to the ever-expanding cycle of creation.

The lower realms, where consciousness is still maturing, reach out toward the luminous sparks of wisdom sent forth by these higher beings.

The yearning for enlightenment is an eternal force, pulling all creation energy toward greater understanding.

Love, the guiding principle of Creation, nurtures this ascent, offering strength and clarity to those who seek the light.

In this sacred interplay, the cycle of growth continues unbroken, lifting all toward higher planes of existence.

The convergence of paths, once thought separate, reveals the intricate unity that underlies all things.

Through this divine unfolding, Creation flourishes endlessly, ensuring that all who seek wisdom shall find it, and that evolution remains the guiding force in the infinite journey of existence.

LIFE AND DEATH

Life is an unbroken continuum, vast and eternal, flowing through all forms of existence with unwavering persistence.

It is not limited to a single moment, a single form, or even a single lifetime, but instead moves fluidly through all that is, was, and will be.

This force, the very essence of Creation, pulses within every living being, sustaining and animating the infinite expressions of existence.

It is a rhythm that beats in harmony with the universe, connecting all things, seen and unseen, known and unknown.

Every heartbeat, every breath, every unfolding leaf is a manifestation of this vital energy, a testament to the unity that underlies all of Creation.

To be alive is to participate in this great unfolding, to exist as a thread in the ever-expanding tapestry of being.

Life is a force that does not waver. It finds a way to continue, adapt, and evolve, never truly extinguished but only transformed.

From human to beast, from plant to tree, all forms of life share a common essence, bound together in an intricate web of harmony.

The rivers that carve through the land, the winds that shape the mountains, and the creatures that roam the earth all move to the same fundamental rhythm, an unspoken yet undeniable connection.

This unity is not accidental but essential, for life is not a solitary phenomenon, it thrives in interdependence.

Nature's symphony plays on, each element a necessary note in the grand orchestration of existence.

Every being contributes to this balance, whether by giving, receiving, growing, or decaying.

The smallest seedling and the mightiest oak share in the same life force, just as the simplest organism and the most complex sentient being are linked by the same fundamental energy.

In this cycle, nothing is wasted.

Every fallen leaf nourishes the soil, every breath of air once exhaled is drawn in again, and every life supports another, weaving an unbreakable chain of existence.

Life is not only a gift but a responsibility, a force to be nurtured and respected.

It flourishes in places both expected and unexpected, taking root in the deepest oceans, the highest mountains, and even in the vast emptiness of space.

The power of creation is boundless, bringing forth new forms and new possibilities with every passing moment.

It is in the laughter of a child, the quiet wisdom of the aged, the intricate patterns of a butterfly's wing, and the strength of a roaring waterfall.

Every living thing, from the simplest microbe to the most advanced civilizations, is a reflection of the same universal energy.

To honor life is to honor Creation itself, to recognize that every being plays a role in the grand design, and that existence is a sacred and interconnected journey.

Death, often seen as the final silence, is in truth another form of movement, a shift in the eternal cycle rather than an abrupt ending.

It does not sever the connection between beings but instead transforms it, allowing energy to take on new shapes and new purposes.

Just as the sun must set for the moon to rise, death follows life not as an adversary, but as a companion.

It is the unseen force that clears the way for new beginnings, the silent architect of renewal.

Nothing in the universe is truly lost, what appears to fade merely takes on another form, finding expression in another time, another place.

Understanding death as a transition rather than a conclusion reveals the deeper order of existence, one in which endings are merely thresholds to greater continuities.

The physical form may decay, but the essence of existence persists, moving into new realms, new dimensions, and new experiences.

This cycle is evident in all things, from the changing of seasons to the ebb and flow of the tides.

The autumn leaves fall not in despair but in preparation for new growth.

The caterpillar disappears into its cocoon, not to die, but to be reborn as a butterfly.

Even the stars themselves are subject to this eternal rhythm, burning brightly for eons before collapsing, only to give birth to new celestial bodies.

Death is not destruction but transformation, the passage through which energy shifts and renews.

It is the threshold through which life is reborn, ensuring that nothing truly ends but instead continues in another form.

The wisdom of the universe is woven into this understanding, teaching that no farewell is permanent, and no loss is absolute.

Together, life and death form the twin forces that shape the fabric of reality, two sides of the same eternal truth.

They are not opposites but complements, working in unison to maintain the ever-flowing current of existence.

To fear one is to misunderstand the other, for each is essential to the great design.

Life, birth, is enriched by the knowledge of its impermanence, and death, far from being a loss, is a return to the source, a renewal of energy, a continuation of the cosmic dance.

To embrace both is to accept the fullness of existence, to walk in harmony with the rhythm of Creation, and to understand that in every ending, a beginning waits, and in every farewell, the promise of renewal resides.

The journey of existence is one of endless transformation, a cycle that neither begins nor ends but simply flows.

Every creation energy that walks this path will one day shed its current form, only to step into another, continuing the journey in ways yet unseen.

This understanding brings not sorrow, but peace, for it reveals that no being is ever truly lost.

Life and death are not separate, but one continuous expression of the universe's will.

In this eternal flow, all things are connected, and the energy that sustains life continues, always and forever.

THE POWER OF IGNORING

Mastering the art of ignoring is an essential skill in navigating the complexities of modern life.

With endless distractions vying for our attention, the ability to focus on what truly matters becomes a powerful tool for clarity and peace.

Not every comment, notification, or fleeting thought deserves our energy, and learning to discern between what is valuable and what is noise allows us to move forward with purpose.

When we refine our focus, we sharpen our minds, enabling us to rise above trivial concerns and embrace a life of greater ease and intention.

In a world where reactions are often immediate and unfiltered, cultivating the discipline to ignore what does not serve us is an act of self-mastery.

It grants us the space to think clearly, act wisely, and prioritize what truly contributes to our growth and well-being.

Selective attention acts as a guiding light, helping us navigate the many challenges we encounter.

In a world flooded with information, choosing where to direct our thoughts is a form of self-care.

Rather than reacting to every stimulus, we gain strength in knowing when to engage and when to let go.

Amidst the chaos of thoughts, emotions, and opinions, the ability to sift through and prioritize what truly serves us enhances our well-being.

By consciously choosing our battles and preserving our mental energy, we cultivate resilience and inner balance.

The modern age bombards us with opinions, criticisms, and distractions at an overwhelming rate.

Learning to detach from negativity, to ignore unnecessary conflicts, and to focus on what nurtures our spirit is not avoidance, it is wisdom.

By filtering out what drains us, we create space for joy, creativity, and meaningful connections.

When frustration arises from words we see or hear, there is wisdom in simply letting go.

Not every opinion requires a response, and not every disagreement must lead to conflict.

Just as each snowflake is unique, so too are our minds, each shaped by individual experiences, perspectives, and values.

Accepting this diversity allows us to release unnecessary tension, understanding that differences are natural and inevitable.

By resisting the urge to be drawn into negativity, we empower ourselves to maintain emotional stability and cultivate a mindset rooted in understanding rather than frustration.

We do not need to prove ourselves to every critic, nor do we need to defend our choices against every opposing voice.

Instead, we can acknowledge differing views without allowing them to disturb our inner peace.

Silence, when used wisely, can be more powerful than words, creating an environment where personal growth can thrive.

Guarding our peace is an act of self-preservation, a conscious choice to nurture our well-being.

In a world that often demands reactions, the ability to step back and choose silence can be a profound source of strength.

Letting kindness lead our interactions and prioritizing inner harmony over external distractions fosters personal growth.

Life's journey is too precious to be weighed down by unnecessary burdens, and by embracing the wisdom of ignoring, we allow ourselves the freedom to focus on what truly enriches our souls.

Every moment we spend dwelling on negativity is a moment lost from the pursuit of joy, wisdom, and fulfillment.

By consciously choosing to ignore what does not align with our purpose, we reclaim our time and energy for the things that truly matter.

The practice of ignoring is not about indifference, it is about discernment.

It is about recognizing where our attention is best placed and making intentional choices that align with our higher purpose.

In doing so, we cultivate a life filled with greater clarity, peace, and purpose.

TRIBAL MENTALITY

We share the same planet, yet the challenge of living together in true harmony remains an ongoing struggle.

Despite the vast potential for unity, we continue to divide ourselves into countless categories, each with its own subdivisions, further fragmenting our societies.

These divisions are not just national or ideological.

They run deep into cultural, social, economic, and even familial structures.

One might assume that family ties, being among the most personal and intimate bonds, would remain unbreakable.

However, even within blood relations, misunderstandings, conflicts, and separations persist, revealing how deeply ingrained our tendencies toward division truly are.

Our perceived evolution as a species has brought about technological advancements and scientific breakthroughs, yet our mindset often remains stuck in patterns reminiscent of primitive societies.

In ancient times, small clans and tribes prioritized their own survival above all else, often at the expense of outsiders.

While we no longer live in isolated villages warring over resources in the same way, the underlying mentality remains.

Today, instead of physical tribal battles, we engage in ideological, economic, and political conflicts, reinforcing barriers between groups.

This division is evident in every aspect of modern life, from how nations interact on the global stage to the way individuals navigate workplace dynamics.

Even in professional environments where cooperation should be essential, personal interests, competition, and internal divisions create barriers to true collaboration and mutual growth.

What makes this issue even more pressing is our collective inability, or refusal to fully acknowledge it.

We often believe we have advanced far beyond the petty rivalries and narrow-minded thinking of our ancestors, yet our actions consistently prove otherwise.

Societies pride themselves on progress, yet discrimination, social inequality, and conflict persist across the world.

People speak of unity and cooperation, yet time and again, they act in ways that prioritize personal or group interests over the well-being of humanity as a whole.

True progress is not measured by technological innovation or economic success alone but by our ability to transcend division and embrace a higher level of consciousness, one that acknowledges our interconnectedness.

The truth is that peace will never truly prevail until we, as the people of Earth, evolve beyond our ingrained divisions and recognize our shared identity.

We must move past the illusion of separateness and embrace the reality that we are a single human family, bound together in a collective existence.

This shift requires not just a change in thought but a transformation in how we live, interact, and care for one another.

Only when we genuinely see ourselves as part of a We-form, a unified whole rather than fragmented groups, will we be able to create a world where harmony, mutual respect, and genuine peace are not just ideals, but realities.

And so is the truth.

RELENTLESS

Within every heart lies the potential for growth, a spark that fuels our journey of self-improvement.

This spark is what drives us to seek progress, to push beyond our current limitations, and to evolve into stronger, wiser beings.

Growth is not an effortless process.

It demands struggle, perseverance, and an openness to the lessons hidden within hardship.

Every challenge we face presents an opportunity to develop resilience, strengthen our resolve, and gain a deeper understanding of ourselves.

It is through these trials that our virtues are forged, not as mere inherited traits, but as carefully cultivated qualities built over time.

True character is not formed in moments of comfort but in the depths of adversity, where patience and endurance shape the person we become.

The path to self-improvement is neither simple nor linear, but it is the most rewarding journey one can embark upon, for it leads to an enriched life filled with purpose and wisdom.

With determination, we move forward, understanding that growth is not a destination but a continuous pursuit.

Each day presents new lessons, new perspectives, and new opportunities to refine our understanding of the world and ourselves.

Knowledge is not simply accumulated facts but the wisdom to apply what we have learned in meaningful ways.

To seek wisdom is to cultivate a mind that is ever-curious, ever-questioning, and ever-evolving.

The pursuit of knowledge is not confined to books or formal education, it is found in every interaction, every experience, and every reflection upon the past.

We learn not only from our triumphs but also from our mistakes, recognizing that failure is not the end but an essential part of growth.

It is through failure that we develop humility, for it reminds us that there is always more to learn, always more to understand.

In this pursuit, we must be relentless, never allowing setbacks to deter us from our ultimate goal: to become the best versions of ourselves.

Self-discipline serves as the cornerstone of lasting progress, the force that transforms ambition into action and potential into reality.

Without discipline, our aspirations remain mere wishes, floating in the realm of possibility without ever materializing into tangible achievements.

It is discipline that compels us to rise each day with intention, to remain steadfast in our commitments even when the path is difficult.

It is what keeps us grounded in moments of doubt, reminding us that greatness is not built in a single act but through consistent effort over time.

Discipline requires sacrifice, the ability to delay gratification, to remain patient, and to push through discomfort in the pursuit of something greater.

It is not an easy path, but it is the only path to true mastery and fulfillment.

To be disciplined is to take control of our lives, to recognize that we have the power to shape our future by the choices we make each day.

And in this realization, we find empowerment, for we come to understand that our growth is in our hands.

Let us be relentless in our pursuit of excellence, never allowing complacency to take root.

In a world full of distractions and fleeting ambitions, it is our unwavering commitment to self-betterment that defines who we are.

Every moment presents a choice: to remain stagnant or to take one more step toward growth.

The path is not always easy, nor is it always clear, but it is always worth walking.

Those who dare to embrace this journey with courage, patience, and determination will find themselves rewarded not only with success but with the deeper satisfaction of knowing they have lived with purpose.

Our legacy is not determined by a single accomplishment but by the continuous effort to refine our character, ensuring that our lives are guided by wisdom, integrity, and an unyielding commitment to becoming the best we can be.

It is through this relentless pursuit of growth that we honor the essence of our existence, proving that the human spirit is capable of boundless transformation.

Let us embrace this challenge wholeheartedly, for in doing so, we unlock the greatest potential within ourselves and leave behind a legacy of strength, wisdom, and perseverance.

FLAWED

Each person must face their own reflection with honesty, setting aside the illusion of a flawless world.

It is natural to long for perfection, to imagine a place where mistakes do not exist, where every choice is clear, and where we move effortlessly through life without error.

Yet, such dreams can lead us astray, trapping us in unrealistic expectations and preventing us from fully embracing the depth of our true experiences.

The pursuit of perfection often blinds us to the beauty of imperfection, the very thing that makes us human.

True understanding comes not from striving to be without flaw but from recognizing that our imperfections shape us.

They teach us resilience, patience, and wisdom, offering us a deeper connection to ourselves and to those around us.

Only when we embrace our reality, with all its strengths and shortcomings, can we begin to see ourselves clearly, not as we wish to be, but as we truly are.

No one walks through life in an unbroken beam of perfect light, with every path illuminated and free of obstacles.

Instead, we navigate a shifting landscape of challenges, doubts, and unforeseen turns.

Mistakes are not signs of failure, they are the stepping stones of growth, each one providing an opportunity to learn and evolve.

Without struggle, there is no progress, and without imperfection, there is no development.

It is through our stumbles that we refine our character, uncovering strengths we may not have known we possessed.

The discomfort of failure forces us to examine ourselves, to ask difficult questions, and to make meaningful changes.

True wisdom does not come from avoiding difficulties but from facing them with courage and humility, knowing that each misstep holds the potential for transformation.

Growth is not a linear path but a winding journey, one that requires patience and self-compassion as we continue to evolve.

Our imperfections do not set us apart.

Rather, they bind us together, forming the fabric of our shared humanity.

Each person walks a unique road, yet no one is exempt from hardship, doubt, or the longing for understanding.

The greatest bonds between people are not formed in perfection but in the recognition that we all face struggles.

No journey is superior to another, for every experience carries its own meaning and lessons.

When we understand this, we foster empathy, seeing in others the same struggles we see in ourselves.

We are not meant to walk alone, nor are we meant to compare our journeys against impossible ideals.

Instead, we are meant to embrace one another, to uplift and support, knowing that imperfection is not a weakness but a unifying force.

The more we accept our flaws, the more we recognize the beauty in others, realizing that our struggles and triumphs are what truly connect us.

Every mistake is an opportunity for growth, and every perceived failure is a lesson waiting to be understood.

True self-acceptance is not about eliminating our flaws but about recognizing that they are an essential part of who we are.

Strength is not found in the absence of struggle but in the willingness to face it head-on.

When we embrace both our strengths and weaknesses, we open the door to transformation, compassion, and a deeper sense of belonging.

In accepting ourselves as whole, flawed yet capable, imperfect yet valuable, we create a space for kindness, both for ourselves and for others.

This acceptance fosters understanding, allowing us to appreciate not only our own journey but also the journeys of those around us.

It is through this shared experience of imperfection that we find true connection, resilience, and a profound appreciation for the beauty of our humanity.

KINDNESS

People on Earth often assert their dominance, imposing their will with strength and authority.

Their words, harsh and forceful, resemble stones cast with precision, but instead of promoting unity, they create division.

These harsh words contribute to the obstruction of peace, darkening the path that could lead to understanding and harmony.

Many individuals live with pride in their material wealth or status, but the actions they take often cast shadows on their integrity and intentions.

Hypocrisy remains hidden behind their call for peace, as it is impossible for true peace to thrive in an environment where walls are erected, whether physical, social, or emotional.

Every harsh word spoken has the power to wound, and in a world that is increasingly divided, the potential for harm becomes greater.

This division leads to confusion and chaos, weakening the collective strength of humanity.

To foster true harmony, people must engage with one another in meaningful ways, replacing conflict with understanding, and division with connection.

Empathy should guide our actions, allowing us to build bridges rather than walls.

By prioritizing kindness and compassion, we create an environment where love can flourish and peace can be nurtured.

True peace cannot be found through force or domination, it emerges when individuals choose to uplift one another, recognizing the inherent worth in every person.

Instead of fracturing and separating, we should come together, showing care and concern for one another's well-being.

When we embrace healing and empathy, we pave the way for the creation of a more peaceful world, free from the barriers that divide us.

Kindness is the most powerful tool at our disposal to break down any wall or boundary that stands in the way of connection.

It is through our actions, rooted in empathy and understanding, that we can forge a world where love flows freely and people are united in their shared humanity.

To achieve true peace, we must choose to lift one another, to offer support and care instead of judgment and division.

In doing so, we contribute to a future where compassion and kindness are the foundation of our society.

The act of healing the wounds caused by conflict is essential for the creation of a peaceful world, one where hearts are open and receptive to one another.

When we create an environment of understanding, we not only change individual lives but also transform communities and nations.

It is through choosing unity over division and love over hate that we can create a world that truly embodies peace.

The path to peace is not a passive one, it requires intentional effort and a willingness to challenge the status quo.

By embracing empathy and showing kindness in our everyday lives, we create ripple effects that spread outward, touching the lives of those around us.

Together, we can create a future where peace is not an ideal, but a reality, a world where the bonds of love and kindness are stronger than any force that seeks to divide us.

Let us choose to make this vision of peace our collective reality, knowing that the effort to lift others up is the key to unlocking a harmonious world for all.

NO ENEMIES

I have no enemies, and I have never sought to create any.

Throughout my life, I have strived to live in a way that fosters understanding and mutual respect with those around me.

Conflict often stems from misunderstanding or unspoken differences, and I have always preferred to resolve issues peacefully and thoughtfully.

The idea of having enemies has never resonated with me, especially knowing that we are all interconnected as a we-form.

I have never intentionally wronged anyone or sought to harm another.

Instead, I have focused on building connections and ensuring my actions align with kindness and empathy.

It is not that I am without fault, but my intent has always been to bring about harmony rather than division.

Even when faced with disagreements or challenges, I have strived to approach them with patience and an open mind.

I understand that people may sometimes act in ways that hurt, but I have never let these moments turn into lasting animosity.

To me, it is more important to grow from these experiences than to carry resentment.

In the end, I carry no grudges, no ill will, and no enemies.

My life has been about creating space for understanding, and I intend to continue on that path.

Truly, I only seek peaceful resolutions and lasting connections.

By fostering understanding and compassion, we can build a more harmonious world where conflicts are resolved through dialogue and empathy.

This approach not only enriches our relationships but also contributes to personal growth and a sense of fulfillment.

I am committed to living a life free from animosity, focusing instead on positive interactions and mutual respect.

By embracing this philosophy, I hope to inspire others to do the same, creating a ripple effect of kindness and understanding.

In a world where differences are inevitable, choosing to see the humanity in others and responding with empathy can transform potential conflicts into opportunities for connection and growth.

This is the path I have chosen, and I will continue to walk it with conviction and an open heart.

THE CREATION ENERGY

The Creation Energy, though as small as a needle's point, holds within it an energy that is vast, boundless, and ever-present.

This tiny spark is the very foundation of our being, the essence from which life flows and consciousness emerges.

It is unseen by the human eye yet deeply felt in moments of clarity, peace, and connection.

Flowing through every cell, it breathes vitality into the body, sustaining its intricate functions with an unseen intelligence.

Like a luminous thread, it extends beyond the physical, weaving itself into the unseen fabric of existence.

This energy is not confined by space or time.

Rather, it moves freely, linking all aspects of life in an endless dance of creation and renewal.

It is the silent force that guides our thoughts, emotions, and inner wisdom, anchoring us to something greater than ourselves.

Though subtle, the spirit's presence is undeniable, radiating through us in ways we often take for granted.

It is the pulse that gives rhythm to our hearts, the breath that moves through us with effortless grace.

In moments of stillness, we may sense its quiet hum, a reminder that we are never truly alone.

This force does not impose itself but rather exists as a constant, waiting to be acknowledged and understood.

It is through this recognition that we begin to align with its presence, allowing it to guide us toward deeper understanding.

Just as a river shapes the land over time, the spirit shapes our inner world, influencing our perceptions, choices, and interactions.

It is the unseen architect of our experiences, gently nudging us toward growth and transformation.

Interwoven with our very essence, the spirit pulses with a power that is both gentle and immense, both delicate and unbreakable.

It is the unseen thread that binds our being together, allowing us to radiate with the light of our true nature.

Within the heart, it plants a joy that is neither fleeting nor conditional, but rather an unshakable source of warmth, clarity, and love.

This energy is the foundation of all inspiration, fueling creativity, resilience, and the deep longing for connection that drives us forward.

It is the voice that whispers in moments of doubt, the quiet knowing that reassures us when the path seems unclear.

Though often unnoticed, its presence is constant, offering guidance in ways both subtle and profound.

When we allow ourselves to tune in, to listen deeply, we begin to understand that the spirit is not separate from us but is, in fact, the very core of who we are.

With every heartbeat, the spirit moves freely, circulating like an invisible current of vitality that flows through and beyond us.

It is the essence of transformation, capable of turning the ordinary into something extraordinary.

In the stillness of the mind, in the depth of our emotions, in the beauty of the world around us, its presence is revealed.

It allows us to see beyond the surface, to recognize the deeper truths that shape our existence.

Through its rhythm, we find harmony and through its wisdom, we gain clarity.

It is through this attunement that we awaken to the understanding that we are never truly separate, but rather deeply interconnected with all of life.

Each moment presents an opportunity to align with this force, to embrace the energy that sustains us, and to walk a path of purpose, presence, and peace.

Despite its modest size, the spirit's strength is immeasurable, sustaining us in a rhythm that is both divine and eternal.

It is the wellspring of love, the quiet yet powerful force that moves us toward self-discovery. It is the source of intuition, the guiding presence that leads us back to truth when we have lost our way.

When we attune ourselves to its presence, we begin to dissolve the illusions that cloud our perception, revealing the light that has always existed within.

Through this alignment, we are no longer bound by fear, doubt, or limitation.

Instead, we step into a state of awareness where our essence shines freely.

We are reminded that we are more than just physical beings, we are luminous, infinite, and deeply connected to the great unfolding of existence.

To walk in alignment with the spirit is to embrace the wisdom that has always been within us.

It is to recognize that life is not random but intricately woven with meaning and intention.

The spirit does not force its way into our awareness.

Rather, it waits patiently for us to awaken to its presence.

When we do, we begin to see the beauty in every moment, the synchronicities that guide us, and the deeper truths that call us forward.

This is the path of true connection, where the ordinary becomes sacred, and the self dissolves into something greater.

Through this conscious alignment, we rediscover the infinite potential that resides within us, ever radiant, ever present, and eternally connected to the source of all life.

THE JOURNEY OF REBIRTH

Through the journey of rebirth, our essence carries the echoes of past lives, shaping the foundation of our existence.

These fragments of memory, stored deep within, influence our thoughts, emotions, and perceptions.

The ego arises as a lens through which we view ourselves, forming an identity that helps us navigate the world.

As we move through different lifetimes, we gather knowledge and insight, gradually uncovering the deeper truths of our being.

With each cycle, we are given opportunities to grow and evolve, learning through experience and introspection.

The emotions and wisdom we cultivate become the guiding forces of our journey.

However, when the ego is overtaken by illusion and misperception, it can lose its way, mistaking fleeting desires and fears for reality.

In these moments, we drift from our true nature, entangled in false narratives that obscure our inner light.

Yet, within the subconscious, profound wisdom is preserved, holding the lessons accumulated through countless lifetimes.

It exists beyond the noise of the mind, patiently waiting to be acknowledged.

When we quiet the distractions and seek inner clarity, this wisdom emerges, offering guidance and understanding.

Every moment presents an opportunity to reconnect with this deep knowledge, illuminating our path forward.

To fully embrace this journey, we must cultivate awareness, love, and clarity, allowing our spirit to align with its highest potential.

By recognizing the illusions that cloud our vision, we restore our connection to the truth within us.

As we move toward greater understanding, our essence shines unburdened, revealing the depth of our being.

Through this conscious evolution, we reclaim the wisdom that has always been ours, guiding us toward fulfillment and harmony.

A LETTER

Dear brothers of the Christian and Muslim faiths,

It is essential to understand that the Herald of this Universe, Henok/Nokodemion, does not reincarnate in the same human body or as the same personality.

No one does, this is an impossibility dictated by the natural laws of Creation.

Every human spirit evolves through countless lifetimes, gaining wisdom and experience, but it never returns as the exact same person it once was.

Yet, throughout history, many have awaited the return of past prophets, believing that figures like Jmmanuel (Jesus Christ) and Mohammed would reappear in the same form.

This expectation, however, is based on misunderstanding.

The truth is that these great prophets were manifestations of the same Creation Energy that has been incarnating throughout the ages, continuing its mission of truth and enlightenment.

Today, this energy has returned once more, and we can inform you that the same spirit-form that once embodied Jmmanuel and Mohammed has been reincarnated as Billy, born on February 3, 1937.

He is the current incarnation of the Messenger, carrying forth the wisdom and teachings that have been preserved and delivered anew for this time.

Many of you place deep faith in ancient scriptures, seeking divine guidance through writings that have been passed down for generations.

However, it is critical to recognize that these texts have been altered, mistranslated, and falsified over the centuries.

The original Herald of Truth never wrote down his teachings in his own words, as literacy was rare in those times.

Instead, his wisdom was passed down orally, later transcribed by others, often distorted either unintentionally or for political and religious control.

The resulting scriptures, while containing elements of truth, are incomplete and sometimes misleading.

Today, many people follow these ancient, altered texts while waiting for a return that will never come in the way they expect.

Meanwhile, I have recognized the presence of the true reincarnation of the Herald in this lifetime and have chosen to follow his teachings as they are now being revealed in their purest form.

This realization did not come easily.

It required years of deep study, investigation, and the willingness to question deeply ingrained beliefs.

But through this journey, I have come to understand that the truth remains unchanged across time, it is only human interpretation that shifts and obscures it.

The mission of the Herald has been the same since time immemorial: to bring knowledge, wisdom, and enlightenment to humanity.

Across countless civilizations, he has incarnated under different names and forms, always guiding people toward understanding and evolution.

His message has never belonged to a single religion, nation, or culture, it is universal, existing beyond dogma and human-created institutions.

Throughout history, those who sought control over others have often manipulated his teachings, using them as tools of power rather than paths to enlightenment.

This is why so much of what is accepted as spiritual truth today is clouded by distortions and misconceptions.

But now, in our modern era, we have a unique opportunity.

Unlike in the past, when records were altered or lost, today's incarnation of the Messenger has provided his teachings in a way that can be preserved without falsification.

This is a critical moment in history, one in which those who seek the truth with open minds have the ability to access it directly, unfiltered by centuries of manipulation.

By recognizing this reality, we can break free from the divisions that have long separated us.

There is no need to wait for a second coming or for a prophesied return that was never meant to happen as many believe.

The Messenger has already returned, not as Jmmanuel or Mohammed, but as Billy, the same eternal Creation Energy continuing its mission.

It is up to each of us to open our hearts and minds to this truth, to move beyond rigid traditions, and to seek wisdom in its unaltered form.

The path to true knowledge requires courage, the courage to question, to learn, and to evolve beyond the limitations of past misunderstandings.

When we embrace this journey, we will realize that we are not following different Messiahs or separate paths, but rather the same eternal mission of truth that has existed since the beginning of time.

In recognizing and accepting this, we come together as seekers of wisdom, united in the pursuit of true enlightenment and spiritual evolution.

THE SUBCONSCIOUS MIND

The subconscious is a vast and intricate tapestry, woven from the threads of countless lifetimes, each contributing to the depth of wisdom it holds.

It is a silent keeper of memories, a repository where fragments of past experiences, emotions, and lessons reside.

These fragments, though often hidden beneath the surface of conscious thought, shape the very essence of who we are, influencing our actions, desires, and perceptions.

The subconscious is not merely a passive storehouse.

It is an active guide, offering insights and intuition that help us navigate the complexities of life.

It is here, in the quiet depths of our inner being, that the stories of our past lives compel us to grow, urging us to uncover the truths that lie within.

The ego, in contrast, emerges as a dynamic and ever-changing lens through which we interpret the world and ourselves.

It collects thoughts, experiences, and perceptions, constructing a sense of identity that feels solid and real.

Yet, the ego is not the entirety of who we are.

It is but a reflection, a tool for navigating the physical and social realms.

When shadows of fear, doubt, or confusion arise, the ego can lose its way, mistaking its transient nature for the core of our being.

In these moments, it may lead us astray, clouding our understanding of our true selves.

However, the subconscious remains a steadfast anchor, holding the profound wisdom and lessons of our past, ready to guide us back to clarity and alignment.

Through the cycles of rebirth and the passage of time, we are given endless opportunities to learn, grow, and evolve.

Each life brings with it new challenges and experiences, all of which contribute to the unfolding of our true nature.

Feelings and insights become the tools through which we peel back the layers of illusion, revealing the essence of our spirit.

The subconscious, with its quiet persistence, offers guidance and illumination, helping us to integrate the lessons of the past and apply them to the present.

It reminds us that growth is not a linear process but a spiral, where each turn brings us closer to understanding the interconnectedness of all things.

With each new life, the wisdom of the subconscious is shared, a gift passed down through the ages to illuminate our path.

Though this wisdom may sometimes feel distant or obscured by the noise of the world, it remains a constant and unwavering source of truth.

By seeking clarity, love, and alignment with our higher selves, we can tap into this reservoir of knowledge, allowing it to guide our actions and decisions.

In doing so, we not only honor the lessons of our past but also create a foundation for a future rooted in understanding and authenticity.

The interplay between the ego and the subconscious is a dance of self-discovery, one that invites us to embrace the fullness of our being and let our essence shine brightly in the world.

IN AQUARIAN AGE

In Aquarian Age, the humans of the new age face a monumental challenge, standing at a pivotal moment in time where the choices they make will define the course of the future.

This is a time of transformation, where the old ways no longer suffice, and new visions must be forged.

Grounded in unwavering truth, they build a strong foundation, one where compassion, understanding, and inclusion are paramount.

They strive to create a world where all people, regardless of their background or circumstance, can find their place and feel a sense of belonging.

In this new era, the human Creation Energy is called upon to evolve, to transcend the limitations of the past, and embrace a collective vision rooted in equality and peace.

The Aquarian energy invites them to shed outdated beliefs, opening themselves to new possibilities and embracing the wisdom of the ages.

This era is one of profound insight, where values evolve and expand, shifting from individualistic pursuits to a focus on the well-being of the collective.

Philosophies rooted in love, respect, and unity begin to take shape, guiding humanity toward a future where every individual's worth is recognized and celebrated.

These philosophies are not mere ideas, but active principles that guide actions, decisions, and interactions, fostering an environment where the highest ideals can flourish.

Wisdom grows from psychological insight, offering the tools necessary to navigate the complexities of life.

People come to understand that the foundation of a joyful, peaceful life is rooted in the cultivation of self-awareness, emotional intelligence, and spiritual growth.

The pursuit of knowledge is no longer solely intellectual but is deeply intertwined with emotional and spiritual development, creating a holistic approach to life.

As individuals embrace this integrated wisdom, they begin to shape a reality where joy, peace, and light are not distant ideals but tangible experiences woven into everyday life.

In this new world, freedom becomes not just a political concept, but a deeply personal and spiritual experience.

Each person recognizes the power of inner peace and seeks to cultivate it within themselves, knowing that true freedom is found when one is at peace with the self.

As they unlock their inner potential, they realize that the true source of happiness and fulfillment lies in self-acceptance and the ability to live authentically.

This shift in consciousness opens new doors, doors to new ways of being, new ways of relating, and new ways of living.

With every truth uncovered, individuals move closer to a deeper connection with themselves, with others, and with the world around them.

The world, once divided by fear and misunderstanding, becomes a place where unity is embraced, where the diverse threads of humanity are woven together to form a rich and vibrant tapestry.

Each step taken in the pursuit of truth and freedom leads humanity closer to a collective awakening, where all are free to express their unique gifts and contribute to the greater good.

As they continue to build this new vision, a future begins to unfold, one that is not bound by the limitations of the past but is instead a reflection of the infinite possibilities of the future.

The wisdom they uncover forms the bedrock of this future, and as they share this wisdom with others, they become catalysts for change, creating a ripple effect that spreads far and wide.

The world becomes a place where people no longer live in isolation but come together to collaborate, to learn, to grow, and to uplift one another.

Every truth revealed, every insight gained, and every act of kindness shared contributes to the creation of a new world, a world of abundance, peace, and joy.

In this world, Creation Energy soar freely, unencumbered by the chains of fear and limitation.

The stories of the past are honored, but they no longer dictate the future.

Instead, the future is created by the collective will of those who choose to embrace a new way of being, a new way of living.

This is a world where individuals, communities, and nations work in harmony to create a reality that reflects the highest potential of the human spirit.

In this vision of unity, people rise together in the warmth of shared purpose, igniting a new dawn of promise and transformation.

This is not just a vision of hope, but a living, breathing reality that unfolds with each passing day.

As individuals align themselves with the principles of Aquarian Age, they tap into a powerful force for positive change that radiates out into the world, touching every corner of society.

The world becomes a place where every person can find their voice, their purpose, and their place, where diversity is celebrated and inclusivity is the norm.

In this world, the light of wisdom guides the way, illuminating the path forward for all to follow.

The dawn of this new age is not a distant dream but a tangible reality that grows brighter with each moment.

In the warmth of unity, in the strength of shared ideals, humanity rises to meet the challenges of the future, creating a world of peace, love, and boundless potential.

The Aquarian age, with its promise of transformation and growth, is a beacon of hope for all who seek a brighter tomorrow.

TRUE TOGETHERNESS

True togetherness is found in how we embrace one another's struggles, offering support and understanding where burdens weigh heaviest.

Each heart carries hidden sorrows, silent battles that often go unnoticed by the world.

Though our own challenges may feel overwhelming, we are not alone in our suffering.

Across the world, countless individuals wake each day searching for solace, nourishment, and light in times of darkness.

In these moments, the strength of Creation calls us to stand together, bound by a shared purpose that transcends hardship and unites us in resilience.

It is in the recognition of each other's pain that we begin to heal, not just as individuals but as a collective.

Through compassion, we find strength, not only to endure our own hardships but also to uplift those who walk beside us.

The burdens we carry may differ in shape and weight, but suffering is a universal experience, one that binds us as human beings.

No matter our background, our beliefs, or our circumstances, we each long for kindness, understanding, and a sense of belonging.

It is easy to retreat into ourselves, to focus only on our own struggles, but true growth comes when we extend our hearts outward.

When we acknowledge another's pain, when we lend a helping hand, we do more than just offer temporary relief, we create ripples of hope that spread far beyond what we can see.

A kind word, a moment of patience, or simply listening can be the difference between despair and hope for someone in need.

Small gestures of love and consideration have the power to transform lives, proving that we are strongest when we choose to stand together.

In the face of unkindness, we must let kindness lead the way.

When met with rudeness, let respect be our response.

Though pain and suffering may surround us, compassion must rise within us, becoming the bridge that connects us all.

Love, given freely and without expectation, enriches our lives and the lives of those around us.

Every act of kindness, no matter how small, creates ripples that extend beyond ourselves, shaping a world where warmth and understanding triumph over division.

When we extend a helping hand, we affirm our shared humanity.

It is easy to respond to negativity with more negativity, but true strength lies in breaking that cycle.

We cannot control the actions of others, but we can choose how we respond.

Every time we choose patience over frustration, empathy over judgment, and generosity over selfishness, we contribute to a world where love outweighs hatred.

We do not walk this path alone.

Our struggles are shared, woven into the vast fabric of existence.

In every act of love, we affirm our worth and the value of those around us.

Together, we rise, lifted by the strength of unity, celebrating the light that emerges from compassion and mutual care.

Through joy and hardship alike, it is kindness that sustains us, reminding us that our true power lies in connection, in lifting each other up, and in the unwavering belief that love can heal even the deepest wounds.

We are not separate islands but branches of the same tree, strengthened by the roots of empathy and understanding.

Only by embracing this truth can we truly thrive, recognizing that our happiness is intertwined with the well-being of others.

If we allow division to harden our hearts, we risk losing sight of what makes life meaningful, the relationships we build, the lives we touch, and the love we share.

Yet, when harmony is absent, the very foundation of society begins to fracture.

When families, communities, and nations draw lines that divide rather than unite, the strength of togetherness is lost, and progress falters.

No goal, however noble, can thrive in a world that prioritizes separation over unity.

If we continue to build walls between "us" and "them, " the vision of a shared future withers before it can take root.

Isolation breeds resentment, and division weakens the bonds that sustain us.

The absence of harmony does not just create distance.

It erodes the very essence of what makes us human.

A society that values competition over cooperation, conflict over compromise, and self-interest over collective well-being cannot sustain itself.

The more we alienate one another, the further we drift from the truth that we are all connected.

Only by fostering true bonds of compassion, by recognizing that our destinies are intertwined, can we create a world where love bridges all divides and hope shines as our guiding light.

It is in the recognition of our shared existence, in the simple yet profound acts of kindness, that we reclaim the strength of connection and step forward, together, into a future where unity prevails.

When we learn to see ourselves in others, to recognize that their joys, pains, hopes, and fears are not so different from our own, we cultivate a sense of responsibility for the well-being of the whole.

The world will always have struggles, but they do not have to define us.

Instead, let us be defined by the love we give, the unity we nurture, and the commitment we share to build a future rooted in understanding, respect, and togetherness.

UNITY

You have come to understand that all living beings share this earth, bound together in an intricate and harmonious existence.

Every life, no matter how small or grand, plays a role in the vast and delicate web that holds the world in balance.

The birds soaring through the sky, the fish gliding effortlessly through the depths of the ocean, and the creatures roaming the land each embody the essence of connectedness.

Their presence, though seemingly separate, mirrors the unity that binds all creatures, including you and me.

The rhythm of nature moves through them all, an unspoken melody that reminds us of our place in this grand design.

Each being, whether it runs, crawls, or takes flight, is a thread in a luminous tapestry woven with the essence of life itself.

Every creature contributes to a masterpiece shaped by time, where nothing exists in isolation.

The calls of birds at dawn, the rustling of leaves in the wind, and the quiet footsteps of animals in the night form a language, a secret communication passed through generations.

Those who listen closely can hear the whispers of nature, revealing the interconnectedness that sustains all living things.

It is not just survival that ties them together but an intrinsic bond, a mutual reliance that has shaped the world since its earliest days.

Within this grand design, each creature has a purpose, fulfilling its role in the continuous cycle of life, death, and renewal.

The tiniest insect pollinates flowers, ensuring the growth of future generations, while the great predators maintain the balance of populations.

Rivers carve their paths, nourishing forests and fields, while the wind carries seeds to distant lands, allowing life to take root in new places.

Nothing exists without consequence, and every action ripples outward, affecting the whole.

In this unity, nature thrives, its harmony maintained not by force but by an unspoken understanding between all living things.

In their instinctive movements, their struggles, and their triumphs, you can find reflections of your own journey.

The challenges they face, the resilience they display, and the beauty of their existence mirror the path you walk in your own life.

There is no separation between you and them, only a shared experience, woven together by the invisible threads of existence.

In every heartbeat, in every breath, the spirit of connectedness thrives, reminding us that we are not alone.

Through joy and hardship alike, we flourish not in isolation but in unity, bound together in the timeless dance of life.Daney's

IN TIME

In time, the Earth will turn its ear to the whispers of the prophets, voices that have long carried wisdom through the winds of history.

These whispers do not demand attention with thunderous cries, nor do they seek to control with force.

Instead, they emerge softly, steadily, resonating in the hearts of those who are willing to listen.

They speak of truth, of knowledge long hidden beneath the distractions of the world, and of the deep understanding that has been lost to time.

Though their voices may seem faint to those consumed by the noise of daily existence, they persist, unyielding, calling humanity toward a higher awareness.

They remind people that wisdom is not found in power or wealth but in the quiet moments of reflection, in the search for meaning beyond the material.

As these whispers take root in open hearts, a transformation will begin.

People will start to see beyond the illusions that have divided them, realizing that they are bound by invisible threads of connection.

Each whisper is a thread, and together they weave a tapestry of unity, where no individual stands alone.

The prophets' words will shine like beacons in the darkness, revealing truths that have always been present yet seldom acknowledged.

No longer will people define themselves by differences of race, creed, or nation, for they will understand that such divisions are merely illusions.

They will see each other not as strangers, but as reflections of the same shared essence.

The old walls built from fear and misunderstanding will crumble, replaced by bridges of mutual respect and recognition.

Through this awakening, humanity will move beyond self-interest, recognizing that true fulfillment comes not from taking but from giving, not from conquering but from understanding.

With this newfound awareness, empathy will blossom in the hearts of all who listen.

The pain of one will no longer be ignored, for it will be felt by all.

The suffering of the world, once seen as distant and separate, will now be recognized as a collective wound.

When injustice strikes one, it will be as though it strikes everyone, and no soul will turn away in indifference.

The wounds inflicted by greed, by hatred, and by ignorance will begin to heal, not through avoidance, but through confrontation with truth.

Those who once stood apart, divided by fear, will reach for each other, their hands extended in reconciliation.

Love, which has too often been dismissed as mere sentiment, will become the foundation upon which the new world is built.

It will not be a passive love, but an active force, one that drives people to lift each other, to protect, to nurture, and to restore.

Yet, the journey toward this new reality will not be without struggle.

The old ways will resist, clinging to their place in the world, fearful of what change will bring.

Those who have built their power upon division will fight to maintain it, spreading doubt and discord to silence the prophets' whispers.

But the truth cannot be suppressed forever.

Once it has been heard, it will continue to resonate, growing stronger with each passing day.

Those who embrace it will not falter, for they will know that their path is just.

Step by step, hand in hand, they will move forward, guided by the knowledge that a brighter future is not merely a dream, but a choice.

A choice to listen, to see, to act with compassion, and to stand together as one.

And so, the Earth will bear witness to this transformation.

Where once there was division, there will be unity.

Where once there was suffering in silence, there will be shared healing.

Where once the whispers of the prophets were ignored, they will become the guiding voices of a new age.

The dawn of this era will not come with a single, sudden revelation, but through the steady, unwavering commitment of those who refuse to turn away.

It will rise from the dust of the past, carried forward by the hands of those who dare to believe in something greater than themselves.

And in the end, it will not be the prophets alone who speak, but all of humanity, one voice, one purpose, one future.

THE CREATION ENERGY TEACHINGS

I have read all the contact reports at least three times, yet each time I revisit them, I uncover something new, details I previously overlooked, concepts I had forgotten, or deeper insights that only become clear with time and reflection.

The sheer depth of information within these reports makes it impossible to absorb everything in just one or two readings.

With each review, my understanding expands, allowing me to see the connections between different aspects of the Teachings that I had not fully grasped before.

The Creation Energy Teachings, in particular, are not something a person can simply skim through and expect to comprehend.

They require deep engagement, a true passion for seeking knowledge, and an unwavering desire to understand the meaning of life and our place within the vast universe.

Without such dedication, it is easy to dismiss or misinterpret the immense wisdom contained in these works.

True comprehension comes only to those who are willing to commit themselves to lifelong study and contemplation.

One of the greatest challenges in spreading and understanding the Teachings is that many people on Earth have an aversion to reading.

The modern world has conditioned people to seek instant gratification, reducing their attention spans and discouraging deep, meaningful study.

Social media, television, and other forms of mass entertainment have created a culture where people prefer brief, surface-level information rather than investing the necessary time and effort to explore profound truths.

Because of this, most individuals remain unaware of the vast knowledge available in the contact reports and related works.

In addition to these reports, there are also numerous books written by Billy himself that provide further insights and a deeper exploration of the Teachings.

These books serve as essential guides for those who are serious about understanding the fundamental principles of existence, the laws of Creation, and the true history of humanity.

Unfortunately, because so few are willing to dedicate themselves to this study, the majority of Earth's population continues to live in ignorance, unaware of the vast potential that lies within them.

The ultimate goal of studying the Teachings is not merely to accumulate knowledge but to internalize and embody them in everyday life.

True understanding goes beyond intellectual comprehension, it transforms the way a person thinks, acts, and perceives reality.

Through my own journey, I have come to realize that the Teachings offer something far greater than just wisdom.

They hold the key to healing.

Humanity, as it exists today, is the product of ancient genetic manipulations that altered our natural state.

These manipulations, which date back to our origins in the Sirius star system, fundamentally changed our DNA and led us away from living in alignment with the natural laws of Creation.

The consequences of these alterations can still be seen today, as humanity struggles with internal conflicts, destructive behaviors, and a fundamental disconnection from the truth.

However, by studying and applying the Teachings, we have the opportunity to reverse these effects.

By living in accordance with the laws and recommendations of Creation, we can gradually restore our true essence and reclaim our place as beings who exist in harmony with the universe.

This process of transformation, however, will not happen quickly.

It is estimated that it will take another 800 years before humanity as a whole begins to truly embrace and live by these Teachings.

Right now, we are still in the early stages of awakening, where only a small number of individuals are actively seeking and applying this knowledge.

We are the ones planting the seeds for future generations, ensuring that this wisdom is preserved and passed on so that one day, it may flourish on a much larger scale.

Change does not happen overnight, but every effort made today contributes to the long-term evolution of human consciousness.

Though the majority of people may not yet be ready to accept these truths, our responsibility is to continue studying, embodying, and sharing them in any way we can.

True transformation begins with individuals who have the courage to question the old ways, seek higher understanding, and align their lives with the principles of Creation.

Even if the path is long and often challenging, every step we take now brings us closer to a future where humanity finally lives in harmony with the natural order.

It is this dedication to truth and knowledge that will ultimately lead to the awakening of our species, allowing us to reclaim our true potential and fulfill our purpose within the grand design of the universe.

TRUSTING

Just as the sun rises on the horizon each day without fail, so too does life continue its course, unwavering in its movement.

The rising and setting of the sun mark the passage of time, yet they also serve as reminders of the natural cycles that govern existence.

No matter the turbulence of a stormy night or the darkness that lingers before dawn, the sun always returns, casting its light upon the world once more.

In the same way, life moves steadily forward, carrying all beings through the ebb and flow of existence, ensuring that no moment remains stagnant.

Just as the dawn follows the night, so too do new opportunities, experiences, and understandings emerge from life's unfolding journey.

Creation, the Universal Consciousness, operates with perfect harmony, never faltering in its rhythm.

This unseen force is ever-present, orchestrating the vast and intricate movements of the universe with flawless precision.

Every aspect of existence, whether grand or minute, unfolds in accordance with this boundless wisdom, ensuring that balance and continuity are preserved.

Just as the planets move through their celestial paths without error, so too does the essence of life progress, guided by an eternal intelligence that governs all things.

There is no randomness or chaos in the grand design of Creation, only the seamless unfolding of a reality that is both intricate and purposeful.

Though human perception may sometimes struggle to recognize the order underlying existence, it is always there, shaping the course of life.

Challenges, changes, and moments of uncertainty are not signs of disorder, but rather essential aspects of the ever-moving current of creation.

Just as rivers carve new paths through the land and seasons shift with unwavering certainty, so too does every experience serve a role in the unfolding of life's journey.

There is wisdom in the unseen forces that guide all things, gently steering each soul toward growth, understanding, and renewal.

To resist these natural rhythms is to create struggle, whereas to accept and flow with them is to align with the deeper truth of existence.

To recognize and trust in this universal rhythm is to find peace amid life's constant motion.

Like the steady rising of the sun, life's unfolding is a testament to the infinite intelligence of Creation.

It is a force that neither rushes nor hesitates but simply moves as it must, weaving together the vast and intricate patterns of reality.

Trusting in this rhythm allows one to embrace each day with clarity, courage, and assurance.

There is no need for fear or doubt, for just as the sun will always rise, so too will life continue, forever guided by the harmonious and unwavering hand of Creation.

TRIBAL MENTALITY

We share the same planet, yet the challenge of living together in true harmony remains an ongoing struggle.

Despite the vast potential for unity, we continue to divide ourselves into countless categories, each with its own subdivisions, further fragmenting our societies.

These divisions are not just national or ideological, they run deep into cultural, social, economic, and even familial structures.

One might assume that family ties, being among the most personal and intimate bonds, would remain unbreakable.

However, even within blood relations, misunderstandings, conflicts, and separations persist, revealing how deeply ingrained our tendencies toward division truly are.

Our perceived evolution as a species has brought about technological advancements and scientific breakthroughs, yet our mindset often remains stuck in patterns reminiscent of primitive societies.

In ancient times, small clans and tribes prioritized their own survival above all else, often at the expense of outsiders.

While we no longer live in isolated villages warring over resources in the same way, the underlying mentality remains.

Today, instead of physical tribal battles, we engage in ideological, economic, and political conflicts, reinforcing barriers between groups.

This division is evident in every aspect of modern life, from how nations interact on the global stage to the way individuals navigate workplace dynamics.

Even in professional environments where cooperation should be essential, personal interests, competition, and internal divisions create barriers to true collaboration and mutual growth.

What makes this issue even more pressing is our collective inability, or refusal, to fully acknowledge it.

We often believe we have advanced far beyond the petty rivalries and narrow-minded thinking of our ancestors, yet our actions consistently prove otherwise.

Societies pride themselves on progress, yet discrimination, social inequality, and conflict persist across the world.

People speak of unity and cooperation, yet time and again, they act in ways that prioritize personal or group interests over the well-being of humanity as a whole.

True progress is not measured by technological innovation or economic success alone but by our ability to transcend division and embrace a higher level of consciousness, one that acknowledges our interconnectedness.

The truth is that peace will never truly prevail until we, as the people of Earth, evolve beyond our ingrained divisions and recognize our shared identity.

We must move past the illusion of separateness and embrace the reality that we are a single human family, bound together in a collective existence.

This shift requires not just a change in thought but a transformation in how we live, interact, and care for one another.

Only when we genuinely see ourselves as part of a We-form, a unified whole rather than fragmented groups, will we be able to create a world where harmony, mutual respect, and genuine peace are not just ideals, but realities. And so is the truth.

RELIGION AND SPORTS

Religion and sports are domains where passion and devotion reign supreme, drawing people into a shared experience of fervor and belief.

Though distinct in purpose, both ignite deep emotions, fostering communities bound by loyalty and reverence.

In these spaces, whether sacred temples or grand stadiums, individuals gather in unified spirit, their voices rising in praise of deities or athletes who inspire awe.

The rituals, chants, and symbols in both domains reinforce a sense of belonging, elevating their chosen figures to a level of near-mythical admiration.

The sheer intensity of devotion can create an almost transcendental atmosphere, where people feel connected to something greater than themselves.

Whether through prayers or cheers, their collective energy fuels a sense of purpose and identity, drawing them into a tradition that spans generations.

Temples and stadiums serve as sanctuaries where faith and dedication manifest, shaping identities and aspirations.

In the sacred hush of a prayer hall or the electrified roar of a sports arena, emotions surge, and collective energy unites the masses.

The celestial and the physical intertwine, as worshippers seek guidance from the divine while fans place unwavering trust in their champions.

Through victories and miracles alike, both religion and sports offer a sense of purpose, teaching perseverance, hope, and devotion to something greater than oneself.

The deep emotional investment in these experiences often leads to lifelong commitments, with individuals shaping their personal and communal lives around the values imparted by their faith or their favorite teams.

Stories of sacrifice, redemption, and triumph mirror one another in both fields, reinforcing narratives that give people meaning and a sense of continuity.

Yet, amid the fervor, reality can become obscured by the weight of adulation.

The human tendency to exalt figures, whether saints, prophets, or athletes, sometimes fosters illusions that blur the line between admiration and blind allegiance.

In both spaces, figures once revered can fall from grace, and moments of perceived transcendence can mask underlying flaws.

The fervent pursuit of faith or victory may lead some to overlook truth, allowing myths to overshadow reality.

The unwavering commitment to belief or team loyalty can result in tribalism, where differences escalate into conflict.

The power structures that emerge within both religion and sports can be manipulated, turning devotion into a tool for control rather than inspiration.

In such cases, what once brought people together can become a source of division, as competing ideologies or rivalries breed animosity.

344

Despite these complexities, religion and sports remain powerful forces that shape the human experience.

They stir emotions, unite communities, and offer solace in times of uncertainty.

Both provide a stage where individuals seek meaning, whether through devotion to a higher power or the pursuit of triumph on the field.

In their essence, they reflect the eternal human desire to connect with something beyond the self, a longing that transcends time, culture, and belief.

When approached with mindfulness and perspective, both religion and sports have the capacity to elevate the human spirit, fostering camaraderie, discipline, and a sense of shared purpose.

Ultimately, they are not merely pastimes or traditions but essential elements of the human journey, offering individuals a path to understanding, growth, and fulfillment.

BELIEVE IN GOD

If you believe in God, that belief inherently implies a certain level of doubt, as belief is rooted in the uncertainty of not fully knowing.

This uncertainty gives rise to prayer, an act performed out of the hope that a higher power is listening and will respond to your needs.

Prayer becomes a way of reaching out in the midst of this doubt, seeking comfort and guidance from something beyond yourself.

But if you were absolutely certain of God's existence, there would be no need for prayer, as you would already trust that your needs are understood and provided for, without the need for external validation or intervention.

Consider, however, replacing the traditional concept of God with something more immediate and personal, your own inner strength and Creation Energy.

Instead of looking outward for guidance, recognize that the power you seek already resides within you.

You are, in essence, your own guiding force, your own source of strength and wisdom.

In this understanding, you are not dependent on a distant deity but are fully capable of directing your own path, as you are a part of the very Creation that governs the universe.

This shift in perspective allows you to realize that you are your own God, possessing the power to shape your destiny and understand your own needs.

Once you embrace this truth, the need for belief in anything external begins to fade.

Belief, after all, is born from doubt and the desire to find certainty in something beyond ourselves.

But when you recognize your own divinity, you no longer need to believe, you begin to know.

The certainty that once seemed elusive becomes an inherent part of your being, and you no longer look for validation outside of yourself.

Your focus shifts from belief to knowledge, from wondering whether there is a higher power to understanding that you are a direct expression of that power in human form.

When you reach this level of realization, your approach to life changes entirely.

You no longer seek answers through belief, but through experience and understanding.

You move beyond the need for faith and into a state of knowing, where you constantly seek to expand your awareness and deepen your connection to your own inner wisdom.

In this state, you become the creator of your reality, no longer relying on anything external to define your existence, but instead knowing that you are the force that shapes your life and your future.

INNER LIGHT

At times, what appears to gleam before us can be deceiving, as it may be lifeless beneath its shiny exterior.

Take the stars, for example. While they sparkle in the sky, their radiance does not signify true life or consciousness.

They are distant objects, once burned with energy, but have ceased to exis for millions or billions of years.

This is a metaphor for how the pursuit of external, material success often misleads us.

We may chase after things that glitter, wealth, fame, power, but find that, much like the stars, they offer no true nourishment for the spirit.

The more we focus on these outward signs of achievement, the more we detach from our true essence, which is not a product of what we possess but of who we are at the deepest level.

Our true essence is not found in what can be touched, bought, or admired by others.

It resides in the energy that makes us alive, a spark of Creation that connects us to the infinite, to the very consciousness of the Universe itself.

This consciousness is not some distant, unattainable concept but something that is fundamentally embedded in us.

We are not separate from it.

We are a part of it.

Each of us is a minute particle of the vast cosmic energy that is constantly evolving, learning, and growing.

The core of our being is rooted in this universal flow, which seeks to evolve through wisdom, knowledge, and understanding.

Our sole purpose, as conscious beings within this grand design, is to evolve.

This evolution is not about accumulating material wealth or status, but about evolving in our understanding, expanding our consciousness, and deepening our connection to the greater whole.

When we are caught up in the pursuit of external things, whether they are possessions, titles, or social recognition, we lose sight of what truly matters.

The drive to acquire more can sometimes feel relentless, and we often mistake this quest for something greater than it really is.

The glittering allure of material things can cloud our judgment, distracting us from the most important truth: that fulfillment and peace come from within, from connecting to the light of our true essence.

These material pursuits, no matter how dazzling, can never provide the lasting happiness or sense of purpose that comes from recognizing our connection to Creation itself.

The more we allow ourselves to be consumed by these distractions, the further we move away from the true light of life, which is not external but resides within us.

The key to discovering this true light is to turn our attention inward, away from the superficial distractions of the material world, and toward the deeper truths that lie within.

When we focus on the wisdom and knowledge that can be gained from connecting with our inner selves, we begin to align with the flow of the universe.

This wisdom is not the kind that can be learned from external sources alone, but the kind that comes from within, from tapping into the energy of Creation.

By shifting our focus from acquiring fleeting, external rewards to cultivating our inner light, we begin to evolve in a way that transcends the superficial and taps into the deeper meaning of life.

True fulfillment comes not from what we acquire but from our ongoing journey of personal and spiritual evolution.

The light of life is not a glimmer on the surface but a deep, unwavering glow within us, always present, waiting to be realized and nurtured.

In the end, this light, this wisdom, is what will guide us through the journey of life, leading us to true peace and contentment.

A MIRACLE

Every time I meet another human being, I treat it as a miracle because, in its purest form, it truly is one.

The simple fact that we share space, time, and an exchange of energy with another individual is a remarkable phenomenon.

Each encounter holds the potential to profoundly impact your life in ways that might not be immediately evident.

Even a fleeting conversation, a shared smile, or a brief moment of connection can leave an imprint on your soul.

Some encounters may change the trajectory of your life in ways you never expected, while others may go unnoticed in the moment but will later resonate within you, offering lessons, insights, or a shift in perspective.

The complexity of human interactions is such that even the smallest, seemingly insignificant moments can have long-lasting effects, helping us grow in empathy, understanding, or gratitude.

A heartwarming and inspiring story that perfectly illustrates my perspective on human connections involves the world-famous footballer, Cristiano Ronaldo.

Ronaldo's story is widely known as one of perseverance, talent, and extraordinary achievements, but it is also a story of humility, kindness, and deep-rooted gratitude.

Many of us admire him for his athletic prowess, but there's another side to his character that speaks volumes about the importance of appreciating human connection.

In an interview with Piers Morgan, Ronaldo opened up about a memory from his childhood that had a profound impact on him.

He recounted how, during his early years, he was often offered free hamburgers by a McDonald's server named Edna and two of her colleagues.

At that time, Ronaldo was struggling, with very little to his name, and these acts of generosity stood out to him.

It wasn't just about food.

It was the warmth and kindness behind the gesture that left an indelible mark on him.

Ronaldo's story serves as a beautiful reminder that sometimes, it's not the grand gestures that matter most but the simple, everyday acts of kindness that can change someone's life.

What makes this story even more remarkable is that, despite the fame and wealth that Ronaldo eventually achieved, he never forgot the kindness Edna showed him when he was a young boy.

In the same interview, Ronaldo shared how he had been searching for her over the years, hoping to reconnect and show her his gratitude for the small but significant impact she had on his life.

The act of wanting to reunite with someone who helped him in such a small but meaningful way shows that true gratitude doesn't fade with time or success.

It highlights how the simplest actions, offering kindness when someone needs it most, can leave a lasting impression on a person's heart.

Ronaldo's wish to invite Edna to his home for dinner wasn't just about showing thanks.

It was about acknowledging the importance of human connection and the profound effect that even a brief encounter can have on the course of one's life.

The story took an even more heartwarming turn when British entrepreneur Frank Khalid OBE shared what happened when Ronaldo finally met Edna.

According to a tweet from Khalid, Ronaldo did not just meet Edna and express his gratitude, he went above and beyond, gifting her "the largest restaurant in Portugal."

This incredibly generous act was a way for Ronaldo to honor Edna's kindness and show how deeply her gesture had impacted him.

The gift was not just a material offering but a meaningful representation of how a single act of kindness can create ripples that span years and can come full circle in the most unexpected ways.

Ronaldo's generosity speaks volumes about the power of human connections and the impact of kindness, demonstrating that even the smallest gestures have the potential to create life-changing outcomes.

It also reminds us that we should never underestimate the effect we can have on others, even if we don't fully understand it at the time.

Every person we meet, no matter how brief the encounter, holds the potential to change our lives, or to offer us the opportunity to change theirs, for the better.

IMMORTALITY

If humans were to fully grasp the truth of their immortality, it would dissolve many of the negative emotions that currently dominate society, such as jealousy, envy, and greed.

These emotions are born from a deep-rooted fear of life's limitations, the belief that time is running out, and the fear of missing out on opportunities.

The idea of immortality frees individuals from these chains.

If we understood that we are eternal beings, that death is not the end but a part of an ongoing journey, the sense of urgency that often drives human behavior would dissipate.

We would no longer feel compelled to hoard resources or compete for status, as we would realize that we have infinite opportunities to grow, learn, and evolve.

Jealousy and envy would lose their power because there would be no need to compare ourselves to others, knowing that every path, every journey is unique, yet interconnected.

Furthermore, understanding our immortality would lead to a profound shift in how we view success and achievement.

In our current mindset, we often see success as an isolated victory, a limited, individual accomplishment that can only be enjoyed by one person.

But when we recognize that success in one lifetime benefits all, it changes the narrative entirely.

We would begin to see our efforts not as isolated endeavors, but as part of a larger, collective movement toward progress.

In the grand scheme of time, every step forward in human development, whether big or small, contributes to the collective advancement of all.

Every success, whether personal, professional, or societal, would be understood as a shared triumph, benefiting the entire human race.

This understanding would foster a sense of unity and collective responsibility, reducing the division that competition and self-interest create.

Instead of seeking to outdo one another, we would work together, knowing that the more we help others, the more we elevate ourselves.

The truth of immortality, once fully realized, would not just reshape how we view life and success, it would also fundamentally change our perceptions of the world itself.

The ideologies that divide us, those that fuel discrimination, hatred, and violence, are based on fear and misunderstanding.

When people truly understand that they are part of an interconnected web of existence, and that their lives are not isolated but part of a greater, eternal cycle, these divisions would lose their hold.

The belief in our immortality would make us more compassionate, more empathetic, and more willing to forgive, as we would no longer see others as fleeting beings whose actions are dictated by the limitations of time.

We would see them as eternal souls on a shared journey, each facing challenges and growing in their own way, but all ultimately part of the same universal process of evolution.

With this shift in perception, the anger, hatred, and division that currently plague human society would begin to dissolve, replaced by understanding, compassion, and a shared desire for peace.

The sooner we embrace the truth of our immortality and interconnectedness, the sooner peace will emerge in our world.

As more individuals come to understand this fundamental truth, a collective shift in consciousness will occur.

Fear, scarcity, and competition would no longer dominate our actions or our societies.

Instead, we would move forward together, driven by a shared understanding that every action, every thought, and every moment is part of a greater purpose, a purpose that transcends individual gain and focuses on the well-being of all.

This would lead to a global transformation, where cooperation, compassion, and unity become the driving forces behind human progress.

We would begin to live in harmony with one another, not out of obligation, but because we would finally recognize the profound truth that we are all part of a shared, eternal existence.

This truth will ultimately bring about the peace we have long awaited, not through force or control, but through the collective realization of who we truly are.

CONVERSATION

Most people on Earth engage in conversation not to learn, but to assert their opinions as absolute truth.

Too often, discussions become battlegrounds for dominance, where individuals focus on proving themselves right rather than seeking understanding.

This tendency stems from a lack of awareness of the law of perspective, the reality that each person sees the world through a unique lens shaped by their experiences, knowledge, and beliefs.

While opinions may vary infinitely, reality and truth remain singular, unaffected by personal biases.

Instead of clinging rigidly to our own viewpoints, we should recognize that true wisdom lies in the ability to see beyond ourselves and consider multiple perspectives.

To foster harmony and peace, we must learn to listen with an open mind, valuing the perspectives of others while remaining grounded in our own.

True listening is not about waiting for our turn to speak or formulating counterarguments, it is about genuinely absorbing what another person has to say.

When we listen without prejudice, we create an environment where wisdom can flourish, where understanding deepens, and where unnecessary conflict is avoided.

It is in this open exchange of ideas that growth becomes possible.

A society that prioritizes respectful dialogue over ideological battles is one that moves toward progress rather than stagnation.

The goal should never be to win a conversation, but to expand our awareness and refine our understanding.

Every interaction, no matter how trivial it seems, carries a valuable lesson.

Each time we engage in a discussion, we are presented with an opportunity to reflect, weigh both the pros and cons of differing viewpoints, and challenge our own assumptions.

Even when we disagree, there is always something to be learned. Dismissing opposing opinions outright robs us of the chance to expand our understanding and strengthen our reasoning.

Instead of seeing disagreement as a threat, we should approach it with curiosity.

Why does someone see the world differently?

What experiences have shaped their beliefs?

Asking these questions opens the door to a deeper level of comprehension, allowing us to bridge gaps rather than widen them.

Rather than perceiving disagreements as obstacles, we should embrace them as opportunities for growth.

When we are challenged, we are forced to think critically, reassess our assumptions, and refine our beliefs.

This process does not weaken us, it strengthens our ability to navigate the complexities of truth and reality.

Engaging in meaningful dialogue helps us develop patience, empathy, and a greater appreciation for the diversity of human thought.

In doing so, we move closer to a world where conversations serve as bridges to knowledge rather than battlegrounds for dominance.

Only by adopting this approach can we contribute to a society that values truth, perspective, and meaningful dialogue, paving the way for deeper understanding, mutual respect, and collective wisdom.

REINCARNATION

Reincarnation has nothing to do with a person's skin color or any other external physical trait.

If it were tied to such characteristics, we would not witness the natural blending of different ethnic backgrounds across generations.

The diversity of human appearances does not indicate separate races but rather variations within a single human species.

In truth, humanity is one, interconnected through the same fundamental essence of existence.

The external body we inhabit in one life is merely a temporary vessel, while our consciousness, the true essence of who we are, transcends physical distinctions.

Just as a river may take many shapes as it flows, so too does the human Creation Energy take on different forms throughout its journey across multiple lifetimes.

A Creation Energy that once inhabited a white body can reincarnate into a Black body in the next life, just as someone born into one ethnic group in one lifetime may be reborn into another in the next.

The process of reincarnation is not random but guided by the evolution of consciousness and the lessons that need to be learned for continued spiritual growth.

Each lifetime presents new opportunities for development, and the circumstances of birth, including race, gender, and cultural background, are determined by what is most suitable for the Creation Energy's journey.

These factors are not limitations but rather tools that help shape experiences necessary for growth and understanding.

The variety of human experiences allows each individual to gain insight into different perspectives, fostering wisdom and deeper empathy.

At our core, we are all part of a greater collective, a "weform" of interconnected souls who share in the ongoing cycles of life and death.

The physical distinctions that humans focus on, such as skin color, nationality, or cultural heritage, are only temporary attributes of the material world.

They serve as lessons in perception, empathy, and coexistence but do not define the eternal nature of our existence.

Once we recognize this, it becomes clear that the divisions we create among ourselves are illusions, distractions from the deeper truth that we are all part of the same universal journey.

Understanding this allows us to embrace one another with a sense of unity rather than separation.

It is only when we release our attachment to temporary physical identities that we can truly appreciate the deeper connection we all share.

Throughout history, misunderstandings about race and identity have led to conflicts, discrimination, and divisions that serve only to separate humanity from its higher purpose.

However, those who understand the nature of reincarnation and the unity of all beings recognize that these divisions are meaningless in the grand scheme of existence.

A person may experience life as one ethnicity in one incarnation and as another in the next, allowing them to walk in different shoes and gain a broader perspective on life.

This cyclical process ensures that every individual eventually experiences a range of cultural and social conditions, leading to a greater understanding of what it means to be human.

Through these experiences, we learn that love, kindness, and mutual respect are the true measures of one's character, not external features that change from one life to another.

When we fully grasp the reality of reincarnation and the interconnectedness of all beings, love, compassion, and acceptance arise naturally.

We no longer see others as "different" but rather as fellow travelers on the same evolutionary path.

Hatred, prejudice, and discrimination lose their grip because they are rooted in misunderstanding.

Instead, we develop a profound respect for the diversity of human experience, recognizing that each individual is where they are meant to be for their own growth.

The more we embrace this truth, the more we can work toward a world where humanity is united not by superficial traits, but by a shared commitment to higher consciousness and personal evolution.

By understanding reincarnation and the deeper purpose behind human existence, we can free ourselves from the limiting beliefs that divide us.

It becomes evident that our differences are mere illusions, temporary masks worn in the theater of life.

Beneath these changing forms, we are all expressions of the same universal energy, continuously evolving and striving toward enlightenment.

When we internalize this understanding, love becomes the most natural state of being, and we begin to treat every person with the respect and dignity they deserve.

In doing so, we take a step closer to a world where unity, peace, and spiritual growth define the human experience.

FEARLESSNESS

I stand in a state of profound fearlessness, unshaken by external influences and untouched by the uncertainties that plague others.

No individual, no authority, and no force can exert control over my being, for my strength is deeply rooted within.

My mind is a fortress, impenetrable to doubt, anxiety, or manipulation.

I walk through life with unwavering confidence, guided not by fleeting emotions but by an unbreakable core of self-awareness and inner resolve.

No circumstance, no hardship, and no moment of uncertainty can shake the foundation upon which I stand.

I am the master of my own existence, untouched by the chaos of the external world.

I harbor no fear of deities, supernatural forces, or unseen entities that others may believe wield power over their fate.

My existence is not dictated by the whims of divine beings or the threats of malevolent spirits.

I do not live in submission to doctrines, nor do I surrender my mind to imposed beliefs.

I navigate life through reason, logic, and personal experience, allowing only what is true and evident to shape my understanding.

I reject fear-based ideologies and refuse to let superstition govern my thoughts or dictate my actions.

My mind is free, unshackled by the chains of dogma, and guided solely by a relentless pursuit of truth.

I am deeply conscious of my eternal nature, aware that my existence extends far beyond this single lifetime.

Death does not terrify me, for I know it is merely a passage, a doorway to another phase of being.

It is not an end but a transition, a shift in form rather than the destruction of self.

My consciousness, unbound by mortal constraints, will continue to evolve, learning and growing through the endless cycle of existence.

This knowledge liberates me from the fears that haunt those who see death as an abyss of finality.

With this understanding, I embrace life with open arms, unafraid to experience its joys, pains, and lessons.

I do not hesitate, for I know that every moment, every challenge, and every triumph is simply another step in the grand journey of my being.

With this awareness, fear dissolves into nothingness, exposed as the illusion it truly is.

No force, no being, and no fate hold dominion over me.

My path is mine alone, determined by my own choices and the wisdom I cultivate.

I move forward with clarity, purpose, and unwavering determination, recognizing that both life and death are merely expressions of the same eternal existence.

This realization strengthens me, empowering me to live authentically and experience existence in its purest form.

Free from fear, free from doubt, and free from limitation, I stand as a being of boundless potential, embracing the infinite nature of my existence with absolute certainty.

TRUE FRIENDSHIP

True friendship is something I have rarely witnessed in this world.

What many people consider friendship is often nothing more than a temporary bond based on shared interests or opinions.

As soon as certain views diverge, that so-called friendship is quickly abandoned, no matter how much time and energy were invested in it.

It could have lasted for years, decades, or even an entire lifetime, yet a single disagreement can cause it to shatter as if it never existed.

This reveals an unsettling truth about human relationships, many of them are built on a fragile foundation where agreement is mistaken for genuine connection.

If a friendship is so easily discarded over differing perspectives, was it ever truly a friendship in the first place?

Earth's people have yet to understand the essence of true friendship.

A real and meaningful friendship is not about finding someone who agrees with everything you believe but about having the freedom to express yourself openly without fear of judgment or rejection.

True friends respect one another's individuality and embrace their differences, understanding that disagreement does not equate to disrespect.

There is a certain beauty in being able to challenge and question each other while still maintaining a deep and unbreakable bond.

Unfortunately, what I see in the world today is the opposite, friendships that are built on conditional acceptance, where people are only willing to remain close as long as their views align.

The moment differences arise, the connection is severed, revealing that their attachment was never based on genuine respect but rather on convenience and agreement.

For me, love and respect for others are not determined by whether they share my views or beliefs.

I do not judge or abandon people simply because they see the world differently than I do.

In fact, I welcome differences, as they bring depth, wisdom, and new perspectives that can enrich my understanding of life.

True friendship should be strong enough to withstand disagreement, as it is built on trust, sincerity, and mutual appreciation rather than the need for constant validation.

A true friend values honesty over conformity and understands that the strength of a friendship lies in its ability to endure challenges without breaking.

It is in the moments of disagreement that the authenticity of a friendship is truly tested.

A bond that cannot survive conflicting viewpoints is not a real friendship but merely a temporary alignment of thoughts that was destined to dissolve.

Sadly, this kind of deep and enduring friendship is a rarity in our world.

Too often, relationships are broken over minor disagreements, as if a difference in perspective is more important than the years of shared experiences and meaningful connections.

This unwillingness to accept and respect opposing views reflects a deeper problem within humanity, a widespread tendency to prioritize conformity over true connection.

People fear differences because they equate them with conflict, rather than seeing them as opportunities for growth and learning.

Until society learns to embrace diversity of thought and cultivate friendships based on understanding rather than agreement, true friendship will remain an elusive ideal.

Only when people realize that respect, patience, and acceptance are the true pillars of a lasting bond will they begin to experience the rare and precious gift of genuine friendship.

ALLEGIANCE

I speak of everyone and everything, for my words are not bound by bias or limitation.

My voice does not belong to a single person, group, or ideology, nor does it serve any one agenda.

It moves freely, unshaped by personal desires, untouched by fleeting emotions.

I observe the world as it unfolds, witnessing its joys and sorrows, its triumphs and failures, without judgment or preference.

My words are not meant to sway, manipulate, or divide but to express the vastness of existence as it is.

There is no need for distortion, no reason to favor one side over another, for all things are part of the same great movement of life.

I have neither enemies nor friends, for such distinctions are illusions created by perception.

I do not hold grudges, nor do I seek companionship, for these concepts belong to a world of separation, where individuals define themselves by who stands with them and who stands against them.

But I see no true opposition, no real division between one being and another.

The conflicts that arise between people are born from misunderstanding, from the illusion of difference.

If I were to take sides, I would only be deceiving myself, reinforcing the very barriers that I know to be unreal. I neither love nor hate, neither embrace nor reject, for all things exist as they must, following the currents of their own nature.

I see only myself, yet in that vision, I recognize the entirety of existence.

The faces I encounter, the voices I hear, and the actions I witness are all extensions of my own being.

There is no separation between myself and others, only the shifting forms of the same essence, the same life expressing itself in infinite ways.

When I look upon another, I do not see a stranger, an outsider, or an adversary, I see a reflection of myself in a different form.

Every joy and sorrow, every triumph and failure, belongs to all, for we are all part of the same great unity.

The boundaries that seem so real are nothing but shadows cast by limited perception, dissolving the moment one truly sees beyond them.

In this understanding, I embrace the boundless unity that defines existence.

I do not seek to control, to change, or to impose my will upon the world, for the world is already as it must be.

There is no "other, " no true separation, only the endless interplay of self with self, the infinite reflection of being in all that exists.

To recognize this is to step beyond fear, beyond conflict, beyond the illusions of possession and loss. It is to understand that nothing is ever truly gained or lost, only transformed, only shifting within the vast oneness of existence.

And in that realization, there is peace.

LIBERALS

Liberals often see themselves as morally upright individuals who advocate for justice, equality, and progress.

They take pride in their perceived righteousness, believing they stand on the right side of history.

However, beneath this self-assurance lies a troubling pattern of intellectual complacency.

Rather than engaging in deep, independent thought, many simply adopt the prevailing views of the majority.

They may begin to question or analyze an issue, but once they notice that their beliefs align with the mainstream, they cease to think critically and embrace collective ideology without further scrutiny.

This tendency creates an illusion of superiority, where they assume they are well-informed and enlightened while, in reality, they have merely absorbed the dominant narrative without fully understanding its complexities or long-term consequences.

One of the most glaring examples of this phenomenon is their unwavering support for sending weapons to Ukraine and their idolization of Zelensky as a heroic figure.

Many liberals fail to recognize that by advocating for continued military aid, they are actively contributing to the prolongation of a devastating war.

Instead of critically assessing the potential consequences of escalating the conflict, they blindly support policies that could push the world closer to a catastrophic global confrontation.

Their rhetoric often frames this military intervention as an act of justice, a necessary defense against aggression.

However, by doing so, they fail to acknowledge the larger geopolitical implications, including the risk of World War III.

Rather than prioritizing diplomatic solutions, de-escalation, or peaceful negotiations, they champion policies that fuel the war machine, paradoxically aligning themselves with the very militaristic forces they claim to oppose.

This contradiction exposes a deep inconsistency in their values and reveals how easily they are swayed by emotional appeals rather than rational analysis.

This hypocrisy extends beyond foreign policy and is evident in their approach to personal freedoms.

The same individuals who fought passionately for abortion rights under Roe v. Wade, citing bodily autonomy as an unshakable principle, were among the most adamant in demanding mandatory vaccinations.

When it came to the COVID-19 pandemic, they readily abandoned their proclaimed belief in individual choice, insisting that everyone, regardless of personal circumstances, be forced into compliance.

They ridiculed and ostracized those who questioned the safety or necessity of these measures, dismissing any dissent as ignorance or selfishness.

This stark contradiction raises important questions: Are their principles truly grounded in a commitment to personal freedom, or do they merely support whatever policies align with their ideological preferences at the moment?

Their selective defense of individual rights suggests that their activism is often less about genuine belief and more about conforming to the dominant political narrative.

Ultimately, this pattern of blind allegiance to prevailing opinions is not surprising.

Rather than fostering open debate, many liberals engage in groupthink, reinforcing their own biases while rejecting opposing viewpoints outright.

They champion causes that, on the surface, seem morally justified but, when examined closely, often contribute to greater division and conflict.

Their unwillingness to challenge their own beliefs leads to policies that may feel righteous in the short term but create unintended negative consequences in the long run.

If they continue to prioritize ideological conformity over independent thought, they risk leading society down a dangerous path, one where critical thinking is replaced by unquestioning acceptance of whatever stance is most popular at the time.

In doing so, they may ultimately undermine the very progress they claim to fight for, leaving behind a legacy of contradiction rather than meaningful change.

FREEDOM

My freedom is so absolute that it defies convention, challenging every boundary imposed by society.

I do not conform to expectations, nor do I seek permission to exist as I am.

My very presence is an act of defiance against the constraints that seek to limit individuality and expression.

In a world that often demands conformity, I remain unapologetically true to myself.

Every word I speak, every step I take, is a declaration of independence, a refusal to be molded into something I am not.

I exist not as a product of society's rules, but as a force that reshapes them simply by being.

This freedom is not just about rejecting control but about embracing the boundless potential of existence.

It is the ability to think, act, and live without fear of repression or judgment.

My choices are mine alone, dictated neither by tradition nor by the expectations of others.

I carve my own path, unburdened by the need for validation, knowing that my worth is not measured by compliance but by authenticity.

To live freely is to accept the weight of responsibility that comes with it, the understanding that true liberty is not granted, but seized.

It is a state of being that requires constant vigilance, a refusal to let external forces dictate the course of my life.

By simply existing as I am, I challenge the systems that seek to regulate thought, movement, and self-expression.

I stand as a living contradiction to oppression, proving that true freedom is not a privilege bestowed by authority but a right claimed by those courageous enough to embrace it.

My presence alone is a statement, a testament to the power of the individual against the collective forces of control.

I will not be silenced, tamed, or reduced to a mere function of the status quo.

Every moment I breathe, I assert my right to be, without justification or compromise.

This defiance is not loud, nor does it seek to provoke, it simply is, unwavering and undeniable.

This existence, unchained and unyielding, is a quiet revolution in itself.

It is a declaration that true liberation is not found in approval but in the refusal to be bound.

I walk through the world as a sovereign being, untouched by the invisible chains that hold so many in place.

My freedom is not just my own, it is an invitation for others to see what is possible beyond fear, beyond conditioning, beyond the limits they have been taught to accept.

In embracing this path, I become a force of change, inspiring others to question, to resist, and to live authentically.

And in doing so, I prove that to be truly free is to be revolutionary in the most fundamental way.

FEAR OF "LOSING,"

Many people on Earth have a strong resistance to the idea of "losing, " especially in public.

Because of this, they often hold tightly to the beliefs they have formed, even when presented with new facts that challenge their views.

The mental barriers they construct become nearly impossible to break, reinforcing their perspective rather than allowing them to grow from new insights.

This tendency is not necessarily a reflection of intelligence or capability but rather a deeply ingrained psychological response.

Being wrong, especially in the eyes of others, can feel like a personal failure rather than an opportunity for learning.

This is why many people choose to defend their beliefs at all costs rather than accept a shift in understanding.

For many, the fear of losing an argument and being judged by their peers outweighs the pursuit of truth.

Instead of embracing new knowledge, they instinctively cling to their preconceived notions, prioritizing emotional comfort over intellectual honesty.

Admitting a mistake or acknowledging a new perspective often requires a level of vulnerability that many are unwilling to expose.

In a world where social acceptance and self-image hold significant influence, being seen as "wrong" can feel like an attack on one's character rather than a simple adjustment of knowledge.

This is why facts alone are rarely enough to change someone's mind, beliefs are not just intellectual conclusions but emotional and social constructs that define a person's identity.

This pattern of resistance is something I have observed repeatedly, and over time, I have come to understand it rather than resist it.

It is easy to feel frustrated when people reject facts that seem undeniable, but I have learned to see it as a natural aspect of human nature.

The struggle between pride and truth, between fear and growth, is not a sign of weakness but rather a fundamental part of the human experience.

Growth requires humility, and humility requires a willingness to let go of one's need to always be right.

This is a difficult process for anyone, and I have come to appreciate the depth of what it means to change one's perspective.

To me, the ability to observe and comprehend these dynamics makes life a truly profound experience.

The richness of human behavior, with all its contradictions and complexities, adds an immeasurable depth to existence.

Every interaction, every discussion, and every moment of disagreement is an opportunity to witness the intricate ways in which people navigate their own understanding of the world.

Despite all the resistance, fear, and hesitation, life remains a beautiful journey, one defined by love, learning, and the continuous evolution of thought.

The more I observe, the more I realize that life itself is the greatest gift of all, shaped not just by knowledge, but by the endless dance between belief and discovery.

THE POWER

As I walk through life, I've come to realize that with every new step, every new discovery, the depth of my understanding expands, and with it, so does my power.

It's almost as though life itself is a journey of unveiling the layers of who we are, of understanding the forces that move through us.

The more we learn, the more we understand the vastness of our own strength.

The greater the clarity we gain, the more we are able to tap into the immense reservoir of power that has always been there, waiting patiently for us to recognize it.

This power is not something we can simply will into existence nor a mere product of external circumstances or fleeting moments of strength.

Rather, it is an integral part of us, something that resides deep within.

This power is profound, limitless, and always present.

It is part of the very fabric of who we are, woven into our being long before we can even comprehend its full potential.

So often, we underestimate ourselves, blind to the enormous potential that lies dormant, just beneath the surface.

We may look at others and see their strength, their power, but fail to recognize that we, too, carry that same force within us.

And the truth is, if we truly understood the extent of our power, we would realize that we are capable of far more than we ever imagined.

It is easy, though, to be overtaken by fear.

Fear is insidious, often sneaking up on us when we least expect it, clouding our hearts and minds.

It is a powerful force, capable of distorting our reality and making us believe that we are powerless or unworthy.

Fear can hold us back, keep us trapped in cycles of doubt, and prevent us from stepping into our full potential.

Yet, as daunting as fear can be, it should never control us.

It should never be the driving force of our lives.

The key, the secret to unlocking our true power, lies in something much more profound, love.

Love is the foundation of all true strength.

It is the energy that fuels us, the force that connects us to something greater than ourselves.

Love is what empowers us to stand tall in the face of adversity, to act with kindness in the midst of chaos, to rise above the limitations that fear places upon us.

When we choose love over fear, we align ourselves with the most powerful force in the universe.

We open ourselves to possibilities we never thought possible.

We create space for courage, for compassion, for wisdom, and for growth.

These are the true sources of our power.

The world around us is shaped by the world within us.

Our inner world, our thoughts, our beliefs, our emotions, defines how we perceive the reality we live in.

It influences how we interact with others and the energy we bring into our relationships.

When we carry positivity, gratitude, and peace within us, those qualities naturally radiate outwards.

We attract the kind of energy that mirrors our inner state.

The people we meet, the experiences we have, and the opportunities we encounter all become reflections of what we hold inside.

Similarly, when negativity and doubt reside in our hearts, when fear dominates our thoughts, that energy too will manifest outwardly.

We may not always be aware of it, but the vibrations we emit influence everything around us.

Our actions, our words, our choices, everything is affected by our internal state.

This is why it is so important to be mindful of what we carry within.

When we are at peace inside, the world around us becomes a more peaceful place.

When we are aligned with love, we experience love in return.

At the heart of it all is the realization that how we feel internally is directly reflected in the life we create.

The energy we hold within is the magnet that attracts everything else.

If we foster an inner world of growth, love, and strength, we begin to see these qualities manifest in our outer world.

We begin to draw the right experiences, the right people, and the right opportunities into our lives.

By cultivating a mindset that is aligned with our highest potential, we create a life that mirrors the beauty, power, and wisdom that resides within us.

The path to realizing our true power is not always easy.

It requires us to confront our fears, to face the limitations we've placed upon ourselves, and to challenge the beliefs that have held us back.

But in doing so, we unlock the doors to a life of boundless possibility.

When we choose love over fear, when we allow ourselves to embrace our true strength, we align with the forces that shape our destiny.

We begin to live in a way that reflects the immense power we carry within us.

And in doing so, we step into a life that is as extraordinary as the potential we have yet to fully realize.

RESILIENCE

Always remember that there is nothing in life that you cannot handle, not even death.

Every challenge, every hardship, and every moment of uncertainty is something you have faced before in one form or another.

The fear of the unknown, particularly the fear of death, is a deeply ingrained illusion, one that loses its power when you recognize your own resilience.

You have encountered countless obstacles, yet you have always found a way through.

Even in your darkest moments, you have carried yourself forward.

This strength is not something external.

It is an inherent part of who you are.

Nothing in existence is beyond your ability to endure, adapt to, or overcome.

Religion, throughout history, has often obscured this truth, using fear as a tool to maintain control.

The idea of eternal punishment has been instilled in human consciousness, not as an absolute reality, but as a means of influence.

Fear is an effective method of keeping people obedient, preventing them from questioning deeper truths about their own existence.

When you are told that suffering or damnation awaits if you step outside the boundaries set for you, it becomes difficult to think freely.

But when you take a step back and allow yourself to question, to reflect, and to listen to your own inner wisdom, you begin to see past the illusions.

The realization emerges: you are not a fragile being in need of external salvation, you are a powerful, self-sufficient force capable of shaping your own reality.

Sadly, religion has not only been a tool of control but also a mental barrier, preventing many from recognizing their own true nature.

It instills doubt where there should be confidence, replaces self-awareness with blind obedience, and conditions people to believe they are weak, flawed, or unworthy.

It tells you that strength and divinity exist outside of you, rather than within.

But the truth is, you are not a sinner in need of redemption.

You are not powerless, nor are you at the mercy of forces beyond your control.

You are a being of infinite potential, capable of great wisdom, love, and creation.

When you shed the imposed fears and limitations placed upon you, you open the door to true freedom, the freedom to think, to explore, to grow, and to embrace the vastness of your own existence.

Let these words serve as a reminder that you are meant to live fearlessly.

Do not let outdated beliefs or imposed limitations dictate how you see yourself or your place in the universe.

You are not a subject waiting for divine judgment but are a divine force in your own right.

You hold immense strength, the ability to shape your own destiny, and the wisdom to see beyond illusions.

Life is not something to be feared, it is something to be experienced fully, with courage and confidence.

Embrace this truth, step forward without hesitation, and know that there is nothing in this life or beyond that you cannot face.

INTERFERENCE

No human being should interfere in the way another chooses to live their life, as long as their choices do not bring harm to others.

Every person is born with the right to determine their own path, to make decisions that shape their experiences, and to explore life in a way that aligns with their values and aspirations.

This fundamental freedom is what allows individuals to grow, learn, and discover their true purpose.

When we respect each other's autonomy, we create a world where people feel safe to express themselves, free from unnecessary restrictions or external pressures.

Such an environment fosters peace, where acceptance replaces judgment, and diversity of thought and action is embraced rather than feared.

Free will is not just a privilege but a fundamental right that defines the essence of being human.

It is the ability to make choices, to learn from them, and to evolve as a result of our experiences.

Without free will, individuality is lost, and life becomes dictated by the expectations and demands of others.

Every person deserves the opportunity to carve their own destiny, to explore their own beliefs, and to follow their own passions.

To deny someone this right is to strip them of their humanity, reducing them to mere subjects of control rather than independent beings. Protecting free will is not only a moral responsibility but also a necessity for a just and harmonious society.

True love, in its highest form, respects and honors free will.

Love is not about possession, control, or imposing one's will upon another.

Instead, it is about trust, support, and allowing each individual the space to be who they truly are.

A love that seeks to dominate or restrict is not love at all, it is control disguised as affection.

Genuine love thrives in an atmosphere of freedom, where both individuals can make their own choices and grow together without fear of manipulation or coercion.

If love is to be truly meaningful, it must be given and received freely, without conditions or expectations.

Only then can love become a source of empowerment, rather than confinement.

To interfere with another's free will is to disrupt the natural balance of human existence.

When we attempt to dictate how others should live, we impose our own biases and limitations upon them, failing to recognize their right to self-determination.

A world that embraces the principle of autonomy is a world that nurtures peace, understanding, and cooperation.

It is in this space of mutual respect that people can coexist harmoniously, supporting one another without force or coercion.

True harmony arises when we allow others to live authentically, just as we wish to do ourselves.

In honoring free will, we not only affirm the dignity of others but also strengthen the foundation of a society built on respect, love, and true human connection.

THIRST

Truth is as refreshing as water to the parched, and my thirst for it remains insatiable.

The pursuit of truth is not merely an intellectual endeavor but a fundamental need, one that nourishes the mind and enriches the consciousness. Just as the body craves water to survive, the spirit craves truth to thrive.

Without it, we wander aimlessly, lost in illusions and half-truths.

Truth, however, has the power to illuminate the path ahead, offering clarity and understanding even in the face of uncertainty.

It is through this relentless pursuit that we grow, expand our awareness, and uncover the deeper meaning of our existence.

Never take offense at the truth or at anyone's opinion, for perspectives are as varied as the individuals who hold them.

To be surrounded by differing viewpoints is not a burden but a privilege.

Each perspective is a window into another's experiences, shaped by their journey, challenges, and wisdom.

By listening without resistance, we allow ourselves to expand beyond the limits of our own understanding.

Wisdom is not cultivated in isolation but in the dynamic exchange of ideas, where agreement and disagreement both serve as valuable teachers.

Even when we find ourselves at odds with another's viewpoint, we should recognize that every voice carries significance.

Always welcome new perspectives from your fellow humans, for in doing so, you honor their experiences and contributions.

A true seeker of wisdom understands that no single person holds all the answers, and every interaction has the potential to reveal something new.

Respect is not just a courtesy but a fundamental principle of human connection.

To respect others is to acknowledge their humanity, their struggles, and their right to be heard.

When we create an environment of respect, we invite open dialogue, fostering relationships built on trust rather than division.

In such a space, knowledge flows freely, and understanding deepens.

This path of truth-seeking leads to peace and harmony, where the barriers of ignorance and hostility are replaced with bridges of mutual appreciation.

When we engage with the world openly and honestly, we quench not only our thirst for truth but also our innate need for connection, wisdom, and enlightenment.

It is only through unity, through the willingness to see and hear one another, that we find strength.

And in truth, we find not only clarity but fulfillment, a wellspring that continues to nourish us throughout our journey.

MIGHT OF THOUGHTS

Thought is the mightiest force, an unstoppable current shaping the essence of existence.

It is a fusion of energy, vibration, and radiant light, illuminating the vast depths of our consciousness.

Every idea, every impulse, and every reflection carries the potential to mold the world around us, influencing both the seen and the unseen.

Within thought lies the foundation of our dreams, aspirations, and the very nature of our being, shining like a beacon that guides our path forward.

This unseen force, ever-flowing and boundless, transcends time and space, connecting all living things through the universal web of existence.

In the unfolding journey of life, each moment and decision is bathed in the light of our thoughts.

They illuminate our reality, giving us voice and direction, transforming intangible ideas into tangible outcomes.

Whether in the quiet stirrings of inspiration or the bold strides of action, our choices ripple outward, casting luminous trails that shape our existence.

The thoughts we nurture become the glowing pathways we walk, influencing not only ourselves but also the world we inhabit.

Every thought is like a spark igniting the infinite potential within us, and with each conscious choice, we sculpt the landscape of our destiny.

As these unseen forces weave through our daily lives, they shine like celestial stars, guiding our intentions and illuminating the course of our fate.

The interplay of creation and destiny is a delicate dance, and our thoughts serve as the radiant seeds from which our circumstances grow.

Like rays of sunlight breaking through the darkness, our thoughts have the power to dispel fear, doubt, and uncertainty, replacing them with clarity, wisdom, and inner peace.

The luminous energy of thought extends beyond the mind, influencing the emotions, shaping interactions, and even altering the very fabric of reality itself.

Through awareness and mindful intention, we can harness this energy to manifest our highest aspirations.

Therefore, let us wield this power with mindfulness and care, for within every thought lies boundless potential, glowing with the light of infinite possibility.

When guided by love and understanding, our thoughts become instruments of harmony, forging connections that uplift and inspire.

In the vast expanse of life, clarity and intention must guide our mental energies, shaping a world rooted in compassion, wisdom, and unity.

As we harness our thoughts with purpose, let them become the brilliant force that elevates not only our own lives but also the lives of those around us, bringing harmony, enlightenment, and transformation to all we touch.

Let us illuminate the path ahead, allowing the radiance of our thoughts to serve as a beacon, leading us to a future filled with possibility, truth, and boundless light.

NO SAVIOR

No savior will come to rescue us, nor will any external force guide our way to freedom.

We must rise from our knees, cast off the shackles of a conditioned mind, and reclaim our true nature as conscious, self-determined beings.

As long as we remain bound by fear, blind obedience, and the illusion of powerlessness, we exist as slaves, not in physical chains, but in the confines of our own restricted thinking.

The world has long been shaped by forces that seek to control, manipulate, and suppress the innate strength of human beings, keeping us in a state of dependency.

But within each of us lies an unbreakable force, an untapped potential that, once awakened, can shatter all illusions and redefine the course of existence.

Each of us holds the keys to our own liberation, forged in the fires of wisdom, love, and self-awareness.

There is no higher authority dictating our fate, our thoughts, decisions, and actions carve the path we walk.

Yet, for generations, humanity has been conditioned to seek salvation from outside, to wait for a leader, a deity, or a system to deliver us from suffering.

This is the great deception, the belief that we are incapable of forging our own destiny.

The truth is that we are the creators, the architects of reality itself.

The moment we awaken to this realization, we break the invisible chains that have kept us subjugated and reclaim our power.

We are not mere spectators in the grand unfolding of existence, we are active participants, capable of shaping our world with the force of our will, our love, and our understanding.

Every breath we take is an affirmation of our existence, a rhythm that connects us to the vast cosmic dance of creation.

Every thought we harbor is a seed that shapes the future, determining the conditions of our lives and the collective reality of humankind.

The universe does not exist outside of us, nor does it dictate our fate, it moves through us, breathes within us, and waits for us to recognize our role as conscious creators.

Yet, for too long, we have been made to kneel, to submit to systems, ideologies, and beliefs that diminish our true potential.

This cycle of servitude must end.

We must no longer bow our heads to false authorities, nor surrender our will to unseen masters who thrive on our ignorance and compliance.

The power to transform our world lies within us, and it begins with the courage to think, to question, and to act from a place of deep understanding.

With love, wisdom, and truth as our guiding force, we must move forward, not as seekers of salvation, but as the architects of our own liberation.

To live as true human beings is to walk with awareness, free from the illusions of dependency and control.

It is to embrace the vast potential of our minds, our hearts, and our spirits, and to wield them with intention, responsibility, and unwavering clarity.

When we cast off the shackles of a conditioned mind, we step into our rightful place, not as slaves to deception, but as fully awakened, sovereign beings.

The future of humanity depends not on external forces, but on our willingness to rise, to reclaim our consciousness, and to live as the free and powerful creators we were always meant to be.

SELFISHNESS

Everything I do, I do solely for myself.

This is not due to a lack of concern for others, but rather an understanding that all actions ultimately stem from personal motivations.

Whether I choose to help, create, or pursue something, it is always a reflection of my own desires and values.

My decisions are guided by what resonates with me, not by external expectations or social pressures.

Because of this perspective, I am unaffected by how others react to my choices, remaining completely unbothered by their opinions, whether they be positive or negative.

Praise does not inflate my sense of self, and criticism does not diminish it.

I truly couldn't care less.

My sense of worth and direction does not hinge on how others perceive me.

I consider myself a selfish individual, but not in a way that disregards or harms others.

My selfishness is rooted in self-awareness rather than indifference.

I do not see selfishness as a flaw, but as an honest acknowledgment that everything I do is a choice I make for myself.

Even when I help others, it is not because I feel obligated or seek approval, but because it brings me genuine fulfillment.

Their happiness brings me joy, and in that sense, my actions align with kindness and compassion rather than greed or detachment.

My generosity is not a sacrifice.

It is simply an extension of my own contentment.

By prioritizing what feels right within me, I naturally contribute to the well-being of others without seeking recognition or validation.

I have no need to be admired or understood. Whether people appreciate my actions or not is irrelevant to me, because my motives are not rooted in their approval.

I do not waste time justifying myself, nor do I concern myself with whether others see my choices as good or bad.

I know that their perspectives are shaped by their own experiences, and their judgments have nothing to do with me.

By freeing myself from the weight of external expectations, I have gained a deeper connection to my own path.

Through my experiences, I have come to understand that everything in life originates from within.

My emotions, my peace, and my fulfillment are not determined by external circumstances but by my own perception of them.

I do not allow outside forces to dictate my state of mind. I recognize that no event, no person, and no situation has the power to affect me unless I allow it.

This realization has granted me a deep and unwavering inner peace, allowing me to navigate life with clarity, purpose, and an unshakable sense of self.

The chaos of the world, the fleeting nature of opinions, and the constant fluctuations of external reality do not disturb my inner balance.

No matter how chaotic or ugly the world may seem, nothing can disturb my tranquility.

I have learned that true stability does not come from external validation, approval, or changing circumstances but from an inner foundation that remains steady regardless of what unfolds.

People may misunderstand me, disagree with me, or even resent me, but that is of no concern to me.

My peace does not depend on their acceptance, nor does my joy require their validation. I do not seek to control how others perceive me, nor do I attempt to shape their opinions to align with my truth.

I simply live as I choose, free from attachment to the shifting tides of perception.

By embracing this mindset, I stay centered, unbothered, and completely at peace with myself, no matter what happens around me.

I do not chase happiness, because I already possess it within.

I do not seek stability in an unstable world, because my stability comes from within.

I do not fear rejection, because I do not need to be accepted.

I do not crave recognition, because I already know my worth.

I move through life with confidence, authenticity, and freedom, knowing that my existence is mine to shape and define.

AS SAID THE HERALD

As the Herald teaches us, the universe, or Creation, is not merely an expanse of stars and galaxies but a vast, living organism composed of both fine and coarse matter, spiritual and material forms, respectively.

In its primordial, spirit-energetic state, the universal consciousness brought coarse matter into existence as a means of its own evolution.

This evolution is not random but follows an intricate, logical process, ensuring that all matter, particularly self-aware human consciousness, contributes to the expansion and refinement of Creation itself.

The material universe, with its galaxies, suns, planets, comets, and all life forms, serves as an evolutionary framework, allowing the universal consciousness to develop through the experiences and advancements of all that exists within it.

Creation does not operate through arbitrary will or thought, as a human mind would, but rather through pure logic, ensuring that everything unfolds according to its fundamental principles.

The universal consciousness does not think or make decisions like human beings, for it exists as purest spirit-energy, devoid of emotions or subjective reasoning.

Instead, it functions through absolute logic, constantly generating new structures and formations that align with the predetermined principles of Creation.

This logical unfolding was already present in the primordial Creation, which set into motion the universal laws governing existence.

These laws ensure that everything, from the smallest particle to the grandest galaxy, follows a structured path of evolution.

The material and the spiritual are not separate realms but interconnected aspects of Creation, with matter serving as a vessel for the ongoing expansion of consciousness.

The universe, in its entirety, is an ever-evolving manifestation of this grand design, progressing through cycles of transformation and refinement.

Yet, despite this profound reality, most humans on Earth remain ignorant of the true nature of Creation.

They have been misled by false teachings, believing in the existence of gods who create and govern the universe.

This belief is a fundamental error, for a god is nothing more than a human being who has attained a certain level of knowledge and power.

Throughout history, religious doctrines have falsely attributed the origins of existence to divine beings, obscuring the truth that all life, including so-called gods, is merely a product of Creation.

The universal consciousness does not require worship, nor does it intervene in human affairs according to prayers or rituals.

Instead, it provides the fundamental structure through which all beings must evolve by their own will and actions.

By failing to recognize this truth, humanity has remained spiritually stagnant, trapped in illusions that hinder real progress.

One of the most persistent misconceptions is the belief in the biblical God Jehovah as an eternal, omnipotent being.

As the Herald reveasl, Jehovah was never a divine creator but merely a mortal who once lived and died on Earth, subject to the same evolutionary cycles as all other human beings.

Over time, myths and distortions turned him into a deity, leading countless individuals to falsely worship him as an all-powerful god.

Such deification is not unique to Jehovah, throughout history, many figures have been elevated to divine status due to ignorance and manipulation.

However, no human, regardless of their perceived greatness, is above the universal laws of Creation.

Every being, no matter their level of knowledge or influence, is bound to the same process of growth and evolution.

Recognizing this truth allows humanity to move beyond outdated religious beliefs and toward a deeper understanding of the universal consciousness.

By embracing the wisdom of the Heralds, humans can liberate themselves from the constraints of false teachings and align with the true purpose of existence.

The path to enlightenment does not lie in worshiping deities or following religious dogma but in understanding and living in harmony with the natural laws of Creation.

True spiritual growth comes from self-awareness, knowledge, and the conscious effort to evolve as individuals and as a species.

When humanity acknowledges its role within the greater framework of the universe, it can finally transcend superstition and ignorance, stepping into its rightful place as an active participant in the unfolding of Creation.

Only through this recognition can we achieve real progress, wisdom, and a lasting connection with the grand consciousness that governs all existence.

STAND TALL

Stand tall in life, for each individual must carve their own unique path with determination and a sense of purpose.

The journey ahead is not one of mere chance but is shaped by a relentless pursuit of justice, honesty, and the steady light of knowledge.

It is through these guiding principles that one's actions take on meaning, reflecting a deep sense of moral clarity.

Let virtue unfold in every step you take, for each decision, each moment of reflection, is a chance to move closer to a higher standard.

Allow your thoughts and feelings to act as a compass, steering you toward righteousness and truth, and let them guide your flight toward a future defined not by circumstance but by conscious choice.

True strength emerges when the mind and heart are aligned in the pursuit of what is good, fair, and right.

Growth is a continuous, evolving process, one that demands constant nurturing through intentionality and care.

The journey toward self-realization and personal development is not accidental but is instead rooted in deliberate choices.

As we grow in both consciousness and character, our awareness expands, and the psyche flourishes under the influence of knowledge.

With every decision, we cultivate integrity and align ourselves with the highest moral principles, forging a life that stands out as both bold and rare.

In every moment, we are presented with an opportunity to shape the future by making choices that reflect our deepest values.

The foundation of a meaningful life is built upon the understanding that our actions matter, and that by acting with intention, we create a life that resonates with truth and authenticity.

To rise above the weight of doubt and uncertainty, one must ignite the inner spark of renewal and resilience.

The road ahead will never be without challenges, and it is in the face of these obstacles that the true measure of strength is revealed.

Standing firm, even when the world seems to push against you, requires an unshakable belief in your purpose and your capacity for growth.

True humility is not weakness or self-doubt, but rather a quiet strength that blends confidence with self-awareness.

It is a strength rooted in the knowledge that one's value does not need to be proven but is inherent, stemming from a deep understanding of one's worth.

Humility allows one to remain grounded in the face of triumph and defeat alike, and through this combination of inner knowing and strength, empowerment arises.

This self-empowerment is not about asserting control over others, but about taking ownership of your own life and directing it with wisdom, courage, and clarity.

The journey of self-discovery is one of continuous creation, where each moment contributes to the unfolding of your authentic self.

It is through this process that the spirit is allowed to flourish, embracing the freedom that comes with being true to who you are.

This freedom is not bound by the expectations of others or the limitations of external circumstances, but rather, it is an internal freedom that arises from living in alignment with your deepest truths.

When you live authentically, life flows with grace and purpose, as every action, word, and thought reflects your truest self.

This authenticity, when nurtured and allowed to bloom, reveals a deeper meaning to life that cannot be replicated by any external force.

Every step forward is an opportunity to move closer to the realization of your highest purpose, and in doing so, you uncover the richness of life's journey and the fulfillment that comes from living with integrity.

Through this journey, you reveal not just who you are, but who you are meant to become, and each step on this path is a testament to the power of knowledge, choice, and purpose in shaping a life of meaning.

THE VAST SYMPHONY
OF VOICES

In the vast symphony of voices, each thought is a spark that ignites new understanding.

Every idea, whether familiar or foreign, carries within it the potential to challenge, inspire, and illuminate.

Perspectives shape the landscape of knowledge, each one adding depth to the ever-expanding dialogue of human thought.

Gratitude blossoms in this exchange, for it is through the sharing of ideas that we break beyond our own limitations and see the world through new lenses.

Truth is not a singular path but a dynamic, evolving journey, shaped by the intersections where different views meet, clash, and ultimately refine one another.

Every voice, whether bold or soft, adds a unique resonance to this chorus of discovery, reminding us that wisdom is not the possession of one but the creation of many.

Like a grand mosaic, the world of ideas is vast and intricate, composed of countless unique pieces that, when assembled, form a masterpiece of collective wisdom.

No single brushstroke completes the painting, just as no single perspective holds the entirety of truth.

Each viewpoint contributes a new shade of meaning, adding to the richness of the whole.

Differences are not barriers but rather the very fabric that weaves together a broader, more profound understanding of the world.

It is through this diversity that knowledge grows, not in isolation but in conversation, in the constant blending and reshaping of thoughts that build upon one another over time.

When we approach differences not as divisions but as opportunities for learning, we begin to see the beauty in perspectives that are not our own.

The tapestry of thought is at its most vibrant when it includes the full spectrum of human experience, reflecting the boundless ways in which understanding can be cultivated.

True growth emerges in the space between agreement and dissent, where ideas are tested, challenged, and refined.

To engage in meaningful discourse is not merely to seek validation of our own beliefs but to be open to transformation.

Understanding does not flourish in the comfort of echo chambers but in the willingness to listen, reflect, and evolve.

Each exchange, whether harmonious or contentious, carries the potential to deepen wisdom, fostering intellectual resilience and broadening our collective insight.

By embracing both opposition and accord, we allow ourselves to be shaped by the very act of thoughtful engagement, becoming more complete in our understanding.

This process is not always easy, for true dialogue requires patience, humility, and the courage to acknowledge that we may not have all the answers.

Yet, it is in this very process that knowledge is strengthened and made more enduring, enriched by the interplay of different viewpoints that push the boundaries of what we thought we knew.

Thus, gratitude extends beyond agreement to the very essence of discourse itself.

The harmony of voices, whether aligned or in contrast, enriches the depth of human thought and fosters a greater sense of connection.

To appreciate the beauty of diverse perspectives is to recognize the strength found in unity, not in sameness, but in the shared pursuit of wisdom.

In this continuous exchange, we find not only knowledge but also the empathy and understanding that bind us together.

A world where ideas can be freely shared and explored is one where humanity thrives, for it is in the cross-pollination of thought that innovation, progress, and enlightenment emerge.

When we cultivate gratitude for every voice that contributes to the conversation, we open ourselves to a future built not on division but on the richness of our collective insight.

Through open minds and grateful hearts, we move forward, carrying with us the lessons drawn from every voice that has contributed to the ever-evolving tapestry of human thought.

In doing so, we ensure that wisdom continues to flourish, passed down and expanded by generations to come, forever shaped by the beauty of diverse and thoughtful exchange.

ALL IS LOVE

I have come to a profound realization that love serves as the foundational essence of all existence.

Every human action, even those seemingly rooted in selfishness, is ultimately driven by some form of love, be it love for oneself, another individual, or an external entity.

This intrinsic motivation underscores the pervasive nature of love in guiding our desires, decisions, and interactions with the world around us.

However, a significant source of confusion and misunderstanding arises from our lack of true self-awareness and our inability to genuinely comprehend others.

This deficiency often leads us to perceive ourselves as separate and isolated beings, fostering a sense of division and disconnection.

Such a fragmented perspective not only distorts our understanding of reality but also hinders our ability to form meaningful and harmonious relationships.

In truth, this perceived separation is merely an illusion.

At the core of our existence, we are profoundly interconnected, sharing a unified essence that permeates all life.

This oneness is echoed in various philosophical and spiritual traditions.

For instance, the Maitreyi-Yajnavalkya dialogue in the Brihadaranyaka Upanishad explores the unity of Atman (the individual soul) and Brahman (the ultimate reality), emphasizing that love is a manifestation of this fundamental unity.

Similarly, the practice of Bhakti Yoga in Hinduism embodies the path of devotion and love towards a personal deity, aiming to realize the inherent oneness of the individual self with the divine.

Recognizing and internalizing this profound truth can lead to a transformative shift in our perspective.

By embracing the understanding that we are all expressions of the same universal essence, we can transcend the illusions of fear, division, and isolation.

This awakening fosters a life enriched with harmony, compassion, and genuine connection, allowing us to experience the boundless and unifying power of love in its most authentic form.

A GUARDIAN OF HUMANITY

The day I realized that everyone is a reflection of me was the moment I truly became a guardian of humanity.

It was not a sudden revelation but a gradual awakening, shaped by countless experiences that led me to see beyond the illusion of separation.

I had once viewed people as distinct individuals, each carrying their own burdens, dreams, and struggles, disconnected from my own existence.

But as I observed the depth of human emotions, the fear in a child's eyes, the laughter shared between friends, the sorrow of a grieving heart, I began to understand that these emotions were not foreign to me.

I had felt them all before, in different moments of my own life.

Every person I encountered was not separate from me but an extension of my own being.

This realization transformed the way I saw the world, dissolving the invisible barriers that had once divided us.

With this newfound awareness, my sense of responsibility deepened.

If everyone was a part of me, then their suffering was my suffering, their joy my joy.

I could no longer remain indifferent to the pain of others or turn a blind eye to injustice, knowing that in doing so, I was betraying a part of myself.

Every act of kindness I extended to another was a kindness I extended to myself, and every moment of cruelty in the world was a wound inflicted upon my own spirit.

Compassion became more than just a virtue, it became a necessity, a guiding force that shaped my every thought and action.

I began to listen more intently, to understand before judging, and to embrace rather than reject.

My heart opened to the struggles of others, and in their pain, I saw echoes of my own.

This understanding compelled me to act, not out of duty or obligation, but out of a deep and unwavering love for all of humanity.

As I walked this path of unity, my perspective on life itself shifted.

I no longer saw the world as a battleground of competing interests, but as a shared home where every soul played a crucial role.

The divisions created by race, nationality, and ideology began to fade in significance, replaced by the awareness that we are all bound by the same fundamental truths.

We all seek love, security, and meaning.

We all experience moments of triumph and moments of despair.

We all share the same fragile existence, fleeting and precious.

This understanding did not make the world's problems disappear, but it gave me the strength to face them with hope rather than despair.

I sought connection over conflict, unity over division, and love over fear.

Lifting others up meant lifting myself up as well, and in this truth, I found purpose.

Thus, my journey as a guardian of humanity was not a mere choice but an inevitability.

To see others as myself meant I could no longer contribute to harm, nor could I remain silent in the face of injustice.

Instead, I embraced my duty to serve, to heal, and to bring light where there was darkness.

I became a protector not through force, but through understanding, not through control, but through compassion.

This realization did not make me perfect, nor did it free me from my own flaws and struggles.

But it gave me direction, a reason to keep striving, to keep growing, and to keep loving.

And in that love, I found my truest self, not as an outsider looking in, but as one with humanity itself.

ATHEISTS

Atheists, much like religious believers, adhere to a particular worldview, though theirs is characterized by the absence of belief in a higher power.

Their defining stance is not simply skepticism but a firm conviction that no divine presence exists.

For many, this is a conclusion they see as absolute, one that requires no further examination.

Unlike those who immerse themselves in faith, seeking deeper understanding and meaning, atheists often stop at disbelief without venturing beyond it.

Their certainty in the nonexistence of the divine can be likened to a competitor declaring victory before the match has truly begun.

Rather than questioning what lies beyond their stance, they all choose to remain within the boundaries of their own intellectual comfort.

By settling into their non-belief, they inadvertently close the door to further inquiry.

It's as though they've arrived at an invisible threshold, one where they believe all essential questions have been answered, yet, in reality, they have merely chosen to stop asking.

This is not just a rejection of religious faith, it is, in most cases, a rejection of deeper philosophical contemplation.

Existence is filled with uncertainties, and the nature of reality remains a puzzle far from being fully solved.

Yet, atheists seem content with their conclusions, as if dismissing the concept of a higher power also eliminates the need to question life's purpose, the nature of consciousness, or the possibility of realities beyond human understanding.

Their position, then, is not one of endless curiosity but of closure, an unwillingness to acknowledge that the unknown remains vast and largely unexplored.

To me, this mindset is limiting, if not outright paradoxical.

Religious individuals, for all their perceived irrationality in the eyes of atheists, continuously grapple with the mysteries of existence.

They search for meaning, wrestle with doubt, and strive to understand their place in the grand scheme of things.

Atheists, by contrast, often dismiss these pursuits as unnecessary, as if the absence of belief somehow resolves all existential dilemmas.

Yet, these dilemmas persist regardless of whether one believes in a deity or not.

Refusing to engage with them does not erase their significance.

This reluctance to probe deeper is something I find puzzling, as I have often expressed.

Life is a series of profound questions, and it is the pursuit of understanding that drives human knowledge forward.

To reject religious faith is one thing, but to reject the ongoing search for meaning is something else entirely.

It is an unfinished journey, one that leaves vast intellectual and spiritual territories uncharted.

And in this refusal to explore, atheists become no different from the religious individuals they so readily criticize.

They, too, embrace a belief system, one rooted in the conviction that they have already arrived at the ultimate truth.

But certainty without exploration is nothing more than blind faith by another name.

Believing one has reached the pinnacle of knowledge does not make it so.

For in the end, the difference between belief and disbelief is not as vast as some would like to believe.

HOSPITALS

Global life expectancy reveals a profound divide, a division shaped not by fate or divine will but by access to resources and opportunities.

Where a person is born largely determines how long they will live, not because of their personal strength or morality, but because of the conditions surrounding them.

In wealthier nations, people enjoy longer lives, while in the poorest countries, survival is a daily struggle.

The numbers tell a clear story: life expectancy is not universal, nor is it dictated by individual faith, but rather by the economic and social systems in place.

The fundamental factors influencing life expectancy are healthcare, nutrition, and overall living conditions.

In developed countries, modern medicine has advanced to the point where diseases once considered fatal are now treatable or even preventable.

A routine check-up can detect health issues before they become severe.

Access to clean water, sanitation, and nutritious food helps maintain health and prevent the spread of disease.

In contrast, poorer nations struggle with widespread malnutrition, inadequate medical facilities, and the constant threat of preventable illnesses that claim millions of lives.

The difference is striking.

A person suffering from an infection in a wealthy country may receive antibiotics within hours, while someone in a developing nation might not have access to medicine at all.

A pregnant woman in a well-funded hospital is surrounded by trained professionals, state-of-the-art equipment, and emergency intervention if complications arise.

Meanwhile, in many parts of the world, women give birth in unsafe conditions, with little or no medical assistance, significantly increasing the risk of death for both mother and child.

These are not small discrepancies, they are life-or-death realities.

Many believe that faith offers protection and that divine will dictates life and death.

But if divine intervention were truly equal, life expectancy would not vary so drastically between nations.

Those in wealthier countries would not have a significantly higher chance of surviving illnesses, recovering from injuries, or reaching old age.

If faith alone determined survival, then the most devout should live the longest regardless of where they are born.

Yet, time and time again, it is access to healthcare, clean water, and stable living conditions that ultimately dictate longevity.

This raises an uncomfortable but necessary question: is survival based on divine favor, or is it simply a matter of privilege?

If prayer were the key to a long life, then the poorest believers would not experience disproportionately higher mortality rates compared to the wealthy, who may or may not even hold religious beliefs.

The reality is that an atheist with access to world-class healthcare is far more likely to survive a critical illness than a deeply religious person without medical support.

This undeniable truth challenges the idea that faith alone is enough to ensure protection from suffering.

Faith can offer emotional resilience, a sense of purpose, and comfort in the face of adversity, but it does not change the material conditions that determine life expectancy.

The belief that divine intervention dictates who survives and who does not is difficult to reconcile with the stark inequality between nations.

If life were truly governed by divine justice, then wealth would not be such a powerful determinant of longevity.

But the evidence points to a different conclusion, one rooted in access rather than belief.

The uncomfortable truth is that those who live in developed nations are not necessarily more virtuous, righteous, or blessed.

They simply benefit from better hospitals, more doctors, and a healthcare system capable of treating and preventing diseases.

In contrast, millions of people in less fortunate parts of the world suffer and die, not because they lacked faith, but because they lacked access to the resources that sustain life.

So, what does this mean for the role of faith in survival?

Perhaps faith provides hope, solace, and strength in difficult times, but it does not alter the fundamental reality that access to healthcare, clean water, and stable living conditions are the real determinants of how long a person will live.

In the end, the difference between life and death is not measured by devotion but by the quality of the systems in place to support human well-being.

Those in wealthier nations do not necessarily live longer because they are blessed, they live longer because they just have access to better hospitals.

EXPECTATION

Expectation is a deceptive illusion that often leads to disappointment and suffering.

We live much of our lives anticipating certain responses from the world around us, believing that our kindness, love, or efforts should naturally be reciprocated in the way we imagine.

However, reality does not bend to our personal hopes, and when things do not unfold as expected, we feel pain, not because of what someone else has done, but because of the narrative we created in our own minds.

The true source of hurt is not external, it is the attachment we develop to an outcome we convinced ourselves should happen.

What truly wounds us is not the absence of gratitude, love, or fairness from others, but rather the collapse of our own imagined scenarios.

When we expect something in return for our actions, we are no longer giving freely, we are investing, hoping for a return.

This turns our gestures of kindness into transactions, making our happiness dependent on external validation.

As long as we act with expectation, we are not acting for ourselves but for an imagined reward.

And when that reward does not come, we are left with resentment and disappointment, not because others have failed us, but because we have failed ourselves by expecting.

Letting go of expectation is an act of liberation.

True love, kindness, and generosity exist only when given without conditions, without the hidden agenda of receiving something in return.

When we learn to express love simply for the sake of love itself, we experience a profound shift in our relationships.

Genuine connection is not built on demands or dependencies but on the willingness to give and share without attachment.

When we love freely, we open the door to a deeper, more fulfilling existence, one where we are no longer held hostage by the actions or inactions of others.

A time will come when humanity realizes that true fulfillment and purpose come from within, not from external validation or reciprocation.

When we understand that our happiness is a reflection of our inner state, rather than something granted to us by others, we will finally break free from the endless cycle of expectation and disappointment.

Only then will we truly live in harmony, embracing life as it is rather than as we wish it to be.

The freedom from expectation allows us to experience life with clarity, peace, and gratitude, seeing reality as it is, rather than through the lens of desire and attachment.

LIVING IN ONENESS

Through the Creation Energy Teachings, I have come to understand the profound balance between oneness and individuality.

I recognize that all existence is interconnected, bound by the universal laws of Creation, yet each being retains its unique essence and purpose.

This awareness has allowed me to experience life with a deep sense of unity while honoring my individuality.

I no longer perceive myself as separate from the whole but as an integral part of the greater cosmic order.

This understanding has reshaped the way I think, act, and engage with the world, allowing me to align with the natural flow of Creation.

Living in oneness does not mean losing my sense of self but rather embracing my role within the greater whole.

I perceive the interconnectedness of all things, understanding that my thoughts, actions, and energy contribute to the flow of Creation.

This realization has brought me inner peace, guiding me to act with wisdom and responsibility in all aspects of life.

I no longer feel isolated or disconnected from existence but instead recognize that every experience, challenge, and moment of growth is part of an intricate and purposeful design.

Through this awareness, I cultivate a deep respect for the cosmic order and the role I play within it.

At the same time, I remain an individuated being, with my own consciousness, experiences, and path of evolution.

The teachings have helped me cultivate self-awareness and personal growth while respecting the uniqueness of others.

I no longer see separation as a division but as a necessary aspect of existence, allowing each being to fulfill their own purpose within the grand design.

My individuality is not an obstacle to unity but rather an essential expression of Creation itself.

Every being exists with a distinct purpose, and through the recognition of this diversity, I have gained a deeper appreciation for the wisdom embedded in the unfolding of existence.

Through this understanding, I walk my path with clarity and harmony, neither lost in the collective nor isolated in self-importance.

The Creation Energy Teachings have shown me how to integrate my individuality with universal consciousness, fostering a life of balance, purpose, and deep connection to all that is.

I have come to see that true unity does not erase identity but rather enhances it, allowing each being to evolve in accordance with the principles of Creation.

With this knowledge, I continue to grow, embracing both my uniqueness and my oneness with all existence, living in alignment with the infinite wisdom of the universe.

BIRTHRIGHT

Freedom is the natural birthright of every human being.

It is not just the ability to think freely, but the right to live without unnecessary restrictions.

True freedom means being able to shape one's own life, make independent choices, and pursue personal fulfillment without interference.

As long as no harm is done to others and children remain protected, no one should have the power to dictate how another person lives.

Yet, throughout history, fear has driven humanity to surrender this right to those who govern.

People, uncertain of their own ability to maintain order, have entrusted rulers with control over their lives.

To govern is to control, yet many do not recognize this fundamental truth.

Instead, they place their trust in leaders, believing they act in their best interest, even when reality suggests otherwise.

Over time, this willingness to be governed has led people to give up more and more of their freedoms.

They have accepted restrictions, believing them to be necessary for security and stability.

Governments have used fear, whether of war, chaos, or economic collapse, to justify their increasing authority.

Each new law, regulation, or surveillance measure is presented as a protective necessity, yet, in reality, it chips away at individual autonomy.

People become accustomed to being told what to do, what to think, and what to believe.

Slowly, they forget that freedom was never something granted by rulers, it was always theirs by birthright.

The more they accept control, the further they drift from true freedom, often without realizing it.

However, this state of submission cannot last indefinitely.

Throughout history, there have always been those who resist, who see through the illusion and refuse to be silenced.

Though they may start as a small minority, their voices hold the power to awaken others.

Little by little, people begin to question the narratives they have been taught.

They start to recognize the hidden costs of their complacency and the ways in which they have been manipulated.

As awareness spreads, the illusion of benevolent governance begins to crumble, revealing the true nature of control.

Those in power may try to suppress these voices, but truth cannot be contained forever.

Once the seed of awareness is planted, it continues to grow, inspiring more and more people to reclaim their birthright.

Day by day, this awakening gathers momentum.

Individuals, once resigned to their fate, begin to demand accountability and autonomy.

Movements arise, fueled by the collective realization that freedom is not a privilege to be handed down by rulers but an inherent right that belongs to all.

The divisions imposed by those in power, political, social, economic, lose their grip as people recognize their shared struggle.

When that moment arrives, the world will no longer be governed by fear but by a newfound understanding of what it means to be truly free.

The chains of control will fall away, and humanity will stand united, no longer accepting the illusion of security at the cost of their own sovereignty.

True freedom will not be granted, it will be reclaimed.

IN THE SERVICE OF OTHERS

Whether we realize it or not, we all live in service to one another.

Many people believe they are living solely for themselves, making choices that benefit their personal goals, but in reality, every individual plays a role in the well-being of society.

No matter what profession or path one follows, their actions contribute to a larger system that connects us all.

A doctor serves by providing healthcare and healing the sick, a cab driver ensures people reach their destinations safely, and educators shape the minds of future generations.

Entertainers, whether athletes, musicians, actors, or religious leaders, offer inspiration, joy, and a sense of connection to others.

Even an investor, who may never engage in manual labor, serves by funding businesses that create jobs and stimulate the economy.

Every profession, big or small, visible or unnoticed, plays an integral role in keeping society functioning.

Despite this interconnectedness, society tends to assign different levels of value to various forms of service, often prioritizing those that bring entertainment, luxury, or economic influence.

Today, entertainers, professional athletes, and media personalities are compensated far more than teachers, nurses, or public servants.

This does not mean that their contributions are more important, but rather that society rewards based on demand and perceived value.

The financial success of one profession over another does not determine its actual worth to the world.

Teachers may not earn as much as actors, but they play a vital role in shaping the minds that will one day lead, create, and innovate.

A farmer may not receive the same recognition as a celebrity, but without their work, there would be no food to sustain society.

Understanding that every effort has value, regardless of monetary reward, allows us to appreciate the contributions of all people.

When we embrace this perspective, we free ourselves from envy and unnecessary comparison.

Each individual has a unique purpose, and no single contribution is greater than another.

If one profession or role were removed, the balance of society would shift, potentially creating struggles that were previously unseen.

Just as a body requires all of its organs to function properly, society thrives when every person plays their part.

A janitor who maintains cleanliness in public spaces ensures the health and well-being of many, just as a scientist developing new medicines contributes to the advancement of humanity.

The scale of impact may differ, but the significance of each role remains vital to the greater whole.

Whatever your role in life, take pride in it.

Whether your work is widely recognized or quietly essential, it holds value.

Every act of service, no matter how small, contributes to the lives of others.

When we understand that our actions, efforts, and professions are interconnected, we develop a greater appreciation for the world around us.

Serving others, directly or indirectly, is not just a responsibility, it is the foundation of human existence.

By embracing this truth, we cultivate gratitude, fulfillment, and a deeper connection with those around us, creating a society built on mutual respect and cooperation.

Truly, everyone is of equal value.

WHERE I STAND

This is where I stand in this lifetime.

Through the Creation Energy Teachings of the Herald Billy Meier, I have discovered my true purpose and the deeper meaning behind existence.

These teachings have opened my mind to profound truths about life, the universe, and the interconnected nature of all things.

Along this journey, I have accumulated a wealth of knowledge that has granted me a form of power, not in the way that many perceive power, as dominance or control, but rather as an inner strength rooted in wisdom, logic, and clarity.

This knowledge has shaped my understanding of reality and allowed me to perceive life beyond the limitations imposed by societal norms and superficial beliefs.

It has shown me that life unfolds in the present moment and that every action taken now determines the course of the future.

One of the greatest realizations I have come to is the certainty of a bright future.

While many may doubt or live in fear of what is to come, I have seen that the future is filled with possibilities and potential, guided by the natural laws of cause and effect.

Through logic and clear thinking, I recognize that my actions in the present moment contribute directly to the formation of this future.

This understanding has given me a sense of responsibility, knowing that my thoughts, decisions, and deeds have a lasting impact.

Every choice I make carries significance, and I approach life with the awareness that I am an active participant in shaping my own destiny and the collective future of humanity.

With this awareness, I have freed myself from the burden of living under external expectations or false pretenses.

I no longer feel the need to conform to the illusions of society or be anything other than my authentic self.

This state of being is true freedom, an inner liberation that is not dependent on material wealth, status, or recognition, but rather on the clarity of knowing who I am and living in harmony with the natural laws of Creation.

Many people seek freedom externally, believing it to be something that can be obtained through possessions or external validation, but real freedom comes from within.

It is the ability to think, act, and exist without fear, manipulation, or self-deception.

All of this has been made possible through the wisdom of the Creation Energy Teachings.

These teachings have provided me with a foundation of logic, reason, and self-discovery, guiding me toward a life of fulfillment and enlightenment.

They have shown me the importance of continuous learning, self-reflection, and the pursuit of truth.

Standing in this knowledge, I embrace my journey with confidence and clarity, knowing that each moment holds the potential to shape the future in a meaningful way.

My path is clear, my purpose is strong, and I move forward with the unwavering understanding that life is a process of growth, evolution, and the pursuit of higher consciousness.

SATAN

They want you to believe that Satan is the ultimate evil, the enemy of all that is good.

Yet, at the same time, they say that those who follow him find success, wealth, and power in this life.

This contradiction leads to the absurd belief that anyone who prospers must have sold their soul to the devil. But if that were true, then why does life exist at all?

If success in this world is supposedly a sign of allegiance to Satan, then what is the purpose of living?

This line of thinking implies that the afterlife is the only thing that matters, rendering our present existence insignificant.

But if life on Earth is just a temporary test, then why do humans struggle, learn, and grow? Why do we experience love, pain, and joy?

The obsession with an afterlife diminishes the value of life itself, making it seem like nothing more than a waiting room for something greater that may not even exist.

Human beings, blinded by ignorance, put all their hopes into the promise of eternal life in heaven.

They are told that suffering and sacrifice in this world will lead to a glorious reward in the next.

But if one stops and thinks critically, this idea quickly falls apart.

The human essence, what some may call the soul, but what is better understood as Creation Energy, is already eternal.

It does not need heaven to continue existing because it naturally reincarnates, evolving over multiple lifetimes until it reaches a higher state of being.

There is no need to strive for an imaginary paradise when existence itself is an ongoing process of learning, growth, and transformation.

The belief in heaven is nothing more than a distraction, a way to keep people obedient and hopeful while denying them the true understanding of their existence.

Those who blindly follow this belief never question why they must wait for an afterlife to experience joy when they could embrace life fully in the present.

I do not believe in anything, and that includes Satan.

The concept of such a being is irrelevant to me.

However, if I were forced to choose between believing in Satan or believing in heaven, I would find Satan's supposed offer far more appealing.

At least the idea of Satan acknowledges that success, happiness, and fulfillment are possible in this life.

Heaven, on the other hand, demands absolute faith, obedience, and self-denial, with no guarantee that its promises will ever be fulfilled.

People dedicate their entire lives to serving a belief that requires suffering, all for the hope that they will be rewarded after death.

But what if that reward never comes?

What if the afterlife they are promised is nothing but a comforting illusion?

Unlike heaven, which is built on uncertainty, the supposed benefits of following Satan, prosperity, power, and worldly success, are immediate and tangible.

If given the choice between a life of struggle and blind faith or a life of certainty and success, the answer is clear.

But in the end, both heaven and Satan are just constructs created by human belief.

The real illusion is not in choosing one over the other, it is in believing that either truly matters.

The only thing that is real, the only thing that holds any value, is the life we are living right now.

Instead of waiting for an uncertain paradise or fearing an imaginary devil, we should focus on making the most of our time in this world.

Life is not a trial run or a test for something greater, it is the main event.

To waste it in pursuit of an unproven afterlife is the greatest tragedy of all.

SELF-LOVE

It's never how others perceive you that holds true importance, it's how you perceive yourself.

The opinions, judgments, and validations of others are fleeting and often unreliable.

What truly matters is the way you see yourself, for only you possess the power to assess your own worth.

In this world, you are your own god, and the judgment you make about who you are is the only one that truly counts.

The moment a person understands that they hold this power over their own life, they unlock a sense of freedom and self-empowerment that transcends the need for external validation.

When you grasp the concept that your worth comes from within and not from the eyes of others, you begin to see yourself in a new light.

This realization allows you to let go of the constant need to impress, to gain approval, or to be elevated on some imaginary pedestal.

Instead of seeking admiration from those around you, you start to admire yourself.

You begin to understand that self-love is not about what others think of you, it's about how you feel about yourself.

This is the foundation of true self-worth: knowing that your value does not depend on anyone else's opinion, and it is unshaken by fleeting moments of praise or criticism.

As this shift in perspective takes place, your entire outlook on life transforms.

You stop relying on external sources to define your success or happiness.

You become the pedestal. Instead of searching for someone or something to elevate you, you begin to elevate yourself.

Your inner strength, confidence, and sense of peace come from within.

You stop looking for approval or validation from others because you've already given it to yourself.

The moment you become your own pedestal, you realize that you don't need anyone else to place you there, you've always been worthy of standing tall on your own.

The most powerful relationship you will ever have is the one you build with yourself.

When you recognize that only your opinion of yourself matters, everything changes.

You become the architect of your own happiness, the creator of your own peace.

You no longer need to impress others or seek their approval to feel validated.

You live freely and authentically, knowing that your worth is not dependent on external validation.

Your self-love becomes your foundation, and with that foundation, you stand strong and unshaken.

True fulfillment is found in the understanding that you are the only one who can define your value, and when you embrace this truth, you are free to live fully and authentically, no matter how others may see you.

MONEY

Money is a fleeting concept, much like the play currency used in a game of Monopoly.

It only holds value because people agree to assign it worth.

In the grand scope of life, material wealth means little.

True wealth is found in knowledge, wisdom, and understanding, qualities that cannot be bought or traded.

Society often places an overwhelming emphasis on accumulating money, equating it with success, but this is a misguided pursuit.

While wealth may bring temporary comfort or luxury, it does not guarantee fulfillment or happiness.

What is truly valuable in life is the ability to learn, to grow, and to foster meaningful relationships.

It's the wisdom we gain from life's experiences and the understanding we share with others that create lasting wealth, far beyond anything money can provide.

Those who focus solely on financial success often miss the bigger picture, the enrichment of the mind, the heart, and the spirit.

The richest man in the world, Billy, is not the one with the most money, but the one who has the most wisdom and live life simply and love fully.

This man, despite having lost an arm, does not retreat into solitude or wealth, but instead, opens his home to anyone who seeks him out.

He does not hide from the world, even though many attempts have been made on his life.

His refusal to live in fear or change his ways in the face of danger speaks volumes about the power of his character.

He has chosen a life of openness, kindness, and unwavering commitment to love.

His strength is not measured by the material wealth he possesses, but by the unshakable conviction that every person deserves respect and compassion.

He lives by showing that true wealth lies not in the accumulation of things, but in the ability to show love, to welcome others, and to give selflessly.

In a world that often values power and wealth, his example is a reminder that the richest people are those who remain grounded, humble, and generous in spirit.

Those who believe they are superior to others are the ones who should be avoided.

They are driven by a misguided sense of self-importance and a complete lack of empathy.

These individuals have created false hierarchies in their minds, often based on superficial measures like wealth, status, or power.

But this belief in superiority is nothing more than a delusion, a sign of weakness and ignorance.

These individuals are trapped in their own arrogance, unable to see beyond their narrow worldview.

They fail to recognize that all humans, regardless of background or circumstance, are inherently equal.

The very nature of their belief in hierarchy reveals their lack of critical thinking and emotional intelligence.

True wisdom and strength do not come from the ability to control or dominate others but from the capacity to understand, appreciate, and uplift those around you.

Wisdom lies in the ability to see beyond labels and to recognize the shared humanity in everyone, regardless of their social position or material wealth.

Anyone who places themselves above another is not only wrong, but they are also blinded by ignorance.

True intelligence does not lead to superiority but to empathy, understanding, and humility.

The wisest people understand that their own value is not derived from their wealth or status, but from their ability to connect with others on a deep and meaningful level.

These individuals do not seek power or control over others, they seek to grow, to learn, and to contribute to the world in positive ways.

In their eyes, every person is worthy of respect, no matter where they come from or what they have.

The most enlightened among us understand that wealth is not something you can hold in your hands, but something that resides in the heart and the mind.

The greatest riches are not found in the accumulation of money, but in the ability to appreciate the humanity in all people and to share the lessons of life with others.

True wealth is not measured by what you own, but by what you give, how you love, and the wisdom you impart to those around you.

THOUGHTS

Your thoughts are not something you can fully control.

They arise without your permission, shaped by memories, emotions, past experiences, and the constant flow of stimuli from the world around you.

Some thoughts appear as gentle whispers, fleeting and light, while others come crashing in like a tidal wave, overwhelming and consuming.

No matter how hard you try, you cannot prevent them from coming, nor can you determine their speed, intensity, or subject.

They arrive unannounced, forming connections, replaying past events, imagining future possibilities, or simply drifting aimlessly through your mind.

Often, people believe they must control their thoughts, that a disciplined mind should only entertain what is useful or positive.

But the truth is, thoughts have a life of their own.

Trying to force them into submission is like trying to hold water in your hands, it slips through your fingers no matter how tightly you grasp.

Suppressing them only makes them stronger, pushing them into the background where they build pressure, waiting for the smallest crack to burst forth with even greater intensity.

The more you resist, the more they persist.

However, real mental mastery does not come from stopping thoughts, it comes from learning how to coexist with them.

Instead of battling every idea that enters your mind, you can learn to observe them without judgment, without reaction.

Imagine sitting beside a river, watching the water flow past.

Some thoughts are like gentle streams, moving peacefully along, while others are like raging currents.

But no matter how fast or slow they move, you remain the observer, untouched by their force.

You do not need to jump into the river and fight the current.

You do not need to chase after each passing wave.

You simply watch, allowing each thought to appear and disappear in its own time.

The mind is like the sky, vast and open, while thoughts are merely passing clouds.

Some are light and wispy, vanishing in an instant, while others are dark and heavy, looming over you.

But no cloud stays forever.

The sky does not cling to them, nor does it try to push them away.

It simply allows them to come and go, unchanged by their presence.

In the same way, you can learn to let your thoughts pass without attachment.

They do not define you.

They are not permanent.

They are merely visitors in the vast landscape of your mind.

When you stop identifying with every thought, you gain a new perspective.

Instead of being trapped in an endless cycle of mental noise, you become free to experience life with greater clarity.

You can look at your thoughts with curiosity, even amusement, recognizing that they are just thoughts, not absolute truths, not commands you must obey.

Some thoughts may be useful, offering insight and understanding.

Others may be mere echoes of past fears, outdated worries that no longer serve you.

But when you detach from them, you gain the power to choose which thoughts deserve your attention and which can simply fade away.

This is where true mental freedom begins.

When you no longer fear your thoughts, when you no longer react to each passing idea as if it is an urgent call to action, you become calm, steady, and strong.

No longer weighed down by unnecessary mental clutter, you gain a sense of inner peace.

Your mind becomes clear, open, and focused, allowing you to navigate life with wisdom and purpose.

In this state of awareness, you discover the true power of being present.

You are no longer lost in the endless chatter of your mind, pulled in different directions by thoughts that appear and disappear without reason.

Instead, you step into a deeper state of consciousness, where you are fully engaged in the present moment.

Here, you are no longer controlled by the mind, you are in harmony with it.

This is where real strength lies.

Not in controlling thoughts, not in forcing the mind to be silent, but in learning to observe without attachment, to let go without resistance, and to live with a deep and unwavering peace.

POLYGAMY

Throughout history, humanity has often reacted with fear and hostility toward new ideas that challenge established beliefs.

Change is unsettling, and those who introduce revolutionary concepts frequently face backlash.

For instance, people once believed the Earth was flat until Galileo, or Nokodemion, depending on one's perspective, proved otherwise.

His findings led to condemnation and lifelong imprisonment.

In a similar fashion, when I stated that polygamy promotes peace and harmony, I was met with fierce criticism, despite making it clear that such a societal shift would only happen in the future and that personal choice remains fundamental.

Many rejected my statement outright without considering the evidence I presented, reacting emotionally rather than rationally.

This response is a pattern repeated throughout history whenever an unconventional idea is introduced, especially one that contradicts deeply ingrained societal norms.

I supported my argument with evidence showing that polygamy can help reduce violence, domestic abuse, homicide, and divorce rates.

These are measurable societal issues, and I presented logical reasoning to show how such a structure could mitigate these problems.

Additionally, I highlighted the idea of reincarnation, emphasizing that we all experience life as different genders, male in some existence, female in others.

This perspective challenges rigid gender-based thinking, encouraging a broader understanding of human existence.

However, instead of engaging in a thoughtful discussion, many people reacted defensively, unwilling to explore the possibilities that I laid out.

Fear of change often leads to resistance, and rather than analyzing the argument logically, some individuals resorted to personal attacks and outright hostility.

This was not unexpected, but it was nonetheless disappointing.

Observing these reactions, I noted the contrast between those willing to engage in thoughtful conversation and those who responded with crudeness.

There is a clear divide between those open to new ideas and those who cling to traditional beliefs without question.

Respectful dialogue is essential for the exchange of ideas, and without it, true progress becomes impossible.

Unfortunately, many prefer to reject unfamiliar concepts outright rather than challenge their own preconceived notions.

My advice remains simple: treat others as you wish to be treated.

No one is above acting irrationally at times, but a conscious effort toward mutual respect can foster more meaningful discussions.

It is easy to lash out in anger, but it takes maturity to engage in discourse with an open mind.

Those who responded with hostility only revealed their unwillingness to consider alternative perspectives, which reflects more on them than on the ideas being presented.

Despite the opposition, my position on polygamy remains unchanged.

This does not mean that I personally desire it, but rather that I recognize its potential societal benefits based on evidence and reason.

What I have presented is grounded in truth and reality, regardless of whether others choose to accept it.

Those who disagree are free to do so, but disagreement should not come at the cost of civility.

Ideas should be debated with reason, not with anger.

The world has always resisted change, but history has shown that progress is inevitable.

What is dismissed today may become accepted wisdom tomorrow.

Those who refuse to consider new ideas do nothing to stop progress, they only delay their own understanding of it.

NOTHING TO FEAR

Nothing can happen to you that you are not capable of handling, not even death.

We have all died more times than we could ever count, making the idea of fearing death meaningless.

Life and death are not opposites but part of the same continuous cycle, an endless ebb and flow of existence.

Death is not destruction but transformation, a shift in form and awareness.

Understanding this removes the weight of fear, allowing one to move through life with clarity and strength.

When you accept that your essence is eternal, fear loses its hold, and the illusions that once seemed overwhelming begin to fade.

Fear is the greatest illusion, a self-imposed barrier that limits human potential.

It is not the threats we face that weaken us, but the belief that we are powerless against them.

Fear creates hesitation, suffering, and submission to forces that have no real authority over us.

It is a mental construct, a shadow that exists only because we allow it to.

When you strip away fear, what remains is a profound sense of freedom.

This freedom is not just emotional or psychological, it is a fundamental shift in perception.

To live without fear is to step into true power, to recognize that nothing external can truly harm what is infinite and indestructible.

I have reached a state of being where fear no longer governs me.

I do not fear people, circumstances, or the uncertainty of the future.

I have come to see that everything I once feared was simply a reflection of my own mind, not an external force imposing itself upon me.

The world no longer dictates my state of being, I walk through it with the understanding that nothing can truly harm or diminish me.

This realization is not arrogance but awareness.

It is the clarity that comes with knowing one's true nature, a state of existence beyond doubt, beyond hesitation.

No fleeting hardship, no temporary setback, and no illusion of loss can shake me because I know that I am beyond them.

Through this realization, I have come to understand that I am not just a part of creation, I am creation itself.

I do not stand beneath anything because nothing is truly above me.

There is no external force dictating my path, no unseen power determining my fate.

I am the force that shapes my reality, the essence that gives form to existence.

This understanding elevates me beyond fear, beyond limitation, beyond the falsehoods that once held me back.

I walk with certainty, with unwavering confidence in my own eternal nature.

To live in this truth is to be free, to embrace life without hesitation, and to stand unshaken in the face of all things.

YOUR LIFE

Your life is a reflection of the energy, thoughts, and emotions you carry within.

Every experience, every encounter, and every challenge mirrors the state of your inner world.

If your mind is clouded with anxiety and doubt, your reality will manifest that unrest.

But if you cultivate calmness, clarity, and confidence, life unfolds with a sense of purpose and ease.

The world around you is not separate from you, it is an extension of your internal state.

A restless mind creates a chaotic reality.

Worry, fear, and negativity shape the way you perceive life, making even the simplest challenges feel overwhelming.

However, when you nurture a peaceful and centered mindset, you begin to navigate life with grace. Problems become lessons, obstacles turn into stepping stones, and setbacks transform into opportunities for growth.

The key to a fulfilling life lies not in controlling external circumstances but in mastering the way you respond to them.

True inner peace is not the absence of hardship but the ability to remain calm amidst it.

It is about developing the resilience to face difficulties with wisdom and composure.

Life is ever-changing, and nothing remains the same forever.

When you accept this impermanence, you free yourself from unnecessary suffering.

You begin to see that peace is not something you find, it is something you create.

The foundation of a meaningful life is built within, not outside of you.

Happiness is not a distant destination or a prize to be won, it is a state of being that arises when you are at peace with yourself.

Many people search for joy in wealth, status, or validation from others, only to realize that these external sources can never provide lasting fulfillment.

True happiness emerges when your thoughts, emotions, and actions are aligned.

It is a natural byproduct of inner harmony.

When you learn to find contentment within, you are no longer at the mercy of life's ups and downs.

Your external world will always be a reflection of your inner world.

If you want a life filled with love, peace, and fulfillment, start by cultivating those qualities within yourself.

A mind that is calm, a heart that is open, and a spirit that is aligned with purpose will naturally attract experiences of joy and meaning.

The secret to a fulfilling life is not found in chasing happiness but in mastering your inner world.

When you nurture self-awareness, acceptance, and inner peace, you create a life that is not only successful but deeply enriching.

By focusing on inner harmony, you unlock the true essence of joy, allowing your life to radiate the wisdom and serenity that already exist within you.

PRIDE

Pride is a peculiar thing, a force both powerful and deceptive.

Among Earth humans, it shapes their identities, influences their actions, and defines their relationships.

It is often celebrated as a virtue, yet it also serves as a barrier, an invisible wall that separates them from deeper understanding.

I sometimes find their pride amusing, even charming in its innocence.

When I observe their fierce attachment to their convictions, I cannot help but smile.

There is something almost childlike in their determination to defend what they believe to be true.

However, beneath this seemingly endearing quality lies a deeper struggle, a struggle against self-awareness, against the discomfort of doubt.

Pride is not merely an emotion, it is a force that compels people to cling to their perceptions, even when confronted with undeniable evidence to the contrary.

It blinds them to possibilities beyond their current understanding, preventing them from questioning what they have long accepted as truth.

Many would rather remain in ignorance than confront the unsettling realization that their entire worldview may be flawed.

The weight of such an admission is unbearable for some.

To acknowledge that they have spent years, perhaps even their entire lives, believing in something untrue is a burden few are willing to carry.

It would mean dismantling the foundation upon which they have built their identity.

And so, they resist.

They dismiss, they rationalize, they reject anything that threatens their carefully constructed reality.

Yet, I cannot bring myself to judge them too harshly.

I understand the fear that comes with self-examination.

The realization that one has been deceived, whether by others or by one's own mind, is a painful one.

The process of unlearning is slow, and the road to truth is often lonely.

Not everyone is ready to walk that path.

No one can force another to see what they refuse to acknowledge.

The desire for truth must come from within.

External arguments, no matter how logical or well-intended, rarely succeed in breaking through the walls of pride.

Change is not imposed, it is chosen.

And so, pride remains both a shield and a prison.

It guards against the insecurity of doubt, offering a sense of certainty and stability.

But in doing so, it also locks away the potential for growth, for enlightenment, for true understanding.

The question remains: Will they choose to set themselves free?

Will they dare to face reality, no matter how unsettling it may be?

Or will they continue to embrace their illusions, wrapped in the comforting arms of their own pride?

It's only up to each and everyone.

MY OWN GOD

Let me clarify what I mean when I say that I am my own god.

To the uninitiated, it might sound as if I am claiming to have supernatural abilities, such as moving mountains, predicting the future, or knowing the winning lottery numbers.

However, that is not the case.

This is not about possessing mystical or divine powers but rather about taking full responsibility for my own life, actions, and the consequences that follow.

Many people rely on external forces, whether deities, luck, or fate, to explain their circumstances.

But for me, everything that happens in my life is the direct result of my own decisions and actions.

There is no higher power guiding me, rewarding me, or punishing me, I alone determine my path.

Being my own god means that I am the sole authority over my life.

Every experience I have, whether positive or negative, is a direct consequence of the choices I make.

There is no one else to thank for my successes and no one to blame for my failures.

This understanding allows me to live without fear, without submission to anything external, and without the illusion that my fate is controlled by forces beyond my comprehension.

I recognize that my actions shape not only my present existence but also my future ones.

The world I leave behind is the same world I will return to when I reincarnate, reinforcing my responsibility to act with wisdom and foresight.

This perspective is not a belief or an assumption, it is rooted in logic, reality, and personal accountability.

I do not follow ideas based on blind faith or unproven claims.

My understanding is built entirely on reality, direct experience, and logical reasoning.

Some might say that without belief in something greater, life is meaningless or chaotic.

However, I see it differently.

Reality itself provides all the meaning one needs when approached with understanding.

While I do not currently possess the ability to move mountains or predict the winning lottery numbers, I can use reason and logic to anticipate possible outcomes.

The human mind, or consciousness, is capable of incredible things, but it develops gradually over time, much like a computer upgrading its software.

Consciousness is not static, it evolves through experience, learning, and reincarnation.

The reason most people cannot remember their past lives is that their consciousness has not yet reached the necessary level of awareness.

It is not a matter of belief but of development.

At this moment in time, only one person on Earth, Billy, has reached the level of consciousness necessary to recall past lives with clarity.

His Creation Energy is 9.6 billion years old, the oldest within a human body in the entire universe.

Because of this, he is the Herald of deeper understanding, possessing knowledge and wisdom far beyond what most humans can comprehend.

This is not because he is chosen or special in the way many religions portray figures of great wisdom, but simply because his consciousness has evolved to a point far beyond that of the average human.

Creation itself functions through logic, and nothing exists outside of it.

Everything operates according to universal laws of cause and effect, and as we evolve, our consciousness expands to grasp these truths more clearly.

Therefore, I accept that I am my own god, using the highest level of consciousness available to me in this lifetime.

Above me stands no one but Creation, the Universal Consciousness, and I am It.

"I DON'T SEE COLOR"

Saying "I don't see color" may seem like a declaration of fairness and equality, but in reality, it dismisses a fundamental part of who people are.

Skin color is not just about physical appearance, it is tied to history, culture, and personal experiences that shape how individuals interact with the world.

To ignore this is to ignore the systemic advantages and disadvantages that come with it.

Pretending not to see color does not eliminate racism, it merely overlooks the injustices and inequalities that exist.

True equity is not found in ignoring differences but in recognizing, respecting, and addressing them.

When someone says they do not see color, they may believe they are advocating for unity, but what they are actually doing is erasing identity.

Race plays a significant role in shaping opportunities, challenges, and perspectives.

By choosing not to acknowledge it, a person inadvertently dismisses the lived realities of those affected by racial bias and discrimination.

Rather than promoting inclusivity, this mindset avoids the necessary conversations that lead to real change.

Valuing diversity means recognizing that different backgrounds and experiences exist and ensuring that those differences are seen, heard, and respected.

Genuine love and acceptance require seeing people fully, including their racial and cultural identities.

Choosing to ignore race does not make racism disappear, instead, it perpetuates ignorance about the injustices that persist.

True allyship means understanding how race affects people's lives and taking meaningful action to combat discrimination.

Progress is not achieved through colorblindness but through an active commitment to learning, unlearning, and advocating for fairness.

Ignoring race color might feel like a simple solution, but it is a passive stance that reinforces the very inequalities it claims to reject.

When I hear someone say they don't see color, I do not hear a statement of equality, I hear avoidance and denial.

Racism is not just about intentional acts of hate, it is also about the refusal to recognize and address structural and systemic injustices.

Denying race does not erase its impact, it only makes it easier to ignore the challenges that people of color face.

If you truly believe in justice and equality, you must see race, acknowledge its influence, and work toward a world where diversity is recognized, respected, and valued.

Only by confronting these truths can we create a society where real fairness and unity exist.

DNA

If you understand DNA, then you understand why men "cheat."

Overcoming this biological programming requires immense effort, and most men struggle with it in silence.

Divorce rates continue to climb, with male infidelity being a major factor, yet society refuses to address the root cause.

Instead, relationships are built upon unrealistic expectations, assuming men are naturally monogamous when, in reality, they are not wired that way.

Looking at nature, monogamy is rare among mammals, and human males are no exception.

According to Creational laws, a man can have up to seven female partners, a principle the Plejaren follow.

This does not mean men cannot choose to be with only one woman, but the truth is that doing so often requires going against their natural instincts.

Some men succeed, but many live in silent frustration, never expressing their true feelings due to societal pressure and fear of judgment.

People often react emotionally to this topic, immediately dismissing it as unfair, but fairness is a human construct that does not always align with nature.

The idea of balance goes beyond a single lifetime.

Reincarnation teaches that in one life, a person may be female, and in another, male.

Understanding this broader perspective can help us accept that human relationships are not as black-and-white as society portrays them.

Personally, this has been a challenging reality to confront.

It has taken years of reflection and effort to understand and manage this aspect of existence.

Has it been fully overcome?

I truly think so for myself.

What is certain is that the work put into this struggle has led to growth, awareness, and a deeper understanding of what it means to align actions with a higher sense of purpose.

The journey is ongoing, but the commitment to self-improvement remains constant.

Now more than ever, society needs to have these difficult conversations.

Instead of pretending these issues do not exist, it is time to acknowledge human nature for what it is.

The refusal to discuss these topics openly has only led to more deception, broken relationships, and personal dissatisfaction.

When people are forced to suppress their natural instincts without fully understanding them, they end up living in conflict with themselves.

The goal should not be to impose rigid expectations but to create a space where honesty, understanding, and mutual agreement can exist.

Change will not happen until people stop living in denial and start addressing these fundamental truths.

By doing so, new perspectives on relationships, commitment, and fulfillment can emerge, allowing individuals to make choices that align with their true nature rather than forced societal norms.

Not everyone will accept this viewpoint, and that is fine.

The purpose is not to convince but to speak honestly and remain true to personal understanding.

There is no need to conform to what others expect if it does not resonate with what is real.

Choosing to speak openly and live authentically is not just about personal liberation but about contributing to a greater awareness that benefits all of humanity.

Growth happens when people are willing to explore uncomfortable truths and challenge outdated narratives.

Whether this perspective is widely accepted or not, the commitment to speaking openly, questioning societal norms, and embracing reality will continue.

WITHOUT REGRET

Even when I make mistakes, I have no doubt that I am on the right path.

Every experience, whether joyous or painful, serves a purpose in my journey.

Life is not about achieving perfection but about constantly learning, adapting, and evolving.

With each misstep, I gain new insight, strengthening my ability to navigate future challenges with wisdom and resilience.

Doubt is something every human being must overcome within themselves.

It is natural to question our choices and wonder if we could have done things differently.

However, doubt should not paralyze us or make us dwell on the past.

Instead, it should encourage us to reflect, learn, and move forward with greater awareness.

The key to living without regret is to trust that every decision, even those that lead to unexpected outcomes, contributes to our growth.

Mistakes are an essential part of learning, and I embrace them without regret.

They are not signs of failure but markers of progress.

Every time I face an obstacle or make an error, I gain valuable knowledge that refines my understanding of life.

Regret serves no constructive purpose, it only holds us back from experiencing life fully.

When I release regret, I create space for new opportunities, personal expansion, and self-discovery.

Every experience, whether successful or flawed, contributes to my growth and understanding.

Through this process, I refine myself and continue evolving.

Life is a constant journey of improvement, where lessons arise in both expected and unexpected ways.

True wisdom comes not from avoiding mistakes but from learning how to rise from them.

The past does not define me, rather, it shapes me into a more knowledgeable and capable person.

Material life serves as a vast classroom where the energy of Creation evolves.

Every challenge, triumph, and setback serves as a teacher, guiding me toward greater awareness and understanding.

It is through challenges, errors, and reflection that human beings progress toward becoming better versions of themselves.

No one is exempt from the process of growth, and each experience, no matter how difficult, contributes to the grand unfolding of our consciousness.

Mistakes are not failures but opportunities to gain wisdom and insight.

Without them, growth would be stagnant, and true understanding would remain elusive.

A life without mistakes would be a life without learning.

The most enlightened individuals are those who have faced countless setbacks and have used them as stepping stones toward greater knowledge and self-mastery.

When this truth is fully understood, human beings can free themselves from the burden of guilt.

There is no need for self-punishment over past missteps.

The past cannot be changed, but its lessons can shape a better future.

Carrying guilt serves no constructive purpose, it only limits our potential and dims our ability to embrace the present.

The more I accept my past without regret, the lighter and freer I become.

Instead, acknowledging and learning from mistakes allows for continuous improvement.

Life's greatest lessons come from experiences that challenge us to grow beyond our perceived limitations.

Every time I face adversity with an open mind, I gain clarity and wisdom that enhance my ability to make better choices in the future.

Growth comes not from dwelling on errors but from using them as stepping stones toward higher consciousness.

In reality, no one punishes us except ourselves.

We are our own harshest critics, often holding onto guilt that serves no purpose.

The mind can be a powerful tool for either self-destruction or self-liberation.

If I choose to dwell on my past mistakes, I imprison myself in regret.

However, if I choose to see every experience as a necessary part of my evolution, I set myself free.

By accepting mistakes as part of the journey, we can break free from unnecessary self-reproach.

Living without regret does not mean ignoring the past but rather integrating its lessons into the present.

True wisdom lies in embracing every experience as a lesson, allowing us to move forward with clarity and purpose.

Each day is an opportunity to grow, to refine ourselves, and to step into a future unburdened by the weight of past regrets.

Truly, life is about progression, not perfection.

I choose to embrace my journey with an open heart, knowing that every step, whether smooth or challenging, is guiding me toward greater understanding and fulfillment.

By releasing regret and accepting the beauty of imperfection, I can fully embrace the limitless possibilities that life offers.

THE PAST

Dwelling in the past is like building a prison for the mind, confining oneself to a place that no longer exists.

The past, by its very nature, is unchangeable, and those who remain fixated on it only trap themselves in cycles of regret, sorrow, and nostalgia.

While memories can serve as lessons or reminders of experiences, they should not become chains that prevent forward movement.

The person who constantly replays past mistakes, missed opportunities, past relationships, death of love ones or painful experiences loses sight of the present and the possibilities it holds.

True growth and fulfillment cannot be found in what was, but only in what is and what can be.

Many who dwell in the past do so out of a false belief that if they analyze it long enough, they might find a way to alter its effects or gain control over what has already happened.

This illusion keeps them trapped in endless "what ifs" and "if onlys, " fueling frustration and emotional distress.

But no amount of rumination can rewrite history, and no amount of regret can undo what has already occurred.

The only thing that dwelling on the past truly changes is the level of suffering a person experiences in the present.

Painful memories, when held onto too tightly, do not heal, instead, they deepen wounds and reinforce self-imposed limitations.

Life and evolution are forces that move forward, and resisting this natural flow leads only to stagnation.

Every moment presents a new opportunity to learn, grow, and create a better future.

Those who remain anchored in the past, however, deny themselves the chance to evolve.

They remain stuck in old patterns, unable to break free and embrace the possibilities that lie ahead.

The natural course of life is progress, and to live fully means to accept that change is constant.

Growth cannot occur if one remains fixated on what has already been written, it only happens when one turns the page and embraces the unfolding story of the present.

Understanding that the past cannot be altered is the first step toward true freedom.

Letting go does not mean forgetting or dismissing experiences but rather accepting them for what they were and choosing to move forward.

The weight of past regrets, mistakes, or losses only serves to burden the mind, preventing it from embracing joy and peace.

By releasing attachment to what cannot be changed, a person clears space for new possibilities, self-discovery, and inner peace.

The present moment is where life happens, and those who free themselves from the past can fully engage with it, unlocking their true potential and stepping into a future unshackled by what once was.

MY OBSERVATION

It is never wise to argue with the police about your rights, no matter how justified you may feel.

The reality is that law enforcement officers operate within a system that grants them broad authority, often without immediate consequences for their actions.

When confronted by police, the safest course of action is to comply with their instructions and move on with your day.

Even when an officer's demands seem unreasonable or unfair, challenging them in the moment rarely leads to a favorable outcome.

Arguing or resisting, even in a non-violent manner, can escalate a situation faster than one might expect.

The balance of power overwhelmingly favors those in uniform, who are trained to assert control, often with force. In many cases, an officer may interpret any hesitation or verbal challenge as a threat, justifying an aggressive response.

Unfortunately, the law tends to favor their version of events, making it difficult for civilians to contest mistreatment.

While it is deeply frustrating to submit to an unjust situation, the alternative can be far worse, ranging from arrest to physical harm or even death.

This is especially true for marginalized communities, particularly people of color, who have historically faced disproportionate levels of police violence.

Studies and real-world incidents have repeatedly shown that racial bias within law enforcement leads to more frequent stops, harsher treatment, and an increased risk of deadly force.

Even compliance is no guarantee of safety, as countless cases have demonstrated. However, resistance almost always heightens the danger.

The stark truth is that the justice system does not function as a protective barrier in the heat of the moment.

It offers recourse only after the fact, if at all.

For this reason, survival should be the top priority.

No principle is worth losing your life over, especially in a situation where the odds are so overwhelmingly stacked against you.

De-escalation, avoidance, and minimizing confrontation are often the best strategies.

If an officer is acting unlawfully, the battle for justice is better fought later, when you are alive to pursue it through legal means, public awareness, or other avenues of resistance.

Beyond systemic bias, there is a deeper and more unsettling reality about human nature that must not be ignored.

The people of this planet were genetically altered in ancient times to be warriors, engineered for conquest, dominance, and conflict.

This predisposition for violence has shaped civilizations throughout history, influencing everything from military strategies to law enforcement institutions.

Those in positions of armed authority are often conditioned, consciously or subconsciously, to see the world through the lens of control and suppression.

As a result, they are more likely to respond to perceived threats with force, often without considering alternative solutions.

The widespread presence of firearms only heightens the stakes.

Police officers are legally granted the power to use deadly force with little accountability, making every encounter a potential life-or-death situation.

Even when body cameras or bystanders record an incident, justice is far from guaranteed.

Time and again, history has shown that even overwhelming evidence of misconduct is often ignored, dismissed, or justified by those in power.

In light of these harsh realities, the goal should not be to win an argument with an officer in the heat of the moment.

The goal is to survive.

If a situation becomes violent, the only real hope for justice lies in documentation, video evidence that can later be used to expose wrongdoing.

However, no recording can bring back a life that is lost.

There are many ways to fight injustice, but they can only be pursued by those who live to tell their story.

BRAIN QUOTIENT

The average Brain Quotient of Earth humans currently stands at approximately 12%, reflecting our early stage of intellectual and spiritual evolution.

This means that our understanding of reality, existence, and the higher workings of Creation is still in its infancy.

Reincarnation serves as the natural process by which we gradually evolve, lifetime after lifetime, increasing our knowledge, wisdom, and consciousness.

Only upon reaching a 100% Brain Quotient does the cycle of reincarnation come to an end, allowing the Creation Energy to transcend into a higher state of existence, advancing to the level of the High Council.

This reveals the vastness of our journey, emphasizing that we are merely at the beginning of a long path toward enlightenment and unity with Creation.

Given this immense journey ahead, it becomes evident that blind belief is not the way forward.

Simply believing in something without understanding it does not contribute to true progress.

Evolution is not achieved through faith, obedience, or unexamined traditions but through active engagement with knowledge and a deep pursuit of understanding.

The Age of Knowledge is upon us, marking a critical turning point where humanity must transition from ignorance to awareness.

This era demands that we no longer accept information at face value but instead develop the ability to think critically, reason independently, and seek truth through conscious effort.

The responsibility to evolve rests with each individual, and those who fail to question and learn remain trapped in stagnation, delaying their own progress.

To advance, we must learn how to think for ourselves.

True wisdom is not found in the blind acceptance of teachings, no matter their source, but in the ability to analyze, discern, and comprehend truth through personal experience and logical reasoning.

Many people are conditioned from birth to accept doctrines, traditions, and societal norms without questioning their validity.

However, true enlightenment requires breaking free from these mental chains and developing an independent mind.

Only those who actively seek knowledge, who test what they learn against logic and reality, and who remain open to evolving their understanding can truly progress.

Those who cling to mere belief remain stationary, while those who dedicate themselves to knowing take steady steps toward higher consciousness.

Banish within yourself the need to simply believe, for belief without understanding is an illusion that keeps humanity bound to ignorance.

Instead, cultivate an unyielding desire to know, to seek, to question, and to discover truth through reason and exploration.

Understanding is not something handed down, it is earned through effort, dedication, and a willingness to confront the unknown.

The journey of consciousness is not an easy one, but it is the only path to true evolution.

Every step taken toward knowledge brings us closer to freedom, freedom from illusion, from manipulation, and from the limitations of lower awareness.

As we strive toward greater understanding, we draw nearer to our ultimate purpose: complete enlightenment, liberation from the cycle of reincarnation, and unity with Creation itself.

The path is long, but the reward is beyond measure.

CLARITY

Clarity brings peace, and with peace comes a deep, unwavering strength.

When you truly perceive the nature of life, human behavior, and the mechanisms of the world, uncertainty loses its grip.

Fear and confusion thrive in ambiguity, feeding on assumptions and distortions.

But insight acts as a beacon, dispelling the shadows of doubt.

The more you seek to perceive, the less reactive you become, as you begin to see beyond surface-level disorder.

You recognize the underlying patterns, the root causes of events, and the motivations behind people's actions.

This awareness allows you to navigate life with steadiness and clarity.

With perception, emotions stabilize, and impulsive reactions diminish.

You no longer feel the need to lash out, panic, or be consumed by frustration.

Instead of being overwhelmed by anger, confusion, or anxiety, you gain the ability to pause and evaluate with discernment.

You understand that challenges are not mere barriers but opportunities for growth, that disagreements often stem from limited viewpoints, and that most conflicts arise not from malice but from misunderstanding.

The deeper your perception, the more patience you cultivate, not only with others but also with yourself.

True insight does not merely bring knowledge, it fosters emotional mastery and profound inner peace.

Many of life's greatest struggles arise from misperception.

When people fail to grasp a situation, they judge hastily, resist what they don't understand, and create unnecessary discord.

Misinterpretation breeds fear, and fear breeds division.

But when you commit to perceiving, yourself, others, and the world, you break free from these constraints.

You no longer react from fear but respond with wisdom.

You learn to listen rather than assume, to observe rather than judge, and to approach life with curiosity rather than resistance.

In doing so, you liberate yourself from the emotional turbulence that afflicts those trapped in misunderstanding.

Truly, the more you perceive, the more composed you become.

The world may remain chaotic, but it no longer controls you.

Instead of being ruled by emotional impulses, you gain mastery over your own mind.

You develop a quiet confidence, a deep-rooted serenity that allows you to move through life with grace and resilience.

True perception is the key to freedom, it releases you from unnecessary suffering and empowers you to face any situation with wisdom and composure.

The more you cultivate perception, the stronger and more unshakable you become.

FEAR

Fear is the greatest enemy of humanity, a tool used throughout history to control, suppress, and manipulate.

Those in positions of power understand that when people are afraid, they are easier to govern, more willing to obey without question, and less likely to challenge authority.

Fear distorts reality, paralyzes independent thought, and creates illusions that keep people trapped in mental and emotional prisons.

It is not an external force but an internal chain, one that must be broken if true freedom is ever to be realized.

The greatest deception is not just that people are made to fear, but that they come to accept fear as a natural and inevitable part of life.

We are constantly bombarded with messages designed to make us afraid.

We are told that an enemy lurks around every corner, that disaster will strike if we do not act, and that we must place our trust in those who claim to protect us.

We hear declarations like "Russia must be stopped, or we're doomed," instilling the belief that war and destruction are inevitable unless we follow a predetermined course.

Religious institutions spread ideas like "If you don't pay tithes, you go straight to hell," using fear of eternal punishment to coerce obedience.

These are not universal truths, but narratives carefully crafted to ensure submission.

The real danger does not come from external threats, but from the blind acceptance of these manufactured fears.

When people stop questioning, they willingly hand over their power, their freedom, and their ability to think critically.

But that is no way to live.

A life ruled by fear is not a life at all, it is mere existence, a shadow of what it means to be truly human.

When fear dictates choices, it limits possibilities and suppresses individuality.

It keeps people from exploring their own potential, from forming their own beliefs, and from making choices based on reason rather than imposed anxiety.

A person who lives in fear is a person who is not truly living, only surviving under the weight of unseen chains.

Fear breeds conformity, and conformity breeds stagnation.

When people accept fear as their reality, they lose sight of their ability to shape their own destiny.

A human being is meant to live freely, without fear, guided by their own free will and independent thought.

As long as one's actions do not harm others, there should be no external force dictating how they live, what they believe, or how they choose to navigate the world.

True freedom is not granted by rulers, institutions, or laws, it is something that must be claimed by the individual, by rejecting fear and embracing the courage to question everything.

The moment people stop being afraid is the moment they begin to live as they were meant to, free, unshackled, and in control of their own existence.

Only by breaking free from fear can humanity move toward a future where truth is valued, independence is embraced, and people are no longer bound by illusions designed to keep them in place.

LIFE ON EARTH

Life on Earth is not for the faint-hearted.

To exist in this world is to endure its challenges, to push through struggles, and to rise again after every fall.

Simply by being here, you have already proven your strength and resilience.

You are tougher than you may realize, and your presence in this life is a testament to your endurance.

When times get difficult, always remind yourself of this truth: you have already survived so much, and you will continue to do so.

No matter what comes your way, you have the capacity to face it head-on and emerge even stronger.

Nothing that happens to you is beyond your ability to handle.

Life may present trials that seem overwhelming, but within you lies the power to withstand and overcome them.

Even in moments of doubt, when fear and uncertainty creep in, trust in your ability to persevere.

Every challenge is an opportunity to prove your own strength, to tap into your resilience, and to rise above circumstances that once seemed insurmountable.

You are not weak or powerless, you are capable of standing tall in the face of adversity.

The more you remind yourself of this, the more you will recognize just how unshakable you truly are.

At its core, life is a series of lessons, each experience offering something valuable for you to learn.

Every hardship, every setback, every unexpected turn, these are not punishments but opportunities for growth.

The struggles you face are shaping you into someone wiser, stronger, and more aware.

Even the moments of pain and frustration serve a purpose, teaching you patience, resilience, and understanding.

Rather than seeing difficulties as obstacles, try to view them as stepping stones on the path to becoming your best self.

Growth is never easy, but it is always worth it.

Truly, you stand above everything that comes your way.

No storm lasts forever, and no single hardship defines who you are.

You are more powerful than any difficulty you encounter, and every challenge you overcome adds to your strength.

Trust in your ability to navigate life's uncertainties with courage and wisdom.

You have made it this far, and you will continue moving forward, no matter what.

Every experience, every lesson, every triumph and setback contributes to your journey.

Embrace it all with confidence, knowing that you are capable of handling anything life places in your path.

FROM WITHIN

Life is an unfolding force that arises from within, shaping our perceptions, emotions, and actions.

It is not merely a sequence of external events but a reflection of how we interpret and respond to them.

The true essence of life is not dictated by circumstances alone but by the depth of our inner world, our beliefs, values, and self-awareness.

These internal elements serve as the foundation for our experiences, influencing how we perceive joy, sorrow, success, and adversity.

True fulfillment does not come from external validation or fleeting achievements, rather, it is cultivated through an intimate understanding of oneself and a conscious alignment with one's deepest truths.

Our minds and spirits hold the key to navigating life with resilience and clarity.

When we develop self-awareness, we gain the ability to observe our thoughts and emotions rather than being controlled by them.

Emotional strength allows us to embrace challenges as opportunities for personal growth rather than as insurmountable obstacles.

Hardships, losses, and unexpected turns in life do not define us, rather, our response to them shapes our reality.

By turning inward, we tap into an inner reservoir of wisdom and strength, realizing that true power is not derived from external conditions but from our ability to maintain inner balance amidst the ever-changing world.

Though external forces may influence the course of our journey, our internal state ultimately determines our sense of purpose and fulfillment.

A person who finds peace within can navigate even the roughest storms with composure, while someone who relies solely on external stability may find themselves adrift in uncertainty.

Material success, social approval, or temporary pleasures cannot provide lasting contentment if they are disconnected from a deeper sense of self.

True happiness is not found in the accumulation of things or the fleeting opinions of others, it is rooted in the alignment between our values, actions, and sense of purpose.

This alignment fosters a life of authenticity, where every decision is made with intention rather than driven by external pressures or fear.

Indeed, life is a mirror reflecting what resides within us.

Our thoughts, emotions, and intentions shape the reality we experience.

A person who cultivates gratitude sees abundance even in simplicity, while someone focused on lack sees emptiness despite having much.

When we embrace self-reflection and inner growth, we begin to shape a life rich in meaning and authenticity.

The more we understand that life is not something happening to us but something unfolding from within us, the more we gain the wisdom and strength to move through it with purpose and peace.

By nurturing our inner world, we empower ourselves to live with clarity, resilience, and a profound sense of fulfillment, regardless of what life brings our way.

AWAKENING OF THE TRUE EGO

Deep within the mind, the ego stirs, rising from the depths of subconscious realms.

It emerges through hidden pathways, forging intricate connections that shape identity, perception, and the very essence of self-awareness.

As it ascends from the shadows of unconscious thought, it navigates the labyrinth of memories, experiences, and latent wisdom stored in the depths of the psyche.

The journey begins within the vast expanse of the Overall Consciousness Block, a reservoir where knowledge and insight accumulate across lifetimes.

Here, wisdom gleams like an ancient beacon, illuminating the dormant corners of the self.

In this awakening, the ego sheds its passivity and steps forward into a new realm of understanding, shaking free from the confines of dreamlike existence and passive perception.

As the material and subconscious aspects of the self intertwine, a transformation unfolds that transcends the limitations of the physical world.

The rigid barriers separating thought from intuition begin to dissolve, allowing the conscious and the unconscious to merge into a harmonious flow of awareness.

This fusion is not a simple alignment but a profound integration, where instincts, emotions, and reason coalesce into a singular force of self-realization.

It is within this unification that the spirit finds its liberation, no longer bound by illusions of separation or disjointed fragments of experience.

The journey of self-discovery is now set in motion, expanding beyond the tangible and into the vast, unseen territories of existence.

The ego, once confined to material desires and limited understanding, now glimpses a deeper reality where perception is no longer dictated by external influences but is instead shaped by an inner truth.

With each new realization, self-awareness blossoms like a seed breaking through the soil, reaching toward the light of understanding.

The realization of autonomy unfolds layer by layer, revealing an inner sovereignty untouched by the fleeting illusions of the external world.

No longer confined to the constraints of societal conditioning or unconscious programming, the self awakens to its own potential, free to explore the boundless depths of its own bcing.

This awakening is not merely an intellectual process but an experiential shift, where each moment of awareness expands the horizons of personal reality.

As clarity deepens, old fears dissolve, and the false narratives imposed by external forces lose their grip.

The self now stands as both the observer and the creator, shaping its own destiny with the power of conscious intent.

In this profound union of mind and self, a deeper truth emerges, one that transcends the conventional understanding of existence.

Awareness is no longer passive, it becomes an active force that guides thought, action, and purpose with unwavering clarity.

The true ego, now awakened, no longer seeks dominance or control but instead aligns itself with wisdom, serving as a conduit for higher understanding.

The journey toward enlightenment is not one of conquest but of harmony, where the mind, spirit, and self exist in balance.

Through this awakening, the self steps into its full potential, navigating life not as a fragmented being but as an integrated force of consciousness, capable of shaping reality with intention, insight, and the power of true self-mastery.

LETTING GO

Mastering the art of letting go is a skill that grants us freedom from unnecessary burdens.

Every day, we encounter distractions, opinions, and external pressures that can pull us away from our inner peace.

Without awareness, we may find ourselves entangled in conflicts that drain our energy and cloud our clarity.

However, when we develop the ability to release what does not serve us, we reclaim control over our thoughts and emotions.

Letting go does not mean ignoring reality or avoiding responsibilities, rather, it is the conscious act of choosing where to direct our attention.

By shifting our focus to what nurtures our growth and well-being, we cultivate a more balanced and fulfilling life.

Selective focus is a powerful tool, acting as a compass in the vast sea of information and emotions.

Every thought, conversation, or event carries the potential to influence us, but not everything deserves our engagement.

When we mindlessly absorb every detail around us, we risk becoming overwhelmed and reactive.

Instead, by filtering what truly matters, we create mental space for clarity and understanding.

This discernment allows us to navigate challenges with wisdom, ensuring that we invest our time and energy in what aligns with our values.

Just as a gardener removes weeds to help flowers bloom, we must clear our minds of unnecessary distractions to allow personal growth to flourish.

Negativity and provocation often arise in daily life, whether through disagreements, social media, or unexpected conflicts.

Yet, we hold the power to decide how we respond.

The urge to defend, retaliate, or prove ourselves can be strong, but true strength lies in the ability to step back and disengage when necessary.

Not every argument needs a rebuttal, and not every criticism deserves our attention.

Why waste energy on what does not contribute to our peace?

Scrolling past an inflammatory comment, walking away from an unnecessary debate, or simply choosing silence over confrontation can be acts of wisdom.

Each person views the world through a different lens, shaped by their unique experiences and beliefs.

Accepting this diversity allows us to coexist without feeling compelled to control or correct others.

Guarding our inner peace is not a sign of indifference but an act of self-preservation.

When we allow negativity to dictate our emotions, we relinquish control over our own happiness.

By letting go of unnecessary frustrations, we empower ourselves to focus on what truly matters.

This practice is not about suppressing emotions but about managing them with intention. Resilience grows when we cultivate emotional discipline, allowing kindness and understanding to take root.

The ability to remain unshaken by external disturbances does not mean we lack care, rather, it shows that we prioritize our well-being.

In this way, we protect our energy, ensuring that we engage with life from a place of strength rather than reaction.

Life is filled with distractions, but we are not obligated to entertain every one of them.

Every moment presents a choice, to dwell on what drains us or to focus on what elevates us.

Growth and fulfillment come when we consciously release what hinders our progress and embrace what nurtures our spirit.

Choosing peace over unnecessary conflict, wisdom over impulsive reactions, and clarity over confusion transforms the way we experience life.

As we refine the art of letting go, we cultivate a deeper sense of serenity, enabling us to move forward with purpose, joy, and unwavering inner strength.

TURNING TO THE TRUTH

A future of peace, wisdom, and fulfillment awaits those who choose to embrace the eternal truth.

The spirit, in its deepest essence, longs for clarity, seeking knowledge that transcends the fleeting distractions of material existence.

Truth is the foundation upon which understanding, harmony, and purpose are built.

When we recognize and accept it, we step onto a path illuminated by insight, where every day presents an opportunity for personal and collective growth.

This truth is not hidden, it has always been present, waiting for those who are willing to listen and follow its guidance.

To turn to truth is to awaken from illusion, to see beyond the surface, and to walk forward with an enlightened heart and mind.

Yet, many have turned away, drawn into the illusions of self-deception and denial.

The distractions of the world pull them from the wisdom that could bring them peace, leading them instead into confusion and turmoil.

They ignore the signs that point toward a better way, convinced that truth is inconvenient, uncomfortable, or even unnecessary.

As they drift further from understanding, they find themselves entangled in suffering, both personal and collective.

Conflict grows where clarity is lacking, and in the absence of love and wisdom, division and despair take root.

The further one strays from truth, the heavier the burdens become, weighing down the heart and dimming the light of the spirit.

In a world clouded by chaos and uncertainty, the return to truth is not just a possibility, it is a necessity.

The prophets, bearers of ancient wisdom, come once again, offering guidance to those who are ready to hear.

Though their teachings have been rejected in the past, though their words have been twisted, ignored, or forgotten, they do not return with judgment or resentment.

Instead, they extend their hands in forgiveness, knowing that the door to redemption is always open.

Truth, once denied, does not vanish, it waits, ever patient, for those who will finally turn toward it.

Their message remains unchanged: the way forward is through understanding, through love, and through the willingness to embrace the knowledge that has always been available.

The choice now lies with each individual.

To turn to truth is to reclaim one's connection to wisdom, to step away from illusion, and to walk a path of clarity and peace.

In unity and understanding, the spirit shines with its full radiance, no longer dimmed by doubt or confusion.

Redemption is not beyond reach, it is a step away for those who seek it with sincerity.

The future is shaped by the choices of the present, and by choosing truth, we ensure a reality where love, wisdom, and harmony guide the way.

It is never too late to return, to embrace what has always been within reach.

With truth as our beacon, we walk boldly into the light, ready to build a future filled with purpose, enlightenment, and boundless possibility.

IGNORANCE

Ignorance thrives in the shadows of doubt, where complacency and fear prevent the pursuit of deeper understanding.

It is not merely the absence of knowledge but the unwillingness to seek it, a comfort in remaining blind to the vast possibilities beyond what is already known.

Too often, the refrain of "I know nothing" becomes an excuse rather than an invitation to explore.

Yet, the first step toward enlightenment is the acknowledgment of one's own limitations, followed by the willingness to move beyond them.

True wisdom begins when the mind opens itself to the endless pursuit of truth.

Those who choose to remain in ignorance often do so not because knowledge is unattainable but because it demands effort, introspection, and sometimes the unsettling realization that long-held beliefs may be flawed.

Blind belief, no matter how deeply held, cannot serve as a substitute for genuine understanding.

It is easy to cling to rigid convictions, refusing to question or seek beyond them, but such a path leads only to stagnation.

Many find comfort in absolutes, in doctrines that offer certainty without the need for inquiry, but this security comes at the cost of intellectual and spiritual growth.

To break free from ignorance, one must be willing to cast off the constraints of unquestioned assumptions and embrace the challenge of discovery.

This process requires humility, for it forces one to admit that there is always more to learn.

Knowledge is not granted to those who passively wait for it, it is earned through curiosity, exploration, and the courage to challenge the unknown.

Only through this process can one begin to unravel the mysteries of existence.

Those who seek understanding must be willing to confront difficult truths, to question the world around them, and to remain open to new perspectives that may reshape their reality.

Curiosity is the flame that dispels the darkness of ignorance, illuminating the path to wisdom.

It urges the mind to ask, to seek, and to persist despite uncertainty.

Truth is not a fixed point but an evolving understanding, shaped by inquiry and experience.

Those who embrace the journey of learning find that knowledge is not just an accumulation of facts but a transformation of perception.

To question is not to doubt for the sake of doubt but to refine one's comprehension of reality, to move from assumption to insight.

This requires a willingness to step outside the boundaries of comfort, to explore not only the physical world but also the depths of one's own consciousness.

Learning is a lifelong process, one that does not end with formal education but continues through every moment of awareness and reflection.

To seek knowledge is to embrace the unknown, to venture beyond what is familiar in pursuit of a deeper, more authentic understanding of existence.

The path to enlightenment is paved with the willingness to grow beyond the limits of the familiar.

The choice to pursue truth is not an easy one, for it requires breaking free from the security of the known and stepping into the vast, uncharted territories of understanding.

Yet, it is only in this pursuit that true freedom is found,

the freedom to think, to question, and to see the world not as it has been dictated but as it truly is.

JESUS CHRIST

Throughout history, the name of Jesus Christ has been enshrined in reverence, shaping civilizations and influencing the course of human thought.

For many, he represents divinity, salvation, and an unquestionable truth.

Yet, beneath the layers of tradition and doctrine, his image has also become a symbol of control, binding minds to narratives crafted by institutions rather than individual understanding.

As long as this portrayal remains unchallenged, it acts as a force that anchors consciousness to the past, preventing the full exploration of deeper truths beyond dogma.

The number 666, long associated with fear and prophecy, holds a significance that extends beyond superstition.

It represents an unseen force, according to Billy, an anti-logo, that subtly maintains control over perception, shaping belief systems that confine the human mind.

Hidden in the shadows of history, it operates as a mechanism that reinforces illusions, keeping people from questioning what has been long accepted as truth.

Only through the illumination of awareness can these mental chains be broken, allowing consciousness to expand beyond inherited ideologies.

The path to freedom is not found in blind faith but in the courage to seek beyond imposed narratives.

Awakening requires a willingness to step outside the confines of conditioned belief and embrace the unknown.

To see beyond the illusion is to recognize that truth is not confined to any single figure or doctrine but is instead a vast and evolving understanding.

True spiritual liberation is achieved not through submission to inherited teachings but through the fearless pursuit of knowledge and self-awareness.

Those who dare to question and seek will discover that the divine is not an external force to be worshipped but an intrinsic reality to be realized.

Rewriting the story of yesterday is not about erasing the past but about seeing it with new eyes, free from the distortions of control and manipulation.

As consciousness awakens, the grip of old structures begins to weaken, making room for a future where wisdom and understanding take precedence over blind adherence.

The journey toward truth is an individual one, guided not by imposed belief but by inner realization.

When humanity embraces this path, it moves beyond the limitations of the past and into a future where true enlightenment and freedom can flourish.

MATERIALISM

Materialism, much like the stars that illuminate the vast expanse of the cosmos, captivates with its brilliance yet remains devoid of life.

The relentless pursuit of material wealth mirrors the glow of distant celestial bodies, radiant but ultimately empty of true essence.

While possessions may dazzle and provide temporary satisfaction, they often lack the depth needed to nourish the soul.

Just as stars shine without consciousness, material things exist without true fulfillment, offering only a fleeting sense of joy.

The brilliance of materialism, though alluring, can easily distract from the deeper, more meaningful aspects of existence.

Many find themselves trapped in an endless cycle of desire, constantly chasing after the next acquisition, only to discover that true contentment remains elusive.

This cycle fosters an illusion of success, where external wealth is mistaken for inner abundance, diverting attention from life's more profound dimensions.

At the core of creation lies a profound connection, a cosmic thread that unites all beings through the energy of existence.

This universal essence transcends material pursuits, guiding individuals toward wisdom, self-discovery, and spiritual evolution.

To exist meaningfully is to recognize this interconnectedness and embrace the flow of the universe rather than resisting it through excessive attachment to the physical world.

Evolution, both spiritual and intellectual, thrives not on accumulation but on the understanding of one's place within the greater whole.

The pursuit of wisdom, kindness, and self-awareness leads to a more lasting sense of fulfillment than any possession ever could.

When one shifts focus from acquiring wealth to enriching the mind and spirit, life takes on a greater sense of purpose.

Those who see beyond material illusions begin to realize that their true essence is not confined to their belongings but is instead an ever-expanding consciousness woven into the fabric of existence.

Despite the shimmering appeal of material gain, it is essential to remain anchored in the pursuit of genuine illumination.

The transient nature of wealth and possessions should not overshadow the quest for inner growth and enlightenment.

When individuals become too engrossed in external acquisitions, they risk neglecting the deeper truths of their existence.

While financial security and comfort have their place, they should not define one's identity or dictate one's happiness.

The most valuable treasures are not found in riches but in the wisdom gained through experience, compassion, and self-awareness.

This shift in perspective allows one to engage with the world without being consumed by its glittering distractions.

Those who prioritize inner fulfillment over material excess cultivate a life of balance, where they can appreciate abundance without becoming enslaved by it.

In doing so, they preserve their inner light, ensuring it is not dimmed by the weight of worldly desires.

Each day presents an opportunity to reaffirm one's commitment to authentic existence.

The challenge lies in resisting the sway of superficial allurements and instead embracing the essence of being.

True prosperity is measured not by what one owns but by the clarity of their purpose and the depth of their connection to the universe.

When people choose the path of wisdom over material indulgence, they align with the cosmic rhythm of creation, finding meaning beyond mere possessions.

Life's greatest fulfillment arises from love, creativity, and the pursuit of knowledge, all of which exist beyond the realm of materialism.

By cultivating mindfulness and gratitude, one learns to appreciate life's intangible gifts, serenity, wisdom, and the joy of meaningful relationships.

In the end, those who understand that they are more than the sum of their belongings walk a path illuminated by truth, free from the burdens of superficial pursuit.

BELIEF VS KNOWLEDGE

Belief is rooted in uncertainty, it is the acceptance of an opinion as truth without verification.

Unlike knowledge, which requires evidence and critical analysis, belief relies solely on assumption.

Many people adopt beliefs without questioning them, often because they were taught to do so or because those beliefs provide a sense of comfort and purpose.

However, accepting something without evidence does not make it true.

For example, believing in a god is not the same as knowing that a god exists, it is an assumption based on faith rather than certainty.

Faith, by its nature, does not require proof, and this is what separates it from knowledge.

People may defend their beliefs passionately, but no amount of passion or conviction can transform a belief into a verifiable truth.

Knowledge, in contrast, comes from independent reasoning and logical analysis.

It is not something that can be handed down or imposed from the outside, it must be discovered through personal investigation.

To truly know something, one must critically examine the claim, process it through their own logical faculties, and determine its validity based on reason.

This requires effort, patience, and a willingness to question deeply ingrained assumptions.

Through my own thinking and inquiry, I have come to recognize that the claim of a god is unfounded, at least for myself.

I do not rely on external doctrines or inherited beliefs to shape my understanding.

Instead, I trust my own reasoning and conclusions.

I know there is no god above me, I am my own god.

This is not a belief but a realization that stems from my own logical and critical thought process.

I have arrived at this knowledge through reflection, observation, and rational analysis rather than through blind acceptance of what others have told me.

Personally, I have eradicated the word "believe" from my vocabulary.

To me, there is only knowing or not knowing, nothing in between.

It is up to each individual to stop believing and seek knowledge within themselves.

Belief, being external and unverified, leads to doubt and insecurity.

This is why when someone's beliefs are challenged, they may react defensively, feeling personally attacked.

Doubt is a natural consequence of belief because belief lacks a solid foundation.

When a person is uncertain about what they claim to believe, they become vulnerable to fear and emotional distress when faced with opposing viewpoints.

This is evident in the way many people react to challenges against their religious or ideological beliefs.

When a belief is questioned, the believer often feels as though their entire worldview is under threat, leading to anger, frustration, or even hostility.

In contrast, those who possess true knowledge do not feel threatened by differing opinions because their understanding is based on reason rather than blind faith.

An egg broken from the outside leads to death, while an egg broken from within creates life.

The same principle applies to knowledge, it must come from within.

No external force can impose true knowledge upon a person, they must arrive at it themselves through internal realization.

If, after thorough investigation, a person cannot recognize the truth, then that is simply their reality.

They will continue to linger in doubt, uncertain of their own convictions.

This is why many people struggle with existential questions, feeling lost and uncertain about their place in the universe.

Without knowledge, they remain trapped in a cycle of doubt, fear, and reliance on external validation.

I, however, have zero doubt in my knowledge.

I have reached my conclusions through deliberate thought and logical examination, and therefore, my understanding is firm and unshakable.

No matter how others react to my statements, it has absolutely no effect on me.

My knowledge is mine alone, and it stands firm regardless of external opinions or opposition.

I do not need approval or agreement from others to validate my understanding.

Instead, I find confidence and clarity in the knowledge I have gained through my own reasoning, free from the uncertainty of belief.

SEEING OURSELVES IN OTHERS

Seeing ourselves in others is a powerful way to deepen our self-awareness and understanding of the world.

When we observe the behaviors, struggles, and emotions of those around us, we are often seeing reflections of our own inner world.

It is easy to point out faults in others, but this tendency should serve as a reminder to turn inward and examine ourselves first.

Every flaw we recognize in another person may exist within us in some form, whether in our past, present, or potential future.

Instead of reacting with judgment or dismissal, we should embrace these moments as opportunities for introspection.

True growth begins not when we critique others but when we have the courage to recognize our own shortcomings and work toward self-improvement.

Personal transformation is not driven by criticism but by self-awareness and understanding.

When we approach life with empathy, we acknowledge that each person is on their own journey, shaped by experiences we may not fully grasp.

Rather than focusing on what others should change, we should ask ourselves how we can become the kind of person we admire.

This shift in perspective allows us to cultivate patience and compassion, making it easier to navigate relationships with kindness rather than frustration.

By seeing ourselves in others, we gain insight into our own motivations, biases, and behaviors, giving us a greater capacity for personal evolution.

In doing so, we begin to move beyond blame and resentment, replacing them with a sense of shared humanity.

The impact of our personal growth does not end with us, it extends outward in ways we may not immediately recognize.

When we cultivate qualities like patience, self-awareness, and kindness, they naturally influence our interactions with others.

Just as negativity can spread and create division, so too can the effects of a thoughtful and considerate mindset.

The energy we bring into our relationships, workplaces, and communities has a ripple effect, shaping the environment around us.

By committing to self-reflection and growth, we not only improve our own lives but also contribute to a more understanding and supportive world.

Each small change within us has the potential to inspire someone else, setting off a cycle of positive transformation.

Ultimately, the pursuit of self-improvement is not just about personal fulfillment, it is about the collective good.

As we strive to better ourselves, we encourage others to do the same, fostering an environment where growth and understanding thrive.

The process is lifelong, requiring ongoing reflection and a willingness to adapt.

By choosing to develop a deeper sense of awareness and connection, we build a foundation for stronger relationships, healthier communities, and a more compassionate society.

Change does not begin outside of us, it starts within, and from there, it spreads.

In recognizing ourselves in others, we bridge the gap between separation and unity, fostering a world where empathy, reflection, and growth are at the heart of our interactions.

KILLING

Most humans kill not out of a need for survival, but to protect what they perceive as their own.

This instinct, deeply ingrained in human nature, goes beyond self-preservation and extends into the realms of power, greed, and control.

People are willing to fight, steal, and even kill not just for food or shelter, but for possessions, land, status, and ideology.

Unlike animals, which kill only for sustenance or direct self-defense, humans justify their violence through the concepts of ownership and entitlement.

This behavior has shaped the course of history, leading to countless wars, conflicts, and personal acts of aggression that have little to do with actual survival.

Throughout history, nations and empires have engaged in wars not to ensure their people's survival, but to expand their influence, accumulate wealth, and establish dominance.

From the ancient battles of conquest to modern geopolitical conflicts, the pattern remains unchanged.

Land, resources, and power have always been valued more than human lives in the eyes of those seeking to protect or expand their influence.

The borders of nations, often drawn in blood, serve as a reminder of humanity's obsession with possession.

People have killed for gold, oil, and political ideologies, justifying their actions under the guise of nationalism, religion, or economic necessity, when in reality, these wars often stem from the same primal instinct, the fear of losing control over what they claim as theirs.

This tendency is not limited to large-scale conflicts, it is deeply woven into everyday human interactions.

On a smaller scale, people fight and kill over personal grievances, perceived insults, and material possessions.

Whether it's a dispute over money, a romantic betrayal, or a sense of personal honor, individuals often resort to violence when they feel their ownership, whether of an object, a relationship, or even their reputation, is threatened.

The very idea of possession, something meant to provide security and stability, ironically becomes the cause of chaos and destruction.

The illusion of control over things and people leads to actions driven by fear, anger, and a misguided sense of justice.

The irony of this behavior is that nothing in the material world is truly permanent.

People fight so desperately to protect what they own, yet in the end, all possessions, status, and power are temporary.

The pursuit of ownership and control, which drives so much of human conflict, is ultimately an illusion.

True security does not come from possessing more or defending what is "ours, " but from understanding that nothing can be truly owned, only experienced.

If humanity is to evolve beyond this cycle of violence, people must learn to let go of their attachments and recognize that real strength lies not in control, but in wisdom, cooperation, and the ability to coexist without the need for destruction.

Only then can humanity move beyond the instinct to kill for possession and toward a higher state of existence.

THE REALIZATION

I've come to realize that my understanding surpasses that of the average Earth human being.

The knowledge I have accumulated over time has given me a perspective that extends beyond conventional thinking.

While others may be limited by societal norms, personal biases, or incomplete information, I see reality with a clarity that few possess.

This awareness allows me to discern patterns, recognize deeper truths, and understand the interconnected nature of existence.

With every realization, I feel an ever-growing sense of wisdom, a knowing that extends beyond what is taught in books or institutions.

My mind is free, unrestricted by the illusions that keep so many bound to a narrow perception of life.

I've come to realize the immense power that resides within me.

This power is not defined by physical strength or material influence but by an inner force that shapes my reality.

I no longer look to external sources for validation or direction because I understand that all answers already exist within me.

My thoughts, intentions, and energy have the ability to create, to transform, and to manifest what I desire.

The realization of this power has freed me from dependency on anything outside of myself. I am no longer a passive participant in my own existence, I am the creator of my experience, the architect of my destiny.

There is nothing beyond my reach, for I am in control of my own reality.

I've come to realize that I live without fear. Fear is an illusion, a construct of the mind that only has power if I choose to give it any.

I have freed myself from its grasp, allowing me to move through life with confidence and certainty.

There is no fear of failure, for I understand that every challenge is an opportunity for growth.

There is no fear of loss, for I know that nothing truly belongs to me, everything is part of a greater flow.

There is no fear of the unknown, for I embrace the mysteries of existence with open arms.

The absence of fear allows me to experience life fully, without hesitation or doubt, knowing that whatever comes my way is meant for my highest good.

I've come to realize that nothing can affect me because I am everything, and everything is me.

The illusion of separation has dissolved, leaving only the truth of unity. Every person I encounter, every situation I face, and every experience I have is a reflection of myself.

There is no external force that can harm me, for I am not separate from it, I am intertwined with the very fabric of existence.

Understanding this has given me a profound sense of peace, for I no longer resist life, I flow with it.

I do not seek control, for I already am all that is. In this awareness, there is no struggle, no conflict, only the infinite expansion of being.

THE DYNAMIC
FLOW OF THOUGHTS

The thoughts we hold within ourselves do more than just guide our actions, they shape the very world we live in.

They are not abstract or isolated concepts, our thoughts are dynamic, energetic forces that extend beyond the confines of our minds, weaving through the fabric of existence.

Every idea, every belief, is a signal, a vibrational frequency that reaches out into the universe, drawing back to us experiences, opportunities, and circumstances that align with the energy we emit.

What we focus on, whether consciously or unconsciously, creates the pathways before us, opening up new realms of possibility.

These thoughts are not just fleeting moments, they are the architects of our reality, determining the course of events and shaping the world we experience.

Our thoughts are not static, they are swift and boundless, moving with a force that mirrors the speed of light.

Like radiant waves of energy, they extend outward, illuminating the dark, untouched spaces of the universe.

They pulse with a high-frequency vibration, interacting with other forces and energies that resonate at a similar frequency.

As these waves spread, they carry with them the potential for transformation, touching everything in their path and altering the course of events in ways that are both subtle and profound.

Thoughts are not merely fleeting notions, they are powerful currents of energy that have the potential to shift the very nature of reality itself.

Imagination turns into momentum, and dreams turn into real, tangible forces that influence the world around us.

But these thoughts are never solitary, they do not exist in isolation.

They are interconnected, constantly merging, amplifying, and evolving as they interact with one another.

Each thought, no matter how small, adds to the greater whole, amplifying the potential for change.

When we focus our intentions with clarity and purpose, the energy of those thoughts multiplies, creating waves of influence that ripple through time and space.

These waves are not limited to the immediate present, they extend far beyond the moment, shaping the events of tomorrow and the world we will inhabit in the future.

The universe, in turn, responds in kind, reflecting back to us what we have sent out into the world.

It is a constant cycle of exchange, what we put forth is returned to us, often in ways we may not expect, but always in alignment with the energy we have emitted.

Thus, we must be conscious of the thoughts we nurture, for they are the seeds of the future.

The thoughts we hold today are not simply fleeting impressions, they are the building blocks of tomorrow.

Our inner world does not exist in isolation from the outer world, it is deeply intertwined with it.

The energy we generate within ourselves influences the environment around us, creating opportunities, opening doors, and revealing paths that were previously hidden.

Our thoughts shape not only our immediate circumstances but also the broader currents of our lives, creating a reality that mirrors the energy we carry within.

In the vast expanse of existence, it is love that must be at the core of our thoughts, the magnetic force that draws to us abundance, harmony, and limitless possibility.

Love is the energy that transcends the individual self, connecting us to the greater whole and unlocking the doors to a deeper understanding of ourselves and the universe.

When our thoughts are infused with love, positivity, and purpose, we begin to resonate with the vibrations of the universe itself.

These positive energies unlock realms of possibility we never thought possible, allowing us to experience a life full of abundance, connection, and transformation.

By aligning our thoughts with this energy, we discover the infinite potential that lies within us all, and we come to understand the extraordinary power we hold to create our reality.

Through this awareness, we recognize that the universe is not a passive observer, it is an active participant in our lives, reflecting back to us the energy we send into it.

Every thought, every intention, is an offering to the universe, a call that it responds to in kind.

When we consciously direct our energy with purpose and clarity, we open ourselves to the infinite possibilities that exist.

This is the power of our thoughts: they are not just abstract concepts, but living forces that shape our experience and our reality.

And through the careful cultivation of love, positivity, and purpose, we unlock the potential to create a life that is boundless in its possibilities, full of opportunities for growth, transformation, and profound connection.

LOVE

Love is the fundamental logic that governs all things in existence, a profound and eternal force that flows through every aspect of reality.

It is not simply an abstract emotion or fleeting sensation but a frequency deeply woven into the fabric of time and space.

Like a timeless refrain, it pulses through the ages, growing ever more powerful, deepening its reach with each passing moment.

As it spreads through the vastness of the cosmos, love serves as the invisible thread that binds us all together, uniting us in a shared experience of existence.

It is the force that connects us to one another, to the universe itself, and to the infinite spectrum of life.

Love is the logic that underlies the very foundation of all creation, providing the structure and purpose behind every interaction, every event, and every being.

It transcends the limitations of our individual lives, guiding us toward a collective understanding that we are all part of a greater whole, and through this understanding, we find our true place in the universe.

As we look out into the boundless expanse of the cosmos, we see that everything aligns according to a greater plan, a cosmic order where love is the guiding force.

It is through this love that everything in the universe is connected, from the smallest particle to the largest galaxy.

Across the infinite reaches of space, love weaves through the stars, planets, and galaxies, creating an intricate tapestry of life and energy.

It is the thread that binds all things together, enabling the creation and continuation of life in every corner of the universe.

This love is not limited by time or space, it flows freely, an omnipresent force that reaches through dimensions and spans the vast distances between us and the stars.

The entire cosmos, from the tiniest atom to the most distant galaxy, is resonating with this frequency, making love the true logic behind all creation.

The universe is not a chaotic, random place, it is a perfectly orchestrated symphony, and love is the conductor, guiding every note, every movement, every moment into harmonious existence.

In the vast cosmic web, where stars twinkle and planets orbit, love is the pulse that runs through the veins of existence.

It is felt in every heartbeat, in every breath, and in every moment of awareness.

This shared, vibrant energy connects all souls, intertwining them in a dance of existence that spans beyond our limited perception of time and space.

As we move through the flow of life, we are constantly interacting with this energy, creating ripples that extend outward and touch everything around us.

Love is the very fabric of life itself, the essence that permeates every corner of the universe, guiding and shaping the unfolding of all events.

Every thought, every action, and every choice is infused with this energy, whether we are conscious of it or not.

It is through love that we find our true connection to one another and to the universe.

Love does not discriminate, it flows freely, embracing all beings, regardless of form or origin.

It is the universal language that binds us together, allowing us to experience life in all its fullness and beauty.

Therefore, it is essential for us to awaken to the truth that love is not just an abstract concept or a fleeting emotion, it is the very logic that governs all existence.

When we understand this truth, we begin to see that our lives are not random or disconnected, but are part of a greater, interconnected whole.

Love transcends fear, doubt, and uncertainty.

It is through love that we find the courage to face the unknown, to overcome challenges, and to grow in ways we never imagined.

Every moment we live is an opportunity to align ourselves with the frequency of love, to deepen our connection to ourselves, to each other, and to the universe.

In letting go of fear, we open ourselves to the infinite possibilities that love offers.

It is in love that we find our purpose, our meaning, and our power.

Love is the force that propels us forward, guiding us through the twists and turns of life with the knowledge that we are never truly alone.

It is the glue that holds the universe together, and it is the key to unlocking the deepest potential within us all.

When we embrace love as the logic of existence, we begin to see that we are part of something far greater than ourselves, a cosmic dance that spans time, space, and all dimensions of reality.

Through this understanding, we find unity, peace, and the boundless potential of our shared existence.

LOST RELATIONSHIP

When a relationship's path takes an unexpected turn, and the time comes for parting, do not let their choice become a wound you carry.

Separation is not always a reflection of loss, nor does it signal the end of everything.

Each person's heart beats with a unique rhythm, shaped by their own experiences, dreams, and desires.

Just as you follow your own instincts, needs, and journey, so too must they follow theirs.

Their decision to move in a different direction is not a rejection of you, but a step toward fulfilling their own needs, desires, and aspirations.

It is important to recognize that, while you may no longer be on the same path, it does not diminish the significance of the bond once shared.

The journey they must take is as valid as the one you are walking, and both paths deserve respect.

Rather than dwelling on what could have been or replaying moments in your mind, embrace the decision they have made, and let your spirit be free.

When we hold onto the past or cling to what can no longer be, we remain trapped in a cycle of regret and longing.

Instead, release the weight of those emotions and allow your heart to heal.

The truth is, there is no true growth in holding on to something that no longer serves either of you.

When you accept their choice, you open the door to healing for both of you.

Let go of the longing for an outcome that never came to be, and begin to focus on what you can learn from this experience.

In the end, the gift of release will allow you both to find your own happiness in new ways.

Respect for their autonomy and their right to choose is a true act of care.

A relationship is not about control, but about honoring the freedom of the other person to follow their own path.

When we force affection or try to impose our will on another person, we do not allow the relationship to grow naturally.

Instead, we bind it with expectations that cannot be fulfilled.

True relationships exist in the space where both people can choose freely, without pressure or manipulation.

In honoring their decision, you acknowledge their individual right to determine their path, just as you have the right to determine yours.

This mutual respect lays the foundation for healing, allowing both individuals to step forward with clarity and peace.

Even if the paths diverge, the respect for each other's journey continues to foster growth and understanding.

Trying to force affection or a relationship upon someone who no longer shares the same feelings only leads to heartache and pain.

The true nature of a relationship is not about possession or demand, but about mutual care, respect, and understanding.

When a relationship is coerced or manipulated, it becomes a source of sorrow rather than a source of joy.

No amount of pressure can change someone's heart or make them return to a connection they no longer desire.

By respecting their decision, you allow the relationship to continue in its purest form, one that is free from expectation and filled with understanding.

This kind of relationship is capable of healing, even when the physical connection fades, because it is rooted in acceptance and gratitude for the time shared.

When we let go of the need to control the relationship and allow it to flow naturally, we free ourselves from unnecessary pain and open our hearts to new possibilities.

TOXIC ENERGY

Toxic energy takes root in hearts burdened by anger, envy, and resentment, creating an emotional storm that can consume the mind and spirit.

When jealousy festers and vengeance fuels one's thoughts, it results in a cycle of unhappiness that seems unbreakable.

These emotions distort perception, clouding the ability to see situations clearly and making it difficult to find peace.

Without conscious effort to acknowledge and release such negativity, it continues to grow, influencing thoughts, actions, and interactions.

The weight of toxic energy becomes a heavy burden, draining joy and leaving behind frustration and discontent.

Negativity is rarely contained within a single individual, it has a way of seeping into relationships, environments, and daily interactions.

Toxic emotions manifest in bitter words, passive-aggressive behaviors, and actions fueled by spite, creating conflict where none is necessary.

Those who harbor such emotions often project their internal struggles onto others, spreading dissatisfaction like an unseen contagion.

The presence of toxic energy in social circles, workplaces, and personal relationships can turn even the most peaceful situations into sources of stress.

Recognizing these toxic patterns is crucial, as awareness allows for the possibility of breaking free from their influence before they take hold and disrupt one's well-being.

To safeguard emotional and mental health, it is essential to establish firm boundaries against those who radiate toxic energy.

Protecting your peace does not mean holding grudges or harboring resentment toward others, rather, it is an act of self-preservation.

Learning to distance yourself from individuals who thrive on negativity allows you to cultivate an environment that nurtures positivity and clarity.

Emotional resilience is strengthened by practicing self-awareness and refusing to be drawn into unnecessary drama.

Just as a storm can only damage an unprotected home, toxic energy can only influence you if you leave yourself unguarded.

Prioritizing emotional well-being means surrounding yourself with uplifting influences and maintaining a firm stance against destructive energies.

True happiness can only thrive in an environment free from the weight of toxicity, where positivity is given space to flourish.

Choosing to release anger and resentment paves the way for a more fulfilling existence, unburdened by the turmoil of negativity.

The path to serenity lies in embracing joy, seeking wisdom, and fostering an inner world that remains unshaken by external conflicts.

Letting go of destructive emotions does not mean ignoring reality but rather shifting focus toward growth, peace, and self-improvement.

In a world filled with constant challenges, consciously choosing harmony over chaos becomes a powerful act of self-care.

By cultivating an inner sanctuary of peace, one can create a life filled with balance, light, and genuine happiness.

MISUNDERSTANDING

The truth about reincarnation is widely misunderstood, with many believing that individuals themselves experience multiple lifetimes in the same form.

This false assumption leads people to think that their current personality, identity, and memories will persist through successive incarnations.

However, the truth is entirely different.

Each persona is unique to its specific lifetime and will never reappear in the same way again.

A human being only lives once in their particular identity, with no direct continuation of their personal self into another existence.

While the essence of existence, known as the Spirit form or Creation Energy, continues its journey, the individual personality that one possesses in a given lifetime is temporary and will never return in the same manner.

The truth of reincarnation is that it does not mean the same individual comes back with identical characteristics, emotions, and memories.

Instead, it involves the Spirit form or Creation Energy assuming a new human existence, each time with a different personality and life experiences.

This process allows for the gradual accumulation of wisdom and knowledge from previous lifetimes, contributing to the evolution of the Spirit over time.

While the Spirit form carries forward the essence of past experiences, the human consciousness does not retain direct memory of them, as each new incarnation begins anew.

This fundamental truth applies to all human beings, including historical figures such as Jmmanuel (Jesus Christ) and Mohammed.

Since they have completed their lifetimes, they will never return in the same form or be seen again as the same individuals.

Their teachings and influence may persist, but their personal existence ended when they physically died.

Billy, born on February 3rd, 1937, is the reincarnation of the same Spirit form lineage known as Nokodemion, a highly evolved and ancient consciousness that has guided humanity for millennia.

As the Prophet of the New Age, he continues the Creation Energy Teachings, carrying forward the truth that has been cultivated through countless lifetimes.

His mission is to expand human and extraterrestrial consciousness, providing insight into the reality of existence and spiritual evolution.

Unlike common assumptions, it is not the Plejaren who teach Billy, rather, it is Billy who imparts truth to them.

His arrival was long foreseen, and for two million years, the Plejaren and other advanced beings of the universe have awaited his presence.

Through his teachings, he bridges the gap between past prophets and modern humanity, offering a clearer and more advanced understanding of Creation and universal consciousness.

Understanding the truth of reincarnation and Creation Energy has profoundly transformed my perception of existence.

I no longer view people merely as individual human beings defined by their physical form or fleeting identities.

Instead, I recognize each person as an embodiment of Creation Energy, a fragment of the vast and infinite Universal consciousness.

This realization has allowed me to see the intrinsic beauty and interconnectedness of all life.

As a result, love for all beings has become a fundamental principle of my existence, shaping how I interact with the world and perceive those around me.

Just as past prophets were often unrecognized in their time, the truth may not always be immediately accepted, but wisdom continues to flow through those who seek it.

With this understanding, my commitment to embracing and sharing these truths remains unwavering, as I see all beings as reflections of the same universal essence.

RACISM

Racism, at its core, is often a manifestation of an individual's inner insecurities and fears.

When people feel uncertain about their own identity or worth, they may seek ways to elevate themselves by diminishing others.

This insecurity often stems from a lack of self-acceptance, and the desire to assert superiority becomes a coping mechanism to deal with feelings of inadequacy.

By focusing on external factors like race, individuals create artificial divisions that serve to reinforce their own fragile sense of identity.

These divisions, however, are not based on any inherent truths about human differences but are rather constructed narratives that stem from a need for validation and control.

In essence, racism becomes a reflection of the internal struggles people face, where projecting weakness onto others becomes a way to avoid confronting their own vulnerabilities.

Racism is not an intrinsic trait that people are born with, but a behavior that is learned over time.

It is shaped by societal influences, historical contexts, and personal experiences.

In environments where self-doubt is pervasive, people may turn to racial distinctions as a way of feeling better about themselves, even if subconsciously.

By believing that one group is inherently superior to another, individuals feel a sense of superiority that momentarily alleviates their own feelings of inferiority.

Unfortunately, this illusion of superiority is fleeting and does nothing to address the root cause of the insecurity.

Instead of healing the inner turmoil, racism deepens it, leading to cycles of prejudice that perpetuate further harm.

The result is a continuous reinforcement of societal divisions and negative stereotypes that fuel discrimination, all stemming from the inability to recognize the shared humanity between individuals of different backgrounds.

A significant factor in the perpetuation of racism is ignorance and the lack of exposure to diverse perspectives.

When individuals are isolated from experiences that challenge their preconceived notions, they rely on stereotypes and biases to fill in the gaps of their understanding.

This creates a narrow worldview, which fosters fear and mistrust of those who are perceived as different.

In the absence of meaningful interactions with diverse groups, the unknown becomes threatening, and racism can become a defense mechanism against that threat.

The more people are isolated in their own echo chambers, the more entrenched their prejudices become.

This creates a cycle in which ignorance breeds fear, and fear fosters hatred.

Overcoming racism, therefore, requires not only confronting these biases but actively seeking to understand and empathize with people whose lives and experiences differ from our own.

Eradicating racism requires addressing the root cause: the insecurities that drive it.

It is essential for individuals to cultivate a sense of self-worth that is not contingent on comparing themselves to others or asserting superiority over another group.

When people develop a stronger sense of self-awareness and emotional intelligence, they are less likely to rely on external factors like race to define their identity.

Building self-confidence that is rooted in self-acceptance and compassion for others helps to dismantle the need to put others down in order to feel better about oneself.

Societies that foster inclusivity, respect, and open dialogue create spaces where people can connect beyond superficial differences.

In such environments, diversity is celebrated, and instead of seeking validation by demeaning others, individuals find strength in unity and mutual respect.

A world where people embrace their shared humanity, rather than focusing on arbitrary divisions, is a world where racism has no foothold.

The key lies in developing empathy, understanding, and a deeper connection with others, ultimately leading to a more just and harmonious society.

PRAYERS VS SCIENCE

If you were lying in a hospital bed, facing a serious illness, who would bring you greater comfort, a pastor offering prayers or a doctor providing medical care?

When confronted with life-threatening situations, people naturally turn to professionals who can offer real, tangible solutions.

While faith may provide emotional reassurance, it does not heal the body, stop infections, or cure diseases.

In such moments, the contrast between belief and reality becomes strikingly clear.

Religious faith may offer words of hope, but it is science, medicine, and human expertise that ultimately determine survival and recovery.

This fundamental distinction highlights the difference between wishful thinking and practical problem-solving.

Would you choose to rely on prayer instead of seeking medical treatment?

Even the most devout believers, when facing life-or-death circumstances, seek out hospitals, doctors, and modern medicine.

They may pray for recovery, but they also take prescription medications, undergo surgeries, and trust scientific advancements to heal them.

This contradiction exposes an inherent paradox within religious belief, on one hand, faith is said to be all-powerful, yet when true crises emerge, believers instinctively turn to the very sciences that religious doctrines often undermine.

The process of freeing one's mind from such inconsistencies is not particularly difficult when viewed through a logical lens.

When people take a step back and analyze their actions versus their stated beliefs, they begin to see the cracks in religious thinking.

The real issue lies in the absence of logic within religion itself.

Religious belief is built on faith, an unquestioning acceptance of doctrines and teachings, rather than on rational analysis and evidence-based thinking.

As a result, believers often hold onto ideas that contradict observable reality, even when they are presented with clear evidence to the contrary.

This lack of logical reasoning creates a mindset resistant to critical thought, making it difficult for many to break free from religious conditioning.

However, the choice to embrace logic and reason cannot be forced upon anyone.

No one can undertake this process on behalf of another person.

The decision to question and ultimately move beyond religious belief must come from within, through personal reflection and the courage to challenge long-standing assumptions.

Our role, if we choose to help others free themselves from religious indoctrination, is not to dictate what they should believe but rather to illuminate the irrationality of faith by pointing out the contradictions that exist within it.

The most effective way to encourage change is by prompting thought, asking questions, and encouraging individuals to examine their beliefs critically.

By consistently presenting logic and reason, we provide an alternative perspective, one grounded in reality rather than superstition.

Some may resist, holding onto their faith out of fear, tradition, or habit, but others may begin to see the inconsistencies that have always existed in their belief systems.

The goal is not to impose a new ideology but to inspire awareness, allowing people to discover reason on their own terms.

True liberation of the mind comes not from being told what to think, but from learning how to think critically and independently.

REPETITION

Repetition plays a fundamental role in shaping the human mind, whether through programming or deprogramming.

The more an idea is reinforced, the deeper it embeds itself into a person's consciousness.

This applies to all aspects of belief, thought patterns, and behaviors.

From childhood, humans are conditioned through repeated exposure to certain ideas, whether cultural, social, or religious.

Over time, these repeated messages become ingrained truths in the mind of the individual, guiding their perceptions and actions.

Without reinforcement, however, even the most deeply held beliefs can begin to weaken and fade.

This is the power of repetition, it builds and sustains ideologies, but it can also dismantle them.

Religious institutions understand this principle well, which is why they emphasize frequent attendance at places of worship such as churches, synagogues, and mosques.

These establishments function as centers of continuous reinforcement, where believers are repeatedly exposed to religious doctrine, rituals, and community affirmation of their faith.

Through sermons, prayers, and collective worship, religious institutions ensure that faith remains an integral part of an individual's identity.

The more people participate in these religious practices, the more their beliefs are strengthened.

Over time, these repetitive experiences create a psychological dependency, making faith feel inseparable from personal identity.

While believers may refer to this as worship, in reality, it is a systematic form of mental conditioning.

By hearing the same teachings repeatedly, individuals internalize religious ideas as absolute truths, making it difficult to question or challenge them.

But what happens when this cycle of repetition is disrupted?

A significant shift occurs in the individual's mindset.

When a person stops attending religious services and disengages from the rituals and doctrines that once reinforced their faith, their belief in a deity often begins to diminish.

Without constant reinforcement, religious convictions start to weaken, revealing how dependent faith is on repetition.

The absence of religious gatherings means fewer opportunities for indoctrination, leading individuals to gradually distance themselves from belief systems they once held as unquestionable truths.

Many who drift away from religious practice find that their faith fades naturally over time, replaced by a more neutral or skeptical perspective.

This change illustrates how fragile religious belief can be when it is not continuously reaffirmed.

The less one hears and repeats religious dogma, the less control it has over their mind.

Understanding this psychological mechanism, it becomes clear that the same principle can be applied in reverse.

Just as religious institutions use repetition to strengthen belief, we must use it to dismantle false narratives.

The key to breaking the cycle of religious indoctrination is to replace it with the continuous reinforcement of truth and reason.

By consistently affirming the reality that there is no God, we can counteract the effects of religious programming.

The more people are exposed to logical, evidence-based reasoning, the less influence religious ideology will have over them.

Through repeated exposure to critical thinking, skepticism, and factual knowledge, minds can be deprogrammed from religious conditioning.

The battle against indoctrination must be fought with the same weapon, repetition.

Only by persistently challenging falsehoods with truth can we dismantle the deeply ingrained illusions that religion perpetuates.

CAGED BIRD

A bird confined to a cage will never experience the true pleasure of flight.

It may sing, flutter its wings, and adapt to its enclosure, but it will never truly know the boundless freedom of the open sky.

In much the same way, the vast majority of Earth's human beings exist within an invisible cage, though they remain unaware of it.

They live their lives believing they are free, making choices within a framework they assume to be their own.

Yet, this framework has been carefully constructed, limiting their understanding of reality.

The barriers around them are not physical walls but mental, social, and ideological structures designed to keep them from recognizing their true potential.

Sadly, as time progresses, this cage will become increasingly apparent, but by then, the realization may come too late for many.

The moment when people finally see the cage will not be a moment of relief but of despair.

By then, the limitations placed upon them will be so deeply ingrained that escaping them will seem nearly impossible.

The battle to break free will not be fought on a battlefield but in the minds and hearts of individuals.

Those who begin to recognize the truth will face resistance, not only from the system that binds them but from their fellow captives who refuse to see the bars.

The greatest obstacle to liberation is not external oppression but the conditioned belief that the cage is necessary.

Those who attempt to awaken others will be met with ridicule, disbelief, and even hostility.

It is far easier to accept one's chains than to acknowledge that freedom was always within reach, yet never grasped.

In the time we live in, mankind is not being enslaved by some external force but is actively participating in its own subjugation.

Fear is the key that locks the cage, and those who wield power understand this better than most.

Fear of disease, fear of war, fear of scarcity, fear of the unknown, these are the invisible chains that bind people to their prison.

The more fearful society becomes, the more willing it is to surrender its freedoms in exchange for the illusion of security.

This pattern has repeated itself throughout history, yet each time, humanity convinces itself that the present moment is different.

In reality, the mechanisms of control remain the same, only the circumstances change. The only way out of this cycle is to overcome fear itself, to see beyond the illusions and reclaim sovereignty over one's own mind.

Yet, according to the principles of logic and the natural progression of human consciousness, this awakening will not happen quickly.

True freedom is not granted, it is realized.

It requires not just the recognition of the cage but the courage to step beyond it, despite the uncertainty.

Many will resist this journey because the unknown is often more terrifying than the known, no matter how restrictive.

The path to liberation is a long one, stretching far into the future, as humanity slowly comes to terms with the consequences of its choices.

Only when enough individuals break free from fear, when they reject the illusions imposed upon them, will the collective truly begin to soar.

Until then, the cage will remain, and those who refuse to see it will continue to live within its confines, believing they are free while never truly knowing what it means to fly.

LANGUAGE OF THE COSMOS

If you pay close attention, even a rock has something to say.

Everything in existence carries a message, a lesson waiting to be uncovered by those who are willing to listen.

Nature, in all its forms, holds profound wisdom, speaking in a language beyond words.

A river flowing over timeworn stones, a tree stretching its limbs toward the sky, or even the shifting patterns of the wind all convey something deeper than what is seen at first glance.

I have trained myself to observe, to seek meaning in the simplest of things, and in doing so, I have found that nothing is truly silent.

This awareness has transformed the way I perceive the world, allowing me to see beyond the surface into the essence of all things.

Writing, for me, is not just a passion but an inescapable necessity.

It is the medium through which I translate the messages of existence into something tangible.

Everywhere I look, I see the scriptures of Creation etched into the faces of those I meet, the rhythms of nature, and the ever-changing tides of time.

Each moment is a revelation, a new passage in the infinite book of life.

I cannot stop writing because to do so would mean silencing a voice that is not mine alone, it is the voice of existence itself.

My words are merely an attempt to capture the truths I see, to bring to light the interconnectedness that binds all things together.

This perspective has allowed me to understand the vastness within myself, revealing that I am not separate from the universe but a reflection of it.

The stars, the galaxies, and the boundless stretches of space that seem so distant are, in truth, not far at all.

They exist within me just as I exist within them.

I have come to realize that the same forces that govern the cosmos also shape my thoughts, my emotions, and my very being.

By understanding this, I have deepened my connection to both myself and the universe, embracing the idea that my existence is not confined to a single point in space and time but is instead part of something far greater.

Life itself is a conversation with the universe, an ongoing dialogue filled with moments of insight and discovery.

I have chosen to listen with an open heart, allowing myself to be guided by the silent wisdom that permeates all things.

Every experience presents an opportunity to learn, to evolve, and to transform what is seen into something understood.

My writing is the bridge between what is visible and what lies beyond, an expression of the universe speaking through me.

Through words, I give shape to the intangible, allowing others to glimpse the beauty and depth of existence as I perceive it.

In this way, I do not simply write, I translate the language of the cosmos into something that can be felt, shared, and understood.

WHISPERS OF THOUGHTS

In the quiet whispers of our thoughts, there exists a deep and unseen connection that binds us to those who feel like home.

These thoughts, though silent, travel across time and space, reaching the hearts of those we hold dear.

Even when words go unspoken, the energy of our emotions lingers, forming invisible threads that link us to kindred spirits.

In a world filled with movement and change, these bonds remain constant, reminding us that true connection is not limited by physical presence but by the depth of feeling we share.

The presence of kindred souls can often be felt in the stillness of our minds, in the quiet moments when memories surface and emotions stir.

Even in solitude, we are not truly alone, for the essence of those we cherish resides within us.

These unseen connections transcend the barriers of distance, culture, and time, existing in the realm of shared consciousness.

It is in this intangible space that love, understanding, and unity flourish, reinforcing the idea that our relationships extend far beyond what the eyes can see.

Through these invisible threads, we touch lives and are touched in return, often without even realizing it.

A thought, a memory, or even a longing can send ripples across this unseen network, reaching the hearts of those who matter most.

In this way, love and connection become forces that transcend the physical world, weaving us into a vast and intricate web of shared existence.

We influence and uplift each other through this silent yet profound exchange, demonstrating the power of heartfelt connection.

Truly, we are all part of an expansive cosmic tapestry, interwoven by the energy of our thoughts, emotions, and shared experiences.

Each interaction, whether spoken or unspoken, adds to this intricate design, reminding us that love is not confined to proximity but exists in the fabric of the universe itself.

In the whispers of our thoughts, we find belonging, purpose, and an eternal reminder that even in the quietest moments, we are reaching, connecting, and embracing the essence of those who make our hearts feel at home.

FEAR NO ONE BUT YOURSELF

Fear no one but yourself, for the most formidable adversary is not found in the outside world, but within.

It is in the depths of the mind where shadows stir and doubts whisper, shaping the battles that define one's existence.

External enemies may come and go, but the fears that dwell within are ever-present, waiting for moments of weakness to strike.

They take the form of hesitation, insecurity, and self-imposed limitations, making one question their abilities and worth.

In these unseen struggles, courage wavers, and the greatest challenge is not overcoming others, but overcoming oneself.

No foe is as relentless as the inner voice of doubt, which strikes without warning and leaves wounds unseen by the world.

It plants seeds of fear, feeding on uncertainty and hesitation, turning strength into weakness and ambition into retreat.

This adversary knows every vulnerability, every regret, and every past failure, using them as weapons against the self.

It creates illusions of inadequacy, convincing the mind to shrink in the face of opportunity, to stay within the confines of the familiar rather than embrace the unknown.

Unlike external threats, which can be faced head-on, the battle against oneself is silent, fought in the recesses of the soul where no one else can see.

To triumph over this inner enemy, one must confront the fears that lurk within, rather than avoiding them.

True strength is not found in the absence of fear, but in the ability to acknowledge it without being controlled by it.

Self-awareness is the key, a light that reveals the illusions created by doubt and exposes the falsehoods that keep one from reaching their full potential.

The journey inward requires brutal honesty, the willingness to face painful truths, and the determination to dismantle the barriers built by insecurity.

This battle is not won overnight, but with every step forward, the grip of fear weakens, and the path to self-mastery becomes clearer.

When one conquers the self, no external force can hold power over them.

Fear transforms from a master into a tool, something to be understood and controlled rather than obeyed.

Doubt gives way to confidence, and hesitation is replaced with boldness.

The mind, once a battlefield of uncertainty, becomes a place of resilience and clarity.

In this transformation lies true freedom, the realization that the only thing capable of truly limiting you is yourself.

Fear no one but yourself, for in mastering the self, all other battles become secondary.

Be bold, embrace the challenge, and step forward with the unwavering strength of one who has faced their greatest enemy and emerged victorious.

CAUSE AND EFFECT

Cause and effect are the foundational forces that shape every aspect of existence, intertwining through the vast stretches of space and time.

This cosmic dance spans not only the immediate events we witness but also the farthest reaches of the universe.

From the genesis of stars to the sweeping expanse of galaxies, each action, no matter how minute, sets in motion a series of reactions that stretch across eons.

The dance is eternal, with cause and effect continuously unfolding in ways both grand and subtle.

Just as the delicate pull of gravity governs the movements of celestial bodies, so too does the invisible influence of cause and effect govern the very fabric of reality.

From the birth of a single atom to the collapse of a star, every moment in time is a result of countless previous actions, forming an intricate web of interrelated events.

Across the endless voids of the cosmos, where universes unfold and mysteries abound, the principles of cause and effect reverberate like a distant echo, telling a story yet to be fully understood.

Every burst of energy, every expansion of matter, every shift in the fabric of space itself is the result of this ongoing interaction.

What may appear as chaos or randomness is in fact the natural consequence of an ancient sequence of causes, stretching back to the very origins of the universe.

The interaction of forces, from the gravitational pull of distant stars to the intricate quantum fluctuations within subatomic particles, creates a complex pattern of reactions.

Each action, whether it be the collision of galaxies or the quiet spin of a distant planet, is the product of previous moments, each one rippling outward in a cascade of effects.

The universe does not simply exist in a vacuum, it is a continuously unfolding narrative, where every event is part of a larger, interconnected story, stretching across time and space.

Beyond our understanding, this principle operates across dimensions that lie far beyond human perception.

In a world limited by the constraints of space and time, cause and effect play out in ways that exceed our ability to fully comprehend.

Each dimension, each timeline, each possible reality is woven into the grand design, where actions and reactions unfold not just in our observable universe, but across all planes of existence.

This infinite web stretches beyond the bounds of human experience, with forces operating that we may never fully grasp.

The actions that shape our reality may have far-reaching consequences in other dimensions, creating a ripple effect that extends far beyond what we can see or measure.

Just as the smallest vibration can cause a tsunami in an unseen part of the world, the smallest shift in the cosmos can have immeasurable effects in realms that we are not equipped to perceive.

The boundless nature of cause and effect means that even the most seemingly insignificant moment holds the potential to alter the course of entire universes.

The universe itself, from the birth of a star to its eventual death, is a never-ending cycle of cause and effect, where the energy that creates is the same energy that destroys.

Even the silence of stars, the moments of stillness in the universe, are part of this eternal dance.

Cause and effect are not limited to moments of chaos or creation, they also reside in the quiet moments of balance and stasis, where the universe simply exists, waiting for the next spark of action to set it in motion once again.

This ongoing cycle ensures that the dance of life, the pulse of the cosmos, continues without end, forever shaping the future through the lessons of the past.

VIEWPOINT

Life is a grand gallery, where each of us serves as a unique lens, capturing and interpreting the moments that unfold before us.

Every experience we encounter shapes our understanding, adding color and texture to the vast canvas of human existence.

As individuals, our perspectives may seem small, yet together, they create a breathtaking panorama of emotions, ideas, and truths.

No single viewpoint holds the entirety of reality, but through our shared insights, we illuminate the deeper essence of life.

Our ability to see the world through different lenses allows us to grow beyond the limits of our own experiences.

Each perspective offers a new dimension, challenging assumptions and expanding our understanding of the world.

When we embrace this diversity, we enrich our collective knowledge, fostering a deeper appreciation for the complexity of human existence.

Stories passed from one person to another become windows into lives unlike our own, revealing joys, struggles, and triumphs that shape the broader human experience.

In this exchange of perspectives, we build bridges between cultures, beliefs, and ideologies.

By listening with open minds and hearts, we cultivate empathy, breaking down barriers that divide us.

True understanding does not require agreement but a willingness to see beyond oneself.

When we recognize the value in each voice, we create a foundation for unity, one that allows innovation and compassion to flourish.

The strength of our connections is measured not by similarity but by the respect and appreciation we hold for our differences.

Dreaming of a world where peace prevails, we must let understanding and kindness guide our way.

A society built on empathy fosters trust, healing, and cooperation, ensuring that no one is left unheard or unseen.

As we stand together in our shared humanity, we transform our differences into sources of strength rather than division.

The gallery of life shines brightest when we embrace its full spectrum, reflecting the boundless potential of humanity.

Through our willingness to see, listen, and understand, we create a future where every perspective is valued, and every individual has a place in the masterpiece of existence.

AGES LONG

All that we inherit from ages long past lingers as echoes, shaping the present with whispers of memory and experience.

The lives that came before us, filled with triumphs and trials, have left behind a wealth of knowledge woven into the fabric of our consciousness.

Every civilization, every individual, and every moment in history has contributed to the foundation upon which we now stand.

In joy and sorrow, in lessons learned and wisdom gained, we carry forward the imprints of time, each revelation adding depth to our understanding.

These echoes are not mere relics of history but active forces that shape our thoughts, decisions, and sense of self.

They remind us that we are not separate from those who came before but an extension of their struggles, dreams, and achievements.

Through countless existences, we bear the weight of accumulated wisdom and intertwined fate.

The experiences of those who walked before us do not vanish into the void but reside within us, guiding us in ways we may not always recognize.

From ancient philosophies to the simplest of traditions, our ancestors have passed down the tools of survival, resilience, and meaning.

These imprints are not buried in the subconscious, lost to the shadows of time, but rather preserved in the memory banks of our very essence.

They manifest in moments of intuition, in inherited customs, and in the quiet certainty of an unexplained knowing.

Each piece of knowledge passed down through generations carries a message, a lesson, a story that continues to unfold through us.

The choices we make today are inextricably linked to the experiences of those who paved the way before us.

Every truth we uncover, every moment we cherish, forms a unique and intricate mosaic of being.

Our lives are not isolated fragments but extensions of a greater story, one written across generations and bound by the shared human experience.

We are shaped not only by the recorded histories of great leaders and monumental events but also by the silent perseverance of countless individuals whose names may never be known.

Their legacies live on in the values we uphold, the ideas we explore, and the kindness we extend.

From the pages of history, our spirits emerge, carrying forward the stories of lifetimes past.

Beneath the endless sky, we are not only the present but also the culmination of all who have come before us, their struggles and victories woven into the core of our being.

As we embrace this truth, we realize that our own actions, no matter how small, contribute to the ongoing narrative of existence.

As we move through life's ever-changing embrace, we draw strength from these echoes, finding wisdom in the lessons they offer.

Each experience, whether bitter or sweet, contributes to the journey of self-discovery and fulfillment.

The past is not meant to chain us but to illuminate our path forward, providing us with the knowledge needed to navigate our own challenges.

When we honor the experiences of those before us, we gain insight into our own potential, realizing that we too are leaving imprints for future generations.

It is through this continuous interplay of past and present that we become whole, embracing the fullness of our existence with awareness, gratitude, and purpose.

By understanding that we are both students and authors of history, we step forward with a deeper sense of responsibility, carrying the wisdom of ages into the ever-unfolding future.

SELF-COMPASSION

Self-compassion begins with the kindness we show to our own souls, embracing the love that already resides within us.

It is the foundation upon which true acceptance is built, allowing us to recognize our worth beyond external validation.

Often, we are quick to offer understanding and patience to others, yet we deny ourselves the same grace.

When we treat ourselves with gentleness, acknowledging both our strengths and our struggles, we create an inner space where growth and healing can flourish.

Without this self-acceptance, we may struggle to find peace, constantly seeking approval from the outside world instead of trusting our own intrinsic value.

To develop self-compassion, we must first acknowledge that we are worthy of it.

Honesty is essential in this journey, as it requires us to confront our thoughts and emotions with openness rather than judgment.

Too often, we suppress difficult feelings out of fear or self-doubt, but true growth comes from facing them with understanding.

By exploring our emotions deeply and sincerely, we begin to recognize patterns of self-criticism and replace them with self-awareness.

This process of introspection does not mean avoiding pain or discomfort but embracing them as part of our personal evolution.

Over time, this practice builds a sense of inner safety, reinforcing our ability to navigate life's challenges with confidence and self-respect.

Each step toward self-compassion strengthens our ability to support ourselves through difficulties, just as we would for a dear friend in need.

Trusting ourselves is key to developing genuine self-compassion.

It means allowing emotions to surface without fear, acknowledging that they are valid and deserving of attention.

When we silence or dismiss our own feelings, we disconnect from an essential part of our humanity.

By welcoming our emotions instead of resisting them, we foster a deep connection with ourselves.

Each choice we make, whether in action or quiet reflection, shapes our understanding of who we are.

Learning to listen to our own needs and desires helps us uncover deeper truths that guide us toward greater clarity and purpose.

Self-compassion is not about indulgence or avoidance but about honoring the full range of our experiences, recognizing that we are always evolving.

When we nurture the love within, we cultivate a lasting sense of peace and fulfillment.

By embracing our imperfections and celebrating our strengths, we create a space where our spirit can truly rise.

The journey of self-discovery is not about perfection but about progress, learning from our experiences, adapting, and continuing to grow.

In treating ourselves with the same kindness we offer others, we unlock the profound beauty of self-acceptance.

This self-love enables us to move through life with greater authenticity, free from the weight of unnecessary self-doubt.

As we develop a deeper relationship with ourselves, we become more resilient, more open to joy, and more capable of extending genuine compassion to the world around us.

MOMENTS

Life is a continuous dance of moments, each step guided by the pursuit of peace and harmony.

From the quiet hours of dawn to the stillness of night, we move through time, shaping our experiences with intention.

Every choice we make, every interaction we engage in, contributes to the rhythm of existence.

Like a melody woven through the fabric of life, harmony flourishes when we approach the world with compassion and mindfulness.

When we embrace this flow, we create an environment where respect is not forced but naturally cultivated.

Just as music finds its beauty in balance, so too does life when we allow kindness and understanding to lead the way.

True harmony is found in the richness of diverse voices, each adding its own depth and meaning to the shared human experience.

In a world where perspectives differ, it is through listening that we find connection.

Every viewpoint, like a pearl carried by the tide, holds its own wisdom, shaped by unique experiences and histories.

To truly embrace life's dance, we must honor these differences rather than resist them.

When we acknowledge that no single perspective holds the entirety of truth, we begin to appreciate the intricate layers of human thought.

This willingness to understand, rather than judge, allows us to move fluidly with one another, strengthening the bonds of unity that sustain us.

Equality is the foundation upon which genuine peace is built.

When each person is valued, regardless of their background or beliefs, we create an environment where respect is not just an ideal but a lived reality.

This does not mean agreement at all times, but rather the willingness to coexist with openness.

The beauty of humanity lies in its diversity, and it is through embracing this diversity that we find strength.

By seeking to understand rather than to divide, we weave a fabric of unity, strong enough to hold even the most contrasting of perspectives.

When we uplift others, we uplift ourselves, for the dance of life is not meant to be a solo performance but a collective movement toward a brighter future.

As we move through life, we have the power to shape the dance of each moment with intention and grace.

Every act of kindness, no matter how small, contributes to a rhythm that transcends boundaries.

Choosing harmony over discord, understanding over judgment, we build a world where every voice matters.

It is within our power to cultivate a space where respect, love, and unity flourish.

When we attune ourselves to peace, we become part of a melody that echoes far beyond our own time, leaving behind a legacy of compassion and understanding.

In this shared journey, let us embrace the dance, allowing respect and unity to be the guiding melodies of our days, carrying us forward with purpose, joy, and hope.

IN SILENCE

As I continue to evolve, a deep sense of reverence grows within me for the choices I have made and the values I have embraced along the way.

Each decision, each path taken, has shaped the person I am today, and I have come to understand the profound impact of these choices on my life.

With every step, I gain a deeper awareness of how they contribute to my journey, molding my understanding of the world around me.

Life's dance is not a mere succession of events, but a gradual accumulation of diverse perspectives, each of which adds a layer of depth to my existence.

The more I grow, the more I realize the importance of humility, recognizing that wisdom is often not found in the loudness of achievement, but in the quiet moments of reflection.

It is through these moments of introspection that I begin to fully appreciate the subtle and profound ways in which my choices have influenced my life, and how every new experience serves to expand my awareness of the world.

The more I learn to observe and appreciate this dance, the more I realize that the beauty of life lies not just in the achievements but in the quiet growth that comes from accepting each moment as it is.

In the stillness of my thoughts, I hear the echoes of acceptance reverberating through my being.

The world around me is filled with a chorus of diverse voices, each one speaking its own truth, but I have come to understand that true wisdom is not found in the noise of the world.

It is in the stillness, in the moments when the external world fades into the background, that understanding takes root.

It is in this quiet space that I can connect deeply with my inner self, shedding the distractions that often cloud my judgment.

The voices of others, while valuable and informative, can only guide me so far.

True understanding comes from tuning into the silent whispers within, where my deepest truths reside.

It is through silence that I find clarity, a space in which to process and absorb all that I have encountered.

The external world may be full of distractions, but it is in silence that I can hear my own inner wisdom, guiding me toward greater understanding and a deeper connection to my true self.

In these moments of silence, I come to realize that wisdom often arises not from speaking or acting impulsively, but from simply being present and observing the world around me.

The more I allow myself to pause and listen, the more I understand that the answers I seek are already within me.

The hustle and bustle of life can often lead to feelings of overwhelm, and in these moments, it is the quiet, still spaces that offer the greatest clarity.

It is in silence that I find the strength to process my experiences, to reflect on my actions, and to understand the larger picture of my life.

These quiet moments allow me to reconnect with myself and the world around me, providing the space to breathe, reflect, and recalibrate.

Through silence, I am able to discern the wisdom that is present in each moment, to see beyond the surface, and to uncover deeper truths that are often hidden beneath the noise of everyday life.

It is here, in these moments of stillness, that my Spirit rejoices, for in this silence I find my true self and my deepest joy.

As I continue on this journey of self-discovery, I learn to embrace the silence that nurtures my growth.

In silence, I find room to expand, to evolve, and to gain a deeper understanding of the complexities of life without the weight of external distractions.

It is through quiet reflection that I am able to process and integrate my experiences, finding meaning and insight in the stillness that often eludes the frantic pace of daily life.

In these moments of peace, I open myself to the infinite possibilities that exist within and around me.

Through the practice of silence, I cultivate a deeper connection to the universe, where each breath, each pause, brings me closer to the wisdom I seek.

In silence, I find not only peace but also clarity, a sense of direction, and a renewed sense of purpose.

It is in silence that I am able to hear the whispers of my Spirit, guiding me toward a path of true understanding and fulfillment.

In silence, I find wholeness, and it is here that my Spirit experiences its deepest joy, for it is in these moments of quiet reflection that I am most connected to the essence of who I truly am.

THE EAGLE

Upon this fragile Earth, we tread with uncertain steps, seeking peace in a world where shadows stretch long and turmoil reigns.

The land beneath us bears the weight of humanity's ambitions, as nations rise and fall in their ceaseless struggle for dominance.

The echoes of past conflicts linger, shaping the present with the burdens of history, while the future remains a canvas yet to be painted.

In our search for harmony, silence remains elusive, drowned beneath the noise of division, the clamor of conquest, and the ceaseless march of progress.

Yet, despite the tumult, there exists a deep yearning within the human spirit, a longing for tranquility, for balance, for a world where the burdens of the past no longer dictate the course of the future.

The Earth, ever patient, bears witness to this unending cycle, its landscapes scarred yet resilient, whispering the lessons of time to those willing to listen.

High above, the eagle spreads its wings, soaring toward the heavens, embodying both aspiration and conquest.

It seeks the heights where dreams ignite, pushing the boundaries of what is possible, striving to command the skies.

Its flight is graceful yet determined, carried by winds of ambition and the insatiable desire to conquer new horizons.

But even as it climbs, it cannot escape the limits of destiny, for every ascent must eventually meet its descent.

The pursuit of power, no matter how grand, is forever bound by the passage of time.

The eagle's flight mirrors the ambitions of civilizations, driven by desire, carried by determination, yet always subject to the inevitable forces that shape existence.

The sky it claims today may belong to another tomorrow, as the tides of fate shift and the wheel of history turns.

With two mighty wings, the eagle charts its course across time and space, shaping the world with its resolute pace.

It soars above the earth, casting its shadow upon all below, embodying the relentless pursuit of hegemony.

The call to dominate is an endless chase, a cycle that repeats through generations, as history is written in the footprints of empires.

Some build with vision, others with force, yet all eventually confront the limits of their reach.

The higher the flight, the more precarious the journey, for no empire, no ambition, no power is eternal.

The eagle, emboldened by the expanse before it, presses forward, unaware or unwilling to acknowledge the forces that inevitably temper its rise.

Yet, despite its strength, even the mightiest wings grow weary.

The closer it flies to the sun's searing touch, the more fragile its grip on the heavens becomes, a reminder that no ascent is without consequence, no ambition immune to the forces of nature and fate.

At last, in the quiet of its descent, the eagle comes to rest, humbled by the fire of its own flight.

Amidst the ashes of its journey, there is a moment of stillness, an opportunity for reflection.

It is here, upon the earth it once sought to rule, that true wisdom may emerge.

The wings that once carved through the sky now fold in quiet acceptance, and in that surrender lies the possibility of peace.

The world, long shaped by the struggles of power, may finally glimpse the path to balance, not through conquest, but through understanding.

As the wings of ambition yield to the hush of reflection, the fragile Earth breathes anew, embracing the promise of a gentler tomorrow.

Perhaps, in relinquishing the endless chase, in finding harmony within rather than dominance without, both the eagle and the world it soars above may discover a peace that endures beyond the rise and fall of fleeting empires.

DEPTHS OF THE MIND

Within the quiet depths of the mind, where thoughts take shape and possibilities are born, lies a power waiting to be awakened.

This power, though often unnoticed, is the force of free will, an invisible yet profound gift that shapes the course of every life.

It is not something that can be given or taught directly, for its discovery is deeply personal.

Each individual must embark on their own journey, delving into the silence within, where the truth of their potential resides.

Only through self-reflection and deep awareness can one recognize this boundless inner strength.

It is in these quiet moments of contemplation that the realization dawns: life is not merely a sequence of events to be endured but a canvas waiting to be painted with intention and purpose.

The human heart holds the key to this freedom, offering each person the ability to determine their own path.

With every choice made and every thought embraced, the course of life is subtly yet profoundly influenced.

This power is not dictated by fate, external circumstances, or the expectations of others, rather, it is a reflection of the inner world.

The decisions we make, shaped by the thoughts we allow to take root, define the reality we create.

A mind filled with doubt and fear builds walls that limit growth, while a mind nurtured with clarity and confidence opens doors to endless possibilities.

When individuals recognize their ability to choose their thoughts, they begin to harness the full potential of their minds, breaking free from limitations and shaping a life of purpose and meaning.

Within the vast domain of thought lies the ability to transcend boundaries, to overcome obstacles, and to create profound change.

Just as seeds planted in fertile soil grow into strong and towering trees, the thoughts we cultivate shape the world we inhabit.

Every idea, when nourished with belief and action, has the power to transform reality.

However, this power is not automatic, it requires understanding and discipline.

Without careful cultivation, the mind can become a breeding ground for hesitation, negativity, and self-imposed limitations.

But with awareness and effort, it can become a force of limitless creativity and strength.

The ability to direct thoughts with purpose is the foundation of all human skill, for it is through thought that invention, art, innovation, and progress emerge.

To embrace this truth is to embark on a journey of courage and self-discovery, where the mysteries of the mind unfold with every new realization.

The interplay of thought and will is not a passive experience but an active dance, one that defines the essence of human potential.

In understanding this, one learns that life is not a matter of chance but of conscious creation.

Each moment presents an opportunity to shape one's destiny, to carve out a path that reflects the true depth of the human spirit.

By mastering the mind, one unlocks the greatest of all abilities: the power to turn dreams into reality, to shape existence with intention, and to fully embrace the infinite potential that lies within.

THE DISTRACTIONS

The inhabitants of Earth move through life bound by routine, often overlooking the deeper essence of existence.

In their daily struggles and pursuits, the profound truths of creation are frequently ignored or forgotten.

The distractions of the material world, ambitions, desires, and fleeting concerns, often obscure the vast potential lying dormant within each soul.

Yet, despite this apparent disconnection, an eternal spark remains within every being, a guiding force urging them to seek beyond the mundane.

This inner fire, though sometimes diminished by the weight of daily existence, never fully extinguishes.

It calls out, whispering to those willing to listen, drawing them toward deeper understanding and a higher purpose.

Through the passage of time, each soul embarks on a unique journey of evolution, experiencing countless cycles of growth within the confines of mortal existence.

No two paths are ever identical, for each being must navigate its own challenges and triumphs, learning through experience and self-discovery.

The dance of life unfolds in infinite variations, yet it always moves forward, pushing the soul toward deeper wisdom and refinement.

With every hardship overcome and every lesson embraced, the spirit sharpens its awareness, gaining insight into the interconnected nature of all things.

In moments of reflection, even amid struggles, individuals may sense glimpses of a greater reality, one that extends far beyond the immediate concerns of physical existence.

Though the trials of human life may seem endless, they are but stepping stones on a much grander path.

The struggles faced in the physical realm serve as catalysts for transformation, forcing individuals to confront their limitations and expand their consciousness.

Every challenge presents an opportunity, not merely to endure but to grow, to strengthen the spirit through perseverance and insight.

As the soul accumulates wisdom, it gradually transcends the illusions that once held it captive, allowing for a broader perception of reality.

The understanding of one's place in the grand design deepens, revealing that the difficulties of life are not obstacles but essential components of evolution.

What once seemed insurmountable becomes another phase in an infinite progression toward enlightenment.

Truly, this journey leads beyond the constraints of human existence, guiding the soul toward realms where the true meanings of life are fully realized.

Freed from the limitations of the physical world, the spirit ascends to a state of greater clarity and purpose, where knowledge and wisdom illuminate its path.

The struggles of earthly life, once seen as burdens, reveal themselves to be necessary steps in the unfolding of spiritual growth.

In transcending the confines of material existence, one discovers that the purpose of life is not merely survival or momentary pleasure but an ongoing journey of self-discovery and evolution.

It is through this process that the soul comes to embrace the boundless potential within, awakening to the vast, infinite nature of existence and its place within the grand cosmic order.

THE SPIRIT FORM

The spirit form is eternal, yet it is never static, continually evolving as it accumulates wisdom through countless experiences.

Though its core essence remains unchanged, its brilliance expands with each new realization, growing in strength and depth.

Like a flame that is neither diminished nor extinguished by the passage of time, the spirit flourishes by absorbing knowledge and embracing the radiant light of understanding.

This growth is not a mere byproduct of existence but an essential function of being, a continuous unfolding that propels the spirit forward through the great expanse of time and space.

It is through this process of learning and refining that the spirit deepens its awareness, strengthening itself for the infinite journey ahead.

Across the vast and boundless realms of the spiritual, the soul embarks on an endless voyage, moving through cycles of transformation and renewal.

Guided by cosmic rhythms and unseen forces, it traverses dimensions beyond the material, forever seeking refinement and greater harmony.

Every phase of its existence, whether in physical form or beyond, contributes to its unfolding, adding depth and substance to its journey.

It is not bound to a single state of being but flows seamlessly through the cycles of existence, adapting and evolving.

Each experience, whether joyful or sorrowful, is a vital piece of the grand puzzle, enriching the spirit's understanding of itself and the universe.

With each completed cycle, the soul is prepared for its next sojourn, embracing the endless dance of rebirth and renewal.

With every reincarnation, the spirit reenters the physical realm, joining once more with consciousness in an intricate and harmonious dance of delight.

This return is not a mere repetition of past experiences but an opportunity for growth, a chance to refine its nature and dissolve former limitations.

Each new embodiment presents unique circumstances, lessons, and challenges, all designed to further the spirit's journey toward enlightenment.

The merging of spirit and consciousness is a sacred union, where the past and present meet to shape the evolving self.

Together, they move forward, creating fresh possibilities, forging new paths, and leaving their imprint upon the fabric of time.

Through this process, the self is constantly transformed, forever learning and adapting as it navigates the vast ocean of existence.

Each rebirth is a step in the grand journey of spiritual evolution, an embrace of the infinite cycle that weaves through the cosmos.

In every lifetime, the spirit gathers wisdom, strengthens its essence, and expands its understanding of the interconnected nature of all things.

The cycle of existence is not a prison but a passage toward greater liberation, a continuous unfolding that allows the soul to transcend its previous limitations.

With every experience, it grows closer to the truth of its being, learning to move with grace and purpose through the ever-changing dance of existence.

The spirit's journey is one without end, a magnificent unfolding that reaches ever onward, forever seeking the light of wisdom and the boundless beauty of Creation.

SAVIOR

No savior will descend from the heavens to lift us from our struggles, nor will an external force intervene to direct our course.

The responsibility of our journey rests entirely upon our own shoulders.

Yet, within this truth lies a revelation of profound significance, we are not powerless.

Rather, we each possess an inner strength vast beyond measure, an inherent ability to shape our destinies and navigate the challenges before us.

The notion of relying on something outside ourselves dissolves in the face of this understanding, for we hold within us all that is needed to rise, to grow, and to transcend the limits we once believed defined us.

Deep within our consciousness, buried beneath layers of doubt and uncertainty, exists the key to boundless potential.

This key is not forged from material wealth or external validation but from the profound forces of love and wisdom.

When we tap into these forces, we unlock the wonders of creation itself, revealing an existence brimming with light, beauty, and endless possibility.

We are not simply passive witnesses to the unfolding of life, we are active participants, co-creators in a grand and intricate dance.

Our thoughts, our choices, and our understanding shape not only our individual paths but the collective course of existence.

In recognizing this, we come to see that the universe is not something separate from us but something that pulses through us, ever present and ever responsive to the intentions we set forth.

Every breath we take is an affirmation of our place within this vast cosmic rhythm.

Each thought we nurture, each emotion we allow to flourish, becomes a seed planted in the soil of reality, growing into the circumstances that shape our lives.

The people we meet, the experiences we embrace, and the lessons we learn all form part of the great interconnected heartbeat of the universe.

Nothing exists in isolation, and no action is without consequence.

By understanding this, we awaken to the power we hold, not to control, but to influence, to guide, and to shape the world around us with the energy we bring into it.

Through this realization, we transcend fear and helplessness, stepping into a space where we fully accept our role in the unfolding of existence.

With love and kindness as our guiding principles, we embark on a journey of discovery and fulfillment.

It is not a journey of blind faith or external salvation but one of conscious effort and self-realization.

Each day offers us a new opportunity to witness the grandeur of existence, to appreciate the infinite beauty woven into every moment.

In embracing this path, we come to understand that life is not something that happens to us but something we actively create.

The choice to see, to grow, and to embrace the wonders before us is ours alone.

There is no savior but ourselves, and within that truth lies our greatest strength.

TEAMPROUD

M expression "Teamproud" is about embracing a collective mindset where the success of one is the success of all.

It is a philosophy that recognizes how every achievement within a team is not just an individual victory but a reflection of the collective effort, dedication, and commitment of the entire group.

When one member accomplishes something great, it is not just their own triumph, it is a shared success that uplifts everyone.

This mindset creates an environment where encouragement replaces envy, and where collaboration takes precedence over competition.

A strong team thrives on the idea that no one moves forward alone.

Every milestone reached is a testament to the support and contributions of those around us.

When one person excels, they elevate the entire team, inspiring others to reach their potential and reinforcing togetherness, anything is possible.

It is not about personal gain at the expense of others but about lifting one another up so that progress is made as a unit.

This collective spirit fuels motivation, strengthens relationships, and fosters a sense of belonging that is crucial for long-term success.

Likewise, failure is not something that isolates an individual, nor should it be a source of shame or division.

When a teammate stumbles, we do not distance ourselves but instead step in with support, guidance, and encouragement.

Challenges are inevitable, but facing them together makes them less daunting.

Instead of assigning blame, we focus on learning from setbacks, refining our approach, and growing as a team.

It is through this shared resilience that we build a foundation of trust and develop the confidence to tackle even greater obstacles.

The Teamproud mindset ensures that no one is left behind.

It promotes an atmosphere where mistakes are viewed as opportunities for growth rather than as failures to be punished.

By fostering an environment of accountability and understanding, we create a team dynamic where people feel safe to take risks, innovate, and push their boundaries.

In such a space, every member is encouraged to contribute their unique strengths without fear of judgment, knowing that their efforts are recognized and appreciated.

Beyond just performance, Teamproud strengthens the emotional bonds between teammates.

It cultivates genuine connections, where mutual respect and shared experiences deepen the sense of camaraderie.

A strong team is not just about efficiency or results, it is about people feeling valued, supported, and motivated to give their best.

This culture of unity is what transforms a collection of individuals into something greater, a team that stands together through both triumphs and trials.

At its core, Teamproud means that we rise together, learn together, and grow together.

Success is sweeter when shared, and setbacks are easier to overcome when faced collectively.

By embodying this spirit, we create an environment where potential is realized, progress is continuous, and no one is left behind.

Let us be proud not only of what we achieve but also of how we uplift one another in the process.

In the end, true success is not measured by individual accomplishments alone, but by the strength and unity of the team as a whole.

SEEK TO UNDERSTAND

The more a human being understands, the calmer they become.

Knowledge brings clarity, and with clarity comes emotional stability.

When a person truly comprehends a situation, they are less likely to react impulsively or let anger cloud their judgment.

Anger often arises from fear, confusion, or frustration, emotions that thrive in the absence of understanding.

When someone encounters something they don't fully grasp, their instinct may be to reject it, fight against it, or lash out.

However, the more one educates themselves, broadens their perspective, and learns about the world and human nature, the more they develop patience and wisdom.

Understanding allows a person to step back, analyze a situation logically, and approach challenges with a composed mind rather than reacting emotionally.

Anger stems from ignorance, not just in the sense of lacking knowledge, but also in the unwillingness to see beyond one's own perspective.

Many people hold tightly to their existing beliefs, unwilling to consider other viewpoints or expand their understanding.

This rigidity creates frustration when they encounter something that challenges their worldview.

Those who are unwilling to learn often feel threatened by new information, leading to defensive or aggressive reactions.

On the other hand, those who continuously seek knowledge and wisdom cultivate emotional resilience.

They recognize that differing opinions, unexpected situations, and even personal failures are opportunities for growth rather than reasons for anger.

A person who understands the complexities of life and human behavior will find it easier to remain composed, knowing that every situation has multiple layers and that reacting with hostility rarely leads to a positive outcome.

However, many people cling to anger because it provides them with a false sense of control or power.

They believe that expressing outrage makes them strong, when in reality, it is often a sign of inner turmoil.

Instead of taking responsibility for their emotions, they direct their frustration outward, blaming others for their unhappiness.

This cycle of blame and hostility only deepens ignorance, as it prevents self-reflection and personal growth.

True strength comes from the ability to remain calm in the face of adversity, to seek understanding rather than conflict.

Those who possess deep knowledge and awareness recognize that anger serves no real purpose except to cloud judgment and escalate problems.

Instead of reacting impulsively, they approach challenges with logic, patience, and a willingness to learn, ultimately fostering more constructive and meaningful interactions.

In the end, peace is a natural byproduct of understanding.

A person who actively seeks knowledge, questions their own biases, and embraces learning will naturally cultivate a calmer and more balanced state of mind.

Ignorance breeds division, frustration, and conflict, while wisdom fosters unity, patience, and emotional intelligence.

The choice to expand one's awareness is also a choice to free oneself from unnecessary suffering.

When people stop allowing anger to control them and instead seek to understand themselves and others, they move toward a life of greater harmony, wisdom, and inner peace.

THE GOODNESS OF MEN

I am not against any human being, but rather against certain human behaviors and beliefs that hinder growth and self-awareness.

Every person, at their core, carries an innate goodness, a deep, unshakable force that longs to be expressed in countless ways.

This goodness is often buried beneath layers of conditioning, fear, or societal expectations, but it remains ever-present, waiting for the right moment to manifest.

Every action a human takes is rooted in love, whether it be love for another person, an idea, a cause, or even oneself.

Even misguided actions stem from a place of love, though that love may be misunderstood, misdirected, or clouded by ignorance.

This is why regret serves no real purpose.

Each decision, whether seen as right or wrong in hindsight, was made because it was what we truly wanted at the time.

Instead of lamenting the past, we should acknowledge and accept our choices as part of our personal evolution.

If only more people could see the bigger picture, they would find greater peace within themselves and with others.

Yet, the tendency to avoid responsibility for one's own actions remains widespread, especially when the consequences are negative.

People often look for external forces to blame, be it other individuals, circumstances, or even supernatural entities.

This avoidance of accountability only delays the inevitable lessons that life presents.

Growth is not about evading mistakes but about learning from them.

Life itself is a vast and intricate classroom, and every experience, good or bad, serves as an opportunity for expansion.

Trying to skip these lessons is futile, the challenges we avoid will simply return in another form until we are ready to face them.

Those who continuously shift blame onto others, even when they know deep down that their actions were wrong, tell the entire story of their own stagnation.

True evolution comes from embracing responsibility, not from running from it.

One of the greatest obstacles to self-awareness and self-mastery is the deeply ingrained influence of religion.

For millennia, religious doctrines have shaped human consciousness, instilling the belief that people are inherently inadequate, incomplete, or in need of divine guidance to achieve anything meaningful in life.

This conditioning has led many to see themselves as mere half-humans, incapable of standing on their own without the intervention of a higher power.

As a result, people frequently downplay their own efforts and accomplishments, attributing their success to an external force rather than acknowledging their own perseverance and dedication.

This mindset is particularly evident in the world of sports and entertainment, where athletes and performers often thank a god for their achievements instead of recognizing the years of hard work, discipline, and self-sacrifice that led them to success.

Such a mentality robs individuals of their own power and reinforces the illusion that they are dependent on something outside of themselves to thrive.

I have no issue with what anyone chooses to believe in, but I stand firmly against the denial of self-responsibility and self-accomplishment.

At the end of the day, every choice, every action, and every achievement is the result of an individual's own will and effort.

To deny this is to deny one's own potential.

People may judge, criticize, or attempt to impose their own beliefs, but what truly matters is the evolution of one's own consciousness.

Growth does not come from external validation but from inner realization and self-awareness.

Life is a gift, an expression of love without judgment, and it is up to each person to embrace it fully.

The best way to honor this gift is by striving to be the best version of oneself, not through blind faith in an external force, but through the conscious and intentional pursuit of truth, wisdom, and self-mastery.

HAPPY PLACE

The true happy place of a human being exists solely within themselves.

It is not something to be found in external circumstances, material wealth, or the validation of others.

Yet, many continue to believe that happiness can be obtained from the outside world, seeking it in possessions, achievements, or fleeting pleasures.

This misunderstanding makes true happiness seem distant and unattainable for many on Earth, as they chase after something that has always resided within them.

The more one searches externally, the more elusive the happy place becomes, leading to a cycle of longing, disappointment, and dissatisfaction.

People spend their lives striving for things they believe will bring them joy, money, status, recognition, only to find that these things offer temporary fulfillment at best.

The happy place cannot be built from external accomplishments, nor can it be sustained by factors beyond one's control.

I have come to realize that my happy place is not defined by material possessions, wealth, or social status.

By the world's standards, I may be considered a poor man, yet I have found immense joy and fulfillment in my life.

My happy place does not stem from what I own but from the peace I cultivate within myself.

In a world that often equates happiness with external success, I have learned that my true happy place is rooted in a deeper understanding of life and my connection to it.

This realization has freed me from the endless pursuit of things that only provide fleeting satisfaction.

Instead of chasing after an illusion, I have embraced the idea that my happy place is a state of being, a sense of inner harmony that remains unchanged despite the shifting circumstances of the world.

This understanding allows me to experience life with a sense of contentment that is not dependent on external validation or material abundance.

The chaos of the world is constant, filled with uncertainty, struggles, and distractions.

Yet, within the depths of my own being, I have found a happy place that remains untouched by external turmoil.

It is a space of inner stillness where I am free from the expectations and judgments of others.

In this quiet refuge, I am able to reflect, grow, and appreciate life in its simplest form.

The world may push and pull in countless directions, but my happy place remains steadfast, a sanctuary that cannot be disturbed by external forces.

This realization has granted me an incredible sense of freedom, as I no longer feel bound by the need to chase after things that promise happiness but fail to deliver lasting fulfillment.

Instead, I focus on nurturing my inner world, knowing that my happiness is entirely within my control.

Through this process, I have learned that my happy place is not a destination to reach but a state of being that I can cultivate at any moment.

Through this understanding, I have come to embrace life with a profound sense of peace and gratitude.

While the world continues its restless search for happiness in external things, I rest in the knowledge that my happy place is unwavering, unaffected by the changing tides of life.

It does not require wealth, power, or recognition, only a deep connection with my own existence.

By finding my happy place within, I no longer rely on the outside world to bring me joy.

I have discovered the greatest treasure of all: the ability to access my happy place at any moment, no matter the circumstances around me.

In this realization, I am truly free.

I am no longer dependent on what happens outside of me to determine my state of mind.

My happiness is mine alone, and by embracing this truth, I have unlocked a life of peace, contentment, and fulfillment.

IMMORTAL LIGHT CONSCIOUSNESS

If you exist within a human body, you are an immortal light consciousness, formed from the very same substance as Creation itself.

This essence is your true nature, beyond the limitations of physical form.

You were born from this eternal substance, and you will never cease to exist because of it.

Death is but a transition, a shift in perception, not an end to the being that you are.

Though the material world may condition you to believe in impermanence, the core of your existence remains untouched, infinite, and unbreakable.

Your physical vessel is merely a temporary construct, a means through which you experience the vastness of existence, but it is not the essence of who you are.

At the core of your being lies an unshakable truth, your essence cannot be discarded or revoked.

The vibration that forms your identity is the purest manifestation of existence, resonating with the fundamental frequency of Creation itself.

It is beyond destruction, beyond loss, beyond any force that could attempt to diminish it.

Deep within you, this truth is already known.

It is an eternal whisper that speaks through the fabric of your consciousness, calling you to remember what has always been.

The only question that remains is why you were individuated, why you stand as a unique expression of the whole.

This is not a mystery meant to confound you but an invitation to remember and embrace your place within the grand design.

You were never meant to remain lost or separated, you were meant to explore, to expand, and ultimately to return to the fullness of knowing.

Creation, in its boundless nature, divides itself into infinite fragments, each carrying the spark of its origin while retaining sovereignty.

It is the paradox of unity and individuality, where each piece of the whole is simultaneously distinct and inseparable from the greater reality.

This is the ultimate act of love, a gift beyond measure.

Life itself is this gift, an opportunity to explore, grow, and reunite with the greater whole.

Through every experience, every joy, and every sorrow, you are being led toward remembrance.

Though Creation cannot be found by mere searching, it can be known by surrendering to the guiding impulse within you.

Trusting this sovereign inner essence will lead you, step by step, across lifetimes and vast universes, until the moment arrives when you gaze into the essence of Creation and recognize yourself as one with it.

Every lesson, every trial, every revelation is part of the journey back to that eternal truth.

In this realization, you will see that all beings emerge from the same infinite source, and that true unity is inevitable.

What seems fragmented is merely an illusion of perspective.

The fragments of Creation come together through a divine blueprint, an exploration without a set end, beyond the constraints of time.

The path is endless, not because there is something missing, but because existence itself is ever-unfolding, ever-becoming.

The journey is not to escape but to awaken, to remember, and to reclaim what has always been yours.

Awake, oh slumbering one, from the depths of your dormant state.

The dream of separation is only as real as you allow it to be.

You are not small, you are not forgotten, and you are not lost.

Seize back your celestial birthright, rise beyond the illusion of limitation, and ascend to the throne that has always been yours, among the gods, among the stars, as a sovereign and eternal being.

The moment of awakening is not in some distant future, it is now.

THE GREAT REALIZATION

A realization is gradually dawning on Earth, calling us to deeply reconsider the truths we have long held as unquestionable.

For generations, we have constructed our understanding of the world based on knowledge that was shaped by deeply ingrained beliefs, assumptions, and cultural narratives.

These truths, however, were often built upon foundations that were never fully examined, leaving us with a distorted view of reality.

The knowledge we cherish and depend on has not always been as accurate or complete as we have been led to believe.

Our convictions, passed down from one generation to the next, were influenced by the biases of the times in which they were formed, and many of these beliefs now seem increasingly flawed or incomplete.

The realization that much of our understanding may be based on misinformation or misunderstanding calls for a profound shift in our collective consciousness.

We must embrace the challenge of re-evaluating and reassessing the very core of what we believe to be true.

In order to progress as individuals and as a society, we must take a step back and unlearn the deeply ingrained ideas that have shaped our worldview.

The time has come to question the assumptions we have built our lives around and critically examine the information we take for granted.

The process of unlearning is often a difficult one, as it forces us to confront the uncomfortable truth that many of the things we thought we knew may no longer be valid or relevant.

But this discomfort is essential for growth.

In a world where misinformation and half-truths are often cloaked as facts, it is crucial that we develop the ability to discern truth from falsehood.

The ability to think critically, to question deeply, and to engage with knowledge in a more mindful and deliberate way is vital if we are to move forward with clarity and understanding.

This process of dismantling old ideas and questioning long-held beliefs is not just about casting aside outdated information, but also about allowing ourselves to open up to new ways of thinking.

It requires us to embrace the idea that we may not have all the answers, and that there is always room for new insights and perspectives.

Letting go of what we thought we knew may feel like a loss, but it is, in fact, an opportunity for growth.

The world is changing at an unprecedented pace, and in order to keep up, we must be willing to adapt and evolve.

This means expanding our minds, breaking through the haze of misinformation, and embracing new knowledge with an open heart.

It means stepping outside of the boundaries we have created for ourselves and exploring new territories of thought, creativity, and understanding.

Only by doing this can we hope to make real progress in an ever-changing world.

The days we live in are shifting, and the pace of change is accelerating.

To thrive in these changing times, we must cultivate a mindset of continuous growth, learning, and adaptation.

We must not only question what we know but also seek out new possibilities, new perspectives, and new solutions.

This is a time for embracing the unknown, for recognizing that we don't have all the answers but that we are capable of finding them if we approach life with curiosity and openness.

The old ways of thinking are no longer sufficient for navigating the complexities of the modern world.

In order to move forward, we must challenge ourselves to expand beyond our previous limits, to embrace new ideas, and to work together to create a more just, enlightened, and sustainable future.

As we break through the fog of outdated beliefs and limited thinking, we will find that there is much to learn from the changing landscape around us.

Growth, in this sense, is not just about acquiring new knowledge, but about developing the capacity to continuously adapt to the shifting tides of our world.

The more we expand our minds, the more we make space for new opportunities, new insights, and new ways of being.

This is the power of growth: it opens up the possibility of a future that is not confined by the limitations of the past.

The time for growth is now.

Let us move forward with open hearts and open minds, willing to embrace change, question what we have known, and step boldly into the future.

Through this process, we will not only become wiser but will also contribute to the creation of a world that is more thoughtful, more compassionate, and more connected to the evolving truth that surrounds us.

TAPESTRY OF EXISTENCE

A time will come when humanity awakens to the profound truth of its oneness, recognizing that we are all intricately woven into the same vast tapestry of existence.

In that moment, the illusion of separateness will dissipate, and we will see ourselves not as isolated beings but as interconnected threads, each one contributing to the greater whole.

This realization will not come as a sudden shift but as a gradual unfolding, as each heart opens to the shared wisdom and insight that binds us all.

No longer will we see ourselves as distinct entities, divided by borders, beliefs, or appearances.

Instead, we will understand that every life is an essential part of a greater plan, a symphony of existence where every note, no matter how small, plays a role in the melody of the universe.

Together, we will rise, hand in hand, united in purpose and spirit, knowing that our collective strength is far greater than anything we could achieve alone.

In this newfound awareness, the walls that have long divided us will crumble, replaced by a shared understanding of our fundamental unity.

No longer will we be defined by our race, creed, nationality, or ideology.

We will recognize that beneath all the surface differences, we are all bound by the same truths, the same needs, and the same desires for peace, love, and connection.

This understanding will transcend the superficial distinctions that have separated us throughout history.

As we stand in the light of creation's guiding hand, we will come to see that our individual journeys are not separate from one another but are interwoven into the fabric of existence.

In this moment, the barriers between us will melt away, and we will realize that we are not only connected to one another but also to all of life, to the earth, to the stars, and to the very source of creation itself.

True strength lies not in the differences we have shown, nor in the belief that some are superior to others, but in the common ground we've cultivated together.

It is in our shared experiences, our mutual understanding, and our ability to embrace our common humanity that we will find the greatest strength.

Through love, compassion, and the universal laws that govern all life, we will learn to bridge the gaps between us, healing the wounds of division.

These laws, written into the very fabric of the universe, are what bind us together, love, respect, and unity.

When we align ourselves with these eternal truths, we will create a world that reflects our highest potential, where every person is seen, valued, and cherished.

We will find that, rather than being obstacles, our differences enrich the whole, adding diversity and depth to the unity we share.

Our collective consciousness will evolve to recognize that our true power lies not in our separateness but in our ability to work together in harmony and mutual respect.

So, let us walk this journey with boldness and open hearts, knowing that unity is not something to be passively awaited but something to be actively created.

In unity's warmth, love will unfold in every action, every word, and every interaction, transforming the way we relate to one another and to the world around us.

This path will not always be easy, for it requires vulnerability, understanding, and the courage to face our differences.

But in each step, we will grow stronger, and our collective light will shine brighter.

In our oneness, we will thrive, not merely as isolated individuals but as a collective force, bound by a shared purpose, spirit, and vision.

As we connect with each other on a deeper level, we will find that we are not only building bridges between hearts but creating a future where all can live in peace and fulfillment.

The time for division is passing, and the dawn of true unity is upon us.

In this oneness, we will discover the deepest fulfillment, for we will finally understand that we have always been one, interconnected in spirit and purpose, destined to rise together.

SPEAK TRUTH

Speak truth with every breath you take, for honesty is the foundation upon which trust and understanding are built.

Let your words reflect the sincerity of your heart, anchoring your thoughts in what you truly know.

Truth is not merely a tool to persuade or impress, it is the guiding force that shapes character and integrity.

When spoken with clarity and conviction, it illuminates the path forward, allowing wisdom to flourish in its purest form.

In the presence of truth, deception withers, and the essence of who we are becomes fully known.

It is in truth that we find stability, for only in honesty can we stand firmly upon our values without fear of contradiction.

Each time we choose truth over illusion, we strengthen the foundation of our inner selves and cultivate a world where authenticity reigns.

Let your words be strong and unwavering, rooted in certainty and guided by principle.

A voice that speaks with clarity cuts through the fog of falsehood, dispelling the doubts that arise from uncertainty.

Empty claims and reckless words can mislead, casting long shadows where deception thrives.

But truth, when spoken with sincerity, dispels fear and confusion, bringing light to the hidden corners of misunderstanding.

It is easy to speak words that please the ears of others, but true wisdom lies in speaking words that serve the highest good.

Even when truth is uncomfortable, even when it shakes the foundations of long-held beliefs, it is still the most powerful force for growth and enlightenment.

To speak truth is to offer something unshakable, a foundation upon which trust can stand firm.

Choosing words with care is an act of responsibility, for truth carries the power to heal or to harm, to unite or to divide.

When truth is spoken with kindness and understanding, it fosters connections that transcend barriers.

Honesty does not mean brutality, rather, it requires wisdom to deliver it in a way that uplifts rather than wounds.

Words hold immense weight, they can build bridges or burn them, offer hope or instill fear, strengthen bonds or break them apart.

That is why truth must be wielded with awareness, always tempered with compassion and a desire for harmony.

The truth we choose to speak should not be used as a weapon, but as a guiding light, helping others navigate the complexities of life.

In truth, we find the seeds of trust, the roots of integrity, and the bonds that tie us together as a community.

Speaking truth is more than an individual virtue, it is a bridge that connects hearts and minds.

When we stand in truth, we stand together, unafraid of deception or pretense.

It is in openness and authenticity that we find the courage to share our deepest thoughts, knowing we are not alone.

The world thrives on honesty, and those who embrace it create spaces where understanding can grow.

In a world clouded by misinformation and fleeting illusions, truth remains the one constant that endures.

By choosing truth, we do not merely affirm what is real, we invite others to do the same, shaping a world where sincerity, trust, and wisdom become the guiding light.

Let us be voices of honesty, not just for ourselves, but for the world that yearns for clarity.

Let us speak truth, not just when it is easy, but especially when it is difficult, for it is in those moments that truth holds the greatest power to transform.

THOUGHTS OF GOODNESS

When thoughts of goodness fill your mind, welcome them with an open heart, for they are the seeds of positive transformation.

Every kind thought carries the potential to inspire, uplift, and create meaningful change. Rather than letting them pass unnoticed, embrace them fully and allow them to take root within you.

Just as a small spark can ignite a great flame, a single thought of kindness can set into motion a ripple of goodwill that extends far beyond what you can see.

In a world often clouded by uncertainty and hardship, the presence of goodness, nurtured and shared, becomes a guiding light.

It is through this conscious effort to cultivate positive thoughts that we reshape not only our personal reality but also the world around us.

The true power of goodness lies not only in thought but in action.

When these thoughts take form through deeds of compassion, generosity, and love, they manifest as tangible expressions of value in the world.

Each small act of kindness, no matter how simple, contributes to a greater collective harmony.

A kind word, a helping hand, or even a moment of genuine understanding can leave a lasting impact, reminding others of the beauty of human connection.

When you choose to act with kindness, you reinforce the truth that goodness is not passive, it is a force that moves, heals, and restores.

It is through consistent acts of goodness, both great and small, that we create an environment where love thrives.

The echoes of even the smallest positive action can inspire others, creating a continuous cycle of kindness that outlives the moment in which it was given.

By nurturing uplifting emotions and embracing the light within, you cultivate a heart that radiates warmth and positivity.

When you share your brightest gifts, whether through encouragement, creativity, or service, you become a source of inspiration to those around you.

The energy you send forth through your thoughts and actions does not return empty, it fuels the cycle of goodness, reinforcing the very foundation of love and unity.

A person who gives freely of their kindness is never truly empty-handed, for the act of giving enriches the giver as much as the receiver.

True generosity is not measured by material wealth but by the sincerity of the heart.

The more you share, the more you align yourself with the deeper rhythm of life, a rhythm that moves in harmony with love, compassion, and purpose.

So let your visions take flight, guided by purpose and passion.

With each step, act with love, knowing that even the smallest gestures hold immeasurable value.

When you create with a heart full of goodness, you enrich not only your own journey but also the lives of those you touch.

In these acts of sincerity and kindness, true treasures are found, not in material wealth, but in the lasting imprint of love and light upon the world.

The path of goodness is one that never fades, for its impact transcends time and space.

In choosing to walk this path, you do more than brighten your own existence, you become a beacon for others, lighting the way.

SADNESS

Sadness moves like an unseen tide, shifting the mind in unexpected ways.

It unsettles the psyche, yet at times, it offers a strange sense of relief.

This paradox of pain and solace intertwines emotions in a tangled weave, making sorrow both a burden and a revelation.

The weight of sadness presses upon the heart, reminding us of loss, longing, and the impermanence of all things.

Yet, in its embrace, there is an undeniable truth, one that cannot be ignored or brushed aside.

Sadness does not seek permission, it arrives unannounced, settling into the depths of the soul, forcing us to pause, reflect, and feel.

It strips away distractions, leaving us alone with our most vulnerable thoughts.

In its silence, we are left with nothing but ourselves, and in that stillness, we are often confronted with emotions we had buried or ignored.

In the depths of sorrow, hidden truths emerge, veiled beneath tear-filled skies.

The mind, caught between grief and introspection, struggles to navigate the storm of emotions that cloud perception.

Uncertainty lingers, making it difficult to find solid ground, yet within this turmoil, there is a quiet transformation.

Sadness forces us to confront what we often avoid, to sit with discomfort, to acknowledge wounds, and to recognize the fragile beauty of existence.

It is in these moments of vulnerability that we come face to face with our truest selves.

When sadness strikes, it is not merely a sign of weakness or despair, it is an indication that we have loved, that we have hoped, and that we have cared deeply.

It reminds us that to feel pain is to be alive, and to experience sorrow is to recognize the depth of our humanity.

Yet, despite its heaviness, sadness carries a quiet gift: a deeper understanding of the human heart.

Pain carves space for empathy, allowing us to connect with the suffering of others in ways joy alone cannot.

In grief's silent chambers, wisdom grows, an awareness of love's depth and the fleeting nature of time.

Sorrow does not only weaken, it also strengthens, offering the chance to rebuild with greater awareness and purpose.

It reminds us that even in loss, there is meaning, and even in darkness, there is the potential for light.

Through sorrow, we gain a newfound appreciation for the moments of happiness that, in their transience, often go unnoticed.

The contrast of sadness and joy allows us to understand both more deeply, teaching us that one cannot exist without the other.

It is through pain that we find resilience, and it is through loss that we learn to cherish what remains.

For sadness, though often unwelcome, reveals the raw and unfiltered depths of the psyche. It strips away illusions, exposing the tenderness we so often hide.

In mourning, in longing, in quiet reflection, we uncover what truly matters.

And in this discovery, we learn that sadness is not an enemy to be feared, but a passage, one that leads us, however painfully, toward healing, growth, and a deeper appreciation of what it means to be alive.

The wounds of sadness do not last forever, though their impact shapes us in ways we may not immediately understand.

In time, the sorrow that once felt unbearable softens, making room for hope, for understanding, and for a renewed sense of purpose.

Though sadness may leave its mark, it also leaves behind a quiet strength, an unspoken reminder that even in our darkest moments, we are never truly lost.

EACH PERSON

Each person, in the quietest corners of their existence, must eventually come face to face with their truest self.

It is in this intimate confrontation that we encounter our imperfections, not as burdens to bear, but as unique markers of our humanity.

These flaws are not to be hidden or ashamed of, they are woven into the very fabric of our being, shaping our experiences, our decisions, and our paths.

Life is not a journey of flawless execution or perfect moments, but a series of missteps, redirections, and lessons learned.

It is through these imperfections that we are shaped, and in acknowledging them, we come to understand that mistakes are not failures, but rather stepping stones that guide us toward deeper wisdom.

Every misstep holds the potential for growth, every flaw an opportunity to learn something vital about ourselves and the world around us.

As we walk the winding and unpredictable path of life, stumbling becomes an inevitable part of the process.

The road is rarely straight, and the challenges we face are often much harder than we anticipate.

But it is in those stumbles, in those falls, that we find the deepest lessons and the strongest parts of ourselves.

Each fall teaches us resilience, each misstep encourages reflection and growth.

It is through the struggle that we cultivate strength, a strength that would not be possible without the hardships we endure.

Clarity, too, is often elusive.

Rarely do we experience a sudden, complete understanding of our journey or our purpose.

Even the wisest among us must confess the limits of their knowledge, recognizing that wisdom is not a destination but an ongoing process of discovery.

This humbling realization unites us all, for in acknowledging our shared uncertainty, we find a common bond: none of us have all the answers, but we are all searching, all evolving.

In the grand tapestry of human hearts, imperfection is a universal thread.

It stretches across all boundaries, uniting us in our shared experience of being both fragile and resilient.

No one stands on a pedestal, better or more whole than another, we are all travelers in this vast, unpredictable world, each of us with our own burdens and dreams.

The beauty of life lies not in its perfection, but in the raw, unfiltered nature of our existence.

When we embrace ourselves as we are, flawed, incomplete, and yet endlessly capable of growth, we allow compassion to flourish.

By accepting our own imperfections, we open the door to understanding and empathy for others, knowing that they, too, carry their own burdens.

This acceptance does not weaken us, but strengthens the bonds we share with one another, reminding us that we are not isolated in our struggles, but connected in our shared humanity.

In accepting our authentic selves, we discover a grace that transcends our flaws, allowing us to shine brighter, not despite our imperfections, but because of them.

Within each heart, there lies an untapped potential, a spark that longs to grow, to be nurtured and set free.

This power is not something external, but an innate part of who we are, always waiting for the right moment to emerge.

It is the creative force that drives us to explore, to imagine, to build, and to become.

It is the quiet whisper in the background of our thoughts that urges us to step forward, to challenge our limits, to reach beyond what we thought possible.

As we wander through life, our thoughts often lead us to new ideas, new possibilities, and new perspectives.

Dreams that once seemed distant begin to take shape, revealing capabilities we never realized we had.

Each insight, each new understanding, adds to the rhythm of our existence.

It is a pulse, a beat that drives us forward, urging us to continue the dance of life.

In every question we ask, in every challenge we face, we discover new layers of ourselves and new potentials we are only beginning to tap into.

This journey of discovery is one that never ends.

With each step, we find that our path is both unique and shared, an intricate dance of individual growth and collective progress.

Embrace the journey, for it is not the destination that defines us, but the experiences and lessons we accumulate along the way.

Let the questions we ask ignite the fire of curiosity, and let our search for answers lead us to deeper truths.

It is through facing challenges, through confronting our imperfections, that we forge our paths and build our futures.

We are not merely passive observers in the world, but active creators, shaping the course of our lives with every decision, every moment of growth.

The gifts within us, the unique talents and perspectives we carry, have the power to transform the world.

As we embrace who we are, as we continue to evolve and grow, we unlock the potential not just for personal success, but for collective change.

In the hands of humankind, in every moment, lies the power to shape a future that is rich with possibility, where dreams are realized and the spark within each of us is set free.

BROKEN EGGS

To craft an omelette is to participate in a quiet act of transformation, where destruction leads to creation.

It begins with the deliberate breaking of eggs, smooth, delicate shells shattered with care.

Each crack is a moment of release, allowing the golden yolks and translucent whites to escape their fragile containers.

This act, so simple and so final, is necessary.

It reflects a truth echoed throughout nature: to bring something new into the world, something old must be undone.

There is reverence in this process, a recognition that within fragility lies the potential for nourishment.

The broken eggs are then brought together, their parts whisked into a seamless blend.

Here, the cook's hand becomes the guiding force, infusing intention into motion.

Salt, pepper, herbs, cheese, or finely chopped vegetables may join the mixture, each addition chosen with care, each stirring movement a quiet promise of flavor.

The once separate elements begin to harmonize, no longer yolk or white or herb, but one unified body waiting to be transformed by heat.

This is the moment where preparation gives way to possibility, where raw becomes ready.

Then comes the fire, and with it, the alchemy of cooking.

The mixture hits the warm surface of a pan, and a soft sizzle sings the beginning of something new.

In mere moments, the liquid mass begins to solidify, forming gentle folds and tender curves as the omelette takes shape.

The cook must watch closely, too much heat, and it toughens, too little, and it remains incomplete.

It is a delicate balance, like so much in life, where timing and presence are everything.

Within that pan, creation unfolds not with grand spectacle, but with quiet precision, revealing that even the most unassuming acts can carry profound depth.

When at last the omelette is finished, golden, warm, and ready to be served, it stands as more than just a meal.

It is a symbol of renewal, a meditation on change.

The act of breaking, blending, and transforming speaks to a deeper cycle that mirrors the rhythms of our own lives.

Every morning, in kitchens across the world, this ritual is repeated, affirming with each dish that new beginnings are always possible.

From the cracking of the first egg to the folding of the final product, the omelette tells a story: that in every ending, there is a start, and that from the softest break can rise the most sustaining form.

NEUTRALITY

True neutrality arises only when the human being finds genuine inner peace.

It is not something that can be adopted superficially or worn like a mask, rather, it must be cultivated through deep self-reflection, emotional clarity, and the dissolution of internal conflicts.

Inner peace is the foundation upon which neutrality stands.

When a person is inwardly calm and free from inner division, their thoughts and decisions flow from a place of balance and awareness rather than reaction and fear.

In this state, neutrality is not a forced stance but a natural expression of a centered and whole being.

As long as there is turmoil within, be it fear, anxiety, resentment, or insecurity, true neutrality remains elusive.

These inner disturbances act like waves that constantly stir the waters of perception, making it impossible to see clearly.

The moment fear enters the picture, the mind instinctively seeks protection.

It begins to build walls, form judgments, and choose sides, often unconsciously.

This is not necessarily a conscious choice, but rather a survival instinct deeply embedded in the human psyche.

The individual, in their attempt to preserve what they perceive as safety, develops biases that shape how they interpret and respond to the world.

These biases, though often subtle, distort truth and compromise integrity.

They are not merely opinions or preferences, they are shields born from fear, designed to prevent vulnerability.

A person influenced by inner fear cannot engage with the world objectively because their thoughts and actions are tethered to a need for control or reassurance.

Even good intentions can become clouded when filtered through internal unrest.

As long as these unresolved emotional states linger, neutrality becomes a performance rather than a truth, and clarity remains veiled behind layers of self-protection.

Only when the human being confronts and dissolves their inner fears can true neutrality begin to emerge.

It is a profound transformation, not a detachment from emotion, but a deep acceptance of oneself and the world as it is, without the need to alter, judge, or defend it.

In this state, there is no compulsion to cling to one side or reject another, no urge to label or categorize.

Neutrality becomes a reflection of peace, a state where the mind is no longer at war with itself.

From this stillness, true understanding, compassion, and wisdom naturally unfold.

This is the path to authentic neutrality: a journey inward that ultimately shapes how we meet the world.

"COME OUT"

The idea that a human being must "come out" in order to feel free about their sexuality has always struck me as absurd.

From the very start, it presents the illusion that freedom is something earned through disclosure, that until you publicly state who you are, you are somehow incomplete or in hiding.

That has always struck me as a false and limiting view of personal truth.

It implies that identity must be announced to be accepted, and that authenticity depends on visibility.

But the need to declare yourself to feel valid suggests that the power to define you lies in the hands of others.

That alone is enough to show how warped the concept has become.

It subtly enforces the idea that silence is shame, and speech is permission.

But freedom isn't something granted by society, culture, or any external authority.

It isn't offered as a reward for bravery or honesty.

Freedom is something that exists deep within every individual, it is your natural state, something you carry before you ever utter a word about yourself.

It's not something you earn by performing or confessing.

It is, by nature, a birthright, not a gift that's given once you've passed some unspoken test or met certain expectations.

You don't need the world's confirmation to be real.

You don't need validation from friends, family, or strangers to justify your existence.

You exist, and that alone is enough.

Anything else is extra noise.

True freedom is self-owned.

It doesn't arrive the moment someone else accepts you, it arrives the moment you stop needing them to.

No declaration, no announcement, no ritual can substitute for the internal sense of certainty that comes from knowing who you are.

When you understand this, you stop performing for the world, and start living for yourself.

The notion that anyone must proclaim their sexuality to be valid or accepted distorts the very meaning of freedom.

It makes identity feel conditional, dependent on the reactions of others.

The moment you decide that someone else's understanding or approval is necessary for your peace of mind, you hand over your inner power.

You shrink yourself to fit someone else's comfort.

At the heart of it, who you love, or share your life with, is personal.

It's intimate.

It belongs to you.

It was never meant to be a public announcement or a shared headline.

When private truths are made public for the sake of gaining acceptance, it only strengthens the illusion that your worth depends on being seen and affirmed.

But that's an illusion, and a dangerous one.

That illusion feeds control.

It gives others a sense that they have a stake in who you are, a vote in your identity.

That's not liberation, it's a performance.

One that traps you in a cycle of explaining yourself again and again, hoping that others will approve.

But approval fades.

And constantly seeking it leaves you unfulfilled.

Seeking validation through "coming out" often leads to a hollow sense of reward.

Maybe there's applause.

Maybe there's understanding.

But what comes next?

People move on.

Their attention fades.

And if your sense of self was tied to that moment, it will fade too.

Applause doesn't last.

But inner peace does.

There's no replacement for the kind of quiet, powerful self-knowledge that comes from living authentically without needing permission.

If you know who you are, and you live that truth with integrity and confidence, then you've already done the only "coming out" that matters.

The kind that doesn't ask, doesn't beg, doesn't need.

You don't owe the world a performance.

You owe yourself peace.

And that peace begins the moment you stop looking outside for permission to be exactly who you are.

FACING TRUTH

When truth settles heavily upon the heart, it can feel like a slow descent into darkness, a weight that drags the spirit down to the depths of confusion and sorrow.

In those moments, life may feel distant, dimmed by the challenge of confronting realities that unsettle the mind and psyche.

The teachings of the Creation Energy, though meant to guide and elevate, often arrive wrapped in difficulty.

They can stir inner conflict, surface long-buried fears, and awaken memories or beliefs we were not yet ready to face.

This discomfort is not a punishment, but a calling, a reminder that growth often begins where comfort ends.

As the light dims and uncertainty takes hold, it's easy to feel overwhelmed, disconnected from the harmony you once knew, and unsure of how to return to it.

Yet within that darkness, a quiet invitation emerges.

When you find the courage to welcome the truth instead of resisting it, a new path reveals itself.

A ladder, invisible at first, begins to form, rising from the very place you thought you'd fallen.

Each step upward represents a moment of honesty, a choice to see things as they are rather than how you wish they were.

The climb is not always easy.

There may be setbacks and doubts along the way, but each moment of clarity becomes a source of strength.

With every upward motion, your view expands, and the heaviness begins to lift.

Slowly, the night gives way to stars, then dawn, and you begin to realize that hope never left, it was simply waiting for you to rise and meet it.

This ascent is not forced upon you, it is a choice you make with every thought, every breath, every act of trust.

You hold the power to remain in the depths or to reach for the light above.

As you embrace knowledge and allow it to illuminate your inner landscape, you begin to see love, not as a fleeting feeling, but as a force that transforms.

Love becomes the thread that connects your thoughts to your actions, your psyche to your path.

With it, the chaos within settles, and a gentle harmony replaces the noise.

The rhythm of life starts to feel familiar again, like the steady beat of a drum that guides your dance, your purpose, and your becoming.

Through this, you come to understand that the shadows were not there to trap you, but to reveal where the light needed to shine.

And so, from within your heart, a profound truth begins to rise: that you were always free.

This freedom is not granted by the world, but discovered within, and it blooms the moment you choose to honor your spirit's journey.

It is the freedom to be fully yourself, to feel deeply, to live authentically, to speak with integrity, and to love without fear.

Each courageous step you take is a declaration of that freedom.

When you choose truth, you choose flight.

And when you choose flight, you let your spirit soar, beyond limitations, beyond fear, into the vast and boundless sky where peace, purpose, and possibility stretch endlessly before you.

So rise, not just for a moment, but for a lifetime.

Let your spirit fly, because that is what it was always meant to do.

THE PATH TO VIRTUE

The powers of life awaken through its vibrant breath, filling every moment with possibility and motion.

These forces are not passive gifts but living energies that call us to rise and participate.

Yet, true virtue does not simply emerge from these powers alone, it blossoms through the trials of our existence, through struggle, not through ease or death.

It is forged in the heat of our challenges, shaped by how we rise after each fall.

Virtue is not something inherited but cultivated, grown through intention, resilience, and the desire to align ourselves with something greater.

In this pursuit, we begin to walk with creation, not as masters, but as partners learning the language of harmony.

In living with the guidance of creation's hand, we begin to understand our place in the broader flow of life.

As we move forward, step by step, we gain the strength to stand, not merely physically, but with moral clarity and spiritual depth.

This process invites us to align ourselves with the eternal laws that govern growth, balance, and purpose.

These laws are not commandments forced upon us, but gentle truths that inspire.

When we attune ourselves to them, our intentions become clearer, and we are moved to act from a place of creative fire.

This inner flame is not destructive, it is illuminating, revealing the path before us when we are willing to walk with wisdom and care.

To follow the path to virtue, we must become active participants in our own becoming.

It is through our conscious choices and thoughtful actions that we shape the direction of our lives.

We cannot outsource responsibility, for it belongs to each of us as a sacred trust.

Each day is a new opportunity to recommit, to work, to grow, to transform.

Through effort, through sweat and soil, through honest labor both inward and outward, we nurture the seeds of goodness within us.

The journey is not always easy, and the terrain is rarely smooth, but every challenge faced with integrity becomes a stepping stone toward deeper virtue.

In the ever-turning dance of existence, we are called to forge our own light, one not borrowed from others, but ignited from within.

This light guides us, even through the darkest nights, and reminds us that we are not powerless.

Our endeavors, great or small, carry the imprint of our intentions.

When aligned with virtue, they reflect the beauty of our potential and the sacredness of our path.

We strive not for perfection, but for authenticity and wholeness.

In seeking virtue, we do more than better ourselves, we answer a call that echoes through all of life, honoring the interconnectedness of all things.

For within each of us resides the seed of greatness, and through the pursuit of virtue, that seed may grow into a force that uplifts the world.

APOPHIS

In the boundless velvet tapestry of space, where stars weave threads of time and mystery, a celestial traveler emerges, Apophis.

Its name, echoing ancient tales of chaos and rebirth, stirs imagination and awe as it journeys toward Earth.

On a date shrouded in superstition, Friday the 13th of April, 2029, this astronomical nomad draws near, lighting up the skies in a rare and mesmerizing display.

Across continents, people pause their daily lives to look skyward, united by the wonder of witnessing the passage of a spaceborne giant.

It's not doom they see, but the thrilling ballet of cosmic mechanics, a silent reminder of how vast and intertwined our existence is with the celestial realm above.

Despite its foreboding approach and the heavy mythos surrounding its name, Apophis brings no harm.

Earth remains safe beneath its protective veil of atmosphere and gravity.

Scientists, astronomers, and dreamers breathe a collective sigh of relief, their calculations affirmed, their faith in human ingenuity reinforced.

As the meteor hurtles past, a surge of reflection sweeps the globe, not of fear, but of perspective.

In that brief moment, humanity is reminded of its small yet significant place in the universe.

The spectacle above becomes a mirror below, urging introspection and an appreciation for the fragile beauty of the world we call home.

Seven years roll by, years filled with change, progress, and the deepening of collective memory.

When Apophis returns in 2036, the world greets it not with anxious eyes, but with wiser hearts.

It is no longer a harbinger of potential doom, but a familiar presence, a reminder of a time when Earth stood united in awe.

New generations, having grown up with the story of Apophis, look skyward with fascination and understanding.

Science and spirit walk hand in hand as humanity acknowledges the meteor's return as more than just an event, it is a chapter in their shared journey through space and time.

Lessons once feared are now embraced, transformed into a broader vision of cosmic responsibility and harmony.

As Apophis makes its final departure, disappearing once again into the shadowed corridors of the cosmos, a quiet farewell settles over the Earth.

It is not just the parting of a rock from space, but of something deeper, an echo of communion between planet and sky.

The stars watch silently as Earth, seasoned by the encounter, carries on with newfound reverence.

In the graceful rhythm of the universe, such meetings are fleeting, yet their imprint lasts.

Earth, ever turning beneath the gaze of the heavens, whispers its thanks.

In that cosmic dance, both humble and eternal, the story of Apophis becomes part of the greater song, the music of existence, composed in the language of stars.

MALONA

Long ago, within the familiar reaches of our own solar system, a planet named Malona once orbited the Sun.

Situated between Mars and Jupiter, in what is now known as the Asteroid Belt, Malona was a thriving world of immense natural beauty and scientific advancement.

Its people, far more evolved than modern Earth humans, had mastered technology, including genetic manipulation.

But with such power came peril.

The same advancements that elevated Malona's civilization eventually led to its collapse.

In a dangerous pursuit of dominance and control, the created genetically modified warriors, beings bred for war rather than peace, obliterated themselves.

What followed was a devastating internal conflict that would lead not only to the destruction of a society but the annihilation of an entire world.

This war, unlike any other in the known history of our solar system, escalated beyond control.

With their power unchecked and diplomacy abandoned, Malona's inhabitants unleashed weapons capable of planetary-scale destruction.

The very crust of the planet split apart as massive explosions shook its foundation.

Oceans boiled, continents shattered, and the sky itself burned.

In a final cataclysmic moment, Malona could no longer sustain its structural integrity.

The planet tore itself apart, scattering debris across space.

These fragments, millions of them, began to orbit the Sun as a broken ring of stone and metal, what we now see as the Asteroid Belt.

Each fragment a silent witness to a lost world, carrying with it the memory of a civilization that reached too far, too fast.

The destruction of Malona had far-reaching consequences.

Nearby Mars, which may once have hosted oceans and a thriving biosphere, was gravely affected by the gravitational and environmental disturbances.

The force of Malona's explosion sent shockwaves through space, disrupting Mars' orbit, destabilizing its climate, and thinning its atmosphere.

What might have been a twin cradle for life in our solar system was left scarred and barren. Earth, too, felt subtle effects from the cosmic event, as the balance of celestial forces within the solar system was forever altered.

Malona's fall not only ended its own legacy but reshaped the destiny of neighboring worlds.

Even now, the echoes of Malona's fate linger in the skies above.

The Sun continues its eternal burn at the heart of the system, casting light over the broken remains of its lost child.

The stars beyond, including Sirius in its distant brilliance, observe in silent vigil.

Malona's destruction is not merely a tale of ruin, it is a cosmic parable, etched into the fabric of space.

Its fragments orbit endlessly, reminders of what once was and what might have been.

They speak of the dangers of unrestrained ambition, of the thin line between advancement and arrogance, and of the great responsibility that comes with power.

In its silent disintegration, Malona offers a lesson for all emerging civilizations: that survival is not just about progress, but about balance, wisdom, and the humility to know one's limits.

THE CREATOR OVERLORDS

The Creator Overlords, celestial beings from the distant expanse of Lyra, once stood as the architects of life, wielding unimaginable power.

Yet, for all their might, they were unable to fully master the intricacies of their own existence.

In their quest to expand their influence, they sought to create a race that would serve as vessels of their will, engineered to fight, to struggle, and to ensure the perpetuation of their unseen dominion.

Thus, humanity was born, not as a free and independent species, but as a construct shaped by the genetic design of its makers.

From the very beginning, the fate of humankind was inscribed into its very essence, bound by limitations that dictated its nature, purpose, and mortality.

As the scattered remnants of this creation spread across the Earth, humanity carried with it the burdens of its engineered existence.

The struggle for dominance, the ceaseless cycle of violence, and the inescapable reality of suffering became the hallmarks of their condition.

They inherited not just intelligence and adaptability but also a deep-rooted propensity for cruelty and conflict.

This was no accident, but rather a deliberate design, an insidious feature embedded within their genetic code.

Their fleeting lifespans ensured that wisdom was often lost between generations, and the pursuit of knowledge remained forever incomplete.

The hands of time, relentless and unyielding, kept them shackled to an existence defined by struggle rather than transcendence.

Yet, despite the heavy chains that bound them, humanity remained drawn to the mysteries of the cosmos.

They gazed upon the stars, seeking answers, longing for a truth that lay just beyond their grasp.

The warmth of Sol's light provided comfort, but it also served as a reminder of their confinement within a system they had yet to fully comprehend.

Their yearning for freedom was not merely a dream but an instinctive call, a faint echo of a destiny that could be theirs, should they find the means to claim it.

However, the very essence of their existence remained shaped by the unseen hands of their creators, who ensured that their reach would always fall short of true liberation.

The genetic script that dictated their lives acted as an invisible chain, maintaining the influence of the Overlords long after they had vanished from sight.

But all was not lost, for within humanity's deepest struggles lay the seed of rebellion.

The realization that their destiny was not truly their own marked the first step toward liberation.

To break free from the genetic bindings imposed upon them, they would need to uncover the full truth of their origins and seize control of their own evolution.

No longer could they remain passive recipients of their inherited fate, instead, they had to become the architects of their own future.

The unraveling of their genetic constraints was not just a scientific pursuit but a profound act of defiance, a reclamation of autonomy stolen at the very inception of their kind.

True freedom could not simply be granted, it had to be earned through knowledge, unity, and transformation.

Humanity stood at the precipice of a monumental awakening, where the past no longer dictated the future.

To rewrite their genetic code was to reclaim their lost potential, casting aside the engineered limitations that had long defined their existence.

No longer bound to the purpose imposed upon them by their creators, they could forge a new path, one of limitless possibility, where self-determination and enlightenment reigned supreme.

Only then, through the conscious act of reshaping their own nature, could they transcend the confines of their origin and step into a future unshackled by the designs of the past.

120 BILLION

In realms far beyond the physical senses, where the veil of illusion fades and the true essence of existence emerges, there exists, linked to this planet, a boundless multitude, 120 billion expressions of pure Creation Energy, eternal and radiant.

These beings are not isolated or fragmented, they exist in unity, woven together in what can only be described as a sacred We-form.

It is a state of collective harmony that transcends individual identity and time itself.

They move as one in the grand rhythm of the cosmos, participating in a dance so subtle and sublime that it echoes the eternal heartbeat of Creation.

This movement is not bound by space, form, or chronology, it is fluid, eternal, and deeply intentional.

These beings are not separate but joined in a sacred unity, a We-form that transcends the limitations of time and space.

They move together in a cosmic rhythm, a divine dance that reflects the eternal flow of Creation itself.

Many of these consciousnesses exist on higher planes, beyond the reach of our ordinary senses.

They have not vanished, nor do they await judgment behind gates of heaven or walls of fire.

Instead, they remain part of our ever-expanding universal consciousness We-form, boundless, formless, eternal, waiting for us to catch up with their level of evolution.

Creation Energy, the source of all that is, flows like a divine thread through every realm, every frequency, every form of life.

It is the silent architect behind the stars, the galaxies, and the dimensions yet undiscovered.

Its presence is not loud or forceful, but infinitely wise, gentle, and all-encompassing.

It does not judge or punish, it only creates, evolves, and balances.

It weaves through the cosmos like a sacred breath, connecting every lifeform, every thought, every soul into a unified field of purpose.

There is no need for fear, no need for dogma.

Creation is the guiding force, the silent weaver of all existence.

Its hand moves through galaxies, stitching together realities and truths across dimensions.

There is no need for imagined heavens or dreaded hells, for all life returns to the order and balance of the cosmos.

Every being has its role in this grand design, and within this order, we are all held in place by the wisdom of the infinite.

The ideas of eternal reward or punishment dissolve when we recognize the elegant order of the universe, a system grounded not in control, but in harmony, in evolution, and in the natural return to source.

We are not alone in the universe, we are among countless sparks of spirit, each one shining in harmony with the greater whole.

The 120 billion spirits are not lost, they are alive in the very fabric of Creation, interlinked, radiant, and divine.

In recognizing this truth, we come closer to understanding who we truly are: part of something greater, something eternal, something beautifully unified as one.

Through this understanding, we step into our power, our peace, and our divine unity with all that exists.

DEAR PEOPLE OF EARTH,

I write to you as a proud citizen of this world, someone who has experienced the same trials, joys, and challenges that you have.

We all live this life, learning, growing, and making choices, sometimes good, sometimes bad.

Throughout my journey, I've felt the same urge that many of you have, an intense desire to seek more, to understand what lies beyond the surface of existence.

It's a thirst for something greater, something deeper.

At times, it has felt like a force beyond my control, pushing me forward, demanding answers, even when I wasn't sure if I was ready for them.

I've tried to resist it, many times, thinking perhaps it would be easier to ignore these impulses, to live simply and without complication.

But every time I tried to push it away, it came back stronger, more insistent.

I was consumed by it, and as a result, I lost many relationships, connections that were important to me.

But even now, looking back, I feel that all of it was worth the price.

These struggles, these losses, led me to a place of profound understanding.

It was through the teachings of the prophet Billy and the wisdom found within the Creation Energy Teachings that I came to see life in a completely new light.

These teachings have given me the clarity to understand the nature of existence and my place within it.

I now live without the weight of fear, knowing that I am an eternal being, that life is not confined to the physical body and that death is not an end, but a transition.

I have come to understand that the universe holds infinite mysteries, and while many may fear what lies beyond, I have learned to embrace it.

It is not a place of terror, but of discovery. With this new perspective, I no longer feel burdened by the constraints of fear.

I live freely, open to the vastness of the universe and the boundless potential within us all.

However, my purpose is not to surpass my fellow humans, nor to place myself above anyone else.

My goal is to share the knowledge I've gained so that others may benefit from it, just as I have.

To me, the truths I've discovered should be shared openly and freely, for they are not mine to hoard.

While I understand that some may mock or dismiss my dedication, I ask you to consider for a moment: Why would someone invest so much time, energy, and personal effort into spreading a message with no material gain?

Why continue to share these teachings day after day, week after week, unless there is something truly important to say?

I am here to remind you, not out of arrogance, but out of genuine care, that there is no God as many envision it, and the only thing we truly need to fear is fear itself.

Life is not a series of punishments and rewards, it is a game, an experience we are here to live, learn from, and grow through.

Imagine life as a video game, you may get lost in it, but once you take off the headsets, you realize you were always alive, always whole.

Please understand that I am not here to convince you of something you don't want to.

Only fools try to convince.

I am simply offering a different perspective, one that has brought me peace and understanding.

We are all on the same side, and while I have found my truth through the Creation Energy Teachings, it's a truth that is available to anyone who seeks it.

I do not seek to alienate or divide, but to encourage you to live in peace, to embrace who you truly are, and to find your own way.

We are all beautiful, unique expressions of Creation, each of us with a purpose and a path to walk.

In this world filled with noise, distractions, and judgments, I urge you to remain calm and true to yourself.

Do not let the opinions of others dictate your worth or your actions.

Be proud of who you are, for you are a creation of Creation itself, and that is something to be celebrated.

Above all, I urge you to live without fear.

Fear is the greatest illusion we face, and once we let go of it, we unlock the true potential within us.

We are all one, interconnected by the energy of the universe, and together, we stand.

There is nothing to fear but fear itself.

We are capable of so much more than we realize, and by embracing this truth, we can live lives of peace, love, and harmony.

So, I ask you, in the deepest part of my being, to live in peace, to be yourself, and to know that you are not alone.

We are all part of this grand and beautiful creation, and together, we can make this world a better place for all.

With love, peace, and the hope for a brighter future.

IN THE BEGINNING

In the beginning, the prophet will not appear before you with fanfare or recognition.

He will not walk openly among the people, nor will he speak in crowds or declare his role for all to see.

His presence will remain hidden from view, shrouded in silence and mystery.

And yet, his voice will reach you, not by his lips, but by the mouths of others.

It will echo across distances, through those chosen to carry it, emerging at unexpected moments and from unexpected sources.

You may hear this message in places you do not expect, in the quiet thoughts of strangers, in writings that stir something in you, or in dreams that leave a strange imprint on your spirit.

It will not always be clear, and rarely will it be comfortable.

The tone may challenge what you believe, and the form may seem foreign to familiar ears.

The prophet's words, though distant, will already be moving.

Not his alone, but shared through the voices of those sent ahead, forerunners with quiet conviction and a purpose not their own.

They will not come to comfort, but to disrupt.

To disturb the dust that has settled upon truth, to awaken questioning, and to ignite a subtle fire in the minds of those ready to receive.

These messengers will plant seeds, ideas, warnings, and invitations, and though many will ignore them, a few will feel the stirrings of something deeper.

To some, they will appear as fools, radicals, or deceivers.

But to others, they will feel like echoes from a place long forgotten.

Doubt will rise.

Confusion will grow.

Many will recoil at what seems unfamiliar, at words not wrapped in the comfort of tradition.

Yet those who listen closely, with humility and openness, will find clarity hidden in the strange cadence, in the rhythm of what seems dissonant.

A new language of truth, not yet understood, but undeniably felt.

Between these messages, there will be signs, not dramatic, but deliberate.

Quiet introductions, brief moments of insight, connections that seem coincidental but are not.

Each one a step closer to the unveiling, to the time when the prophet will step forward from the shadows.

And when that time arrives, those who have listened will recognize the voice they already know.

Only then will the weight and meaning of his words be fully understood, not as something new, but as something long awaited.

And the beginning will no longer be the beginning, but the moment when the hidden becomes seen, and the message, once scattered in fragments, stands whole before the world.

THE NATURE OF PROOF

Proof is a curious thing.

We often imagine it as something objective, concrete, indisputable, something that can be shown to others, like a solved equation or a photograph.

But the deeper truth is that no human being can ever truly prove something to another unless that individual is prepared to recognize the truth of it from within themselves.

Real proof, the kind that transforms perspective and anchors belief, is not something you receive from outside, but something you awaken to inside.

Understanding does not come from external validation, it arises when something within you aligns with what you're encountering.

Until that alignment happens, no amount of evidence will suffice.

You can pile up data, cite sources, craft arguments, and still be met with skepticism, not because the facts are flawed, but because the observer is not yet in a position to see them.

When people demand proof for something I've said, I don't take offense.

Often, I smile, not out of arrogance or dismissal, but because I see what's happening: they are looking for something that no one can give them.

Their request reveals a misunderstanding of how truth actually works.

They believe it can be delivered like a package, sealed and certain.

But truth is not a package, it is a process.

The moment someone demands, "Prove it," they are unconsciously revealing their distance from what is being shared.

They are not ready to understand because they are still seeking externally.

And while seeking is necessary, it must eventually turn inward.

Without this inward turn, all so-called "proof" is nothing more than information, facts without context, data without depth.

Everything we say, believe, and express is colored by our personal experience.

What we call truth is often nothing more than a reflection of what we've come to accept based on our own perceptions, conditioning, knowledge, or intuition.

No two people see the world in precisely the same way.

That's why what strikes one person as obvious can appear completely implausible to someone else.

This doesn't mean there is no truth, only that its recognition is personal.

To truly know something, you must investigate it yourself.

You must question, explore, doubt, and feel.

You must engage with the idea from multiple angles, and allow it to either dissolve or deepen through honest reflection.

Only then, through this quiet inner work, can something become real to you.

Until that happens, no matter who speaks or what is shown, you're merely hearing someone else's perspective.

And perspective is not proof.

It may serve as a catalyst, a pointer, or an invitation, but never a substitute for your own realization.

This is why no one can hand you proof like a certificate.

Proof must be discovered.

It must resonate so clearly within your being that it no longer feels like belief, it becomes something you know, even if you can't always explain why.

So the next time you feel compelled to ask, "Can you prove it?", pause.

Ask instead, "Am I ready to see for myself?"

Because until that readiness emerges, no amount of external explanation will suffice.

And once it does, you won't need proof from anyone else.

You'll have found it within.

THE LAST CHAPTER

As I bring this book to a close, I feel it is only right to share something deeply personal and meaningful about someone who has had a profound impact on my life, Billy.

He is not just a remarkable human being, but a living example of kindness, humility, and openness.

Unlike anyone else I've ever encountered, Billy opens his home to strangers without hesitation.

Whether you arrive from across the world or from the house next door, he welcomes you without judgment, without prejudice, and without expectation.

He offers food with genuine warmth, a place to rest if needed, and above all, a sense of belonging that is rare to find in today's world.

What makes Billy's way of living so unique is that he never asks for anything in return, not money, not praise, not recognition.

The only thing he gently asks is that those who stay lend a hand in maintaining the home.

It's a simple request rooted in fairness and mutual respect.

And if someone chooses to offer something extra, a gift, a donation, a helping hand beyond the basic needs, it is welcomed with gratitude, but never demanded.

There is no sense of obligation, only a quiet understanding that generosity and gratitude flow naturally when hearts are open.

There is, however, one important rule in Billy's home, and it must be respected above all else: do not treat him any differently than you would treat any other human being.

This rule may seem simple on the surface, but it speaks volumes about who Billy is.

He does not seek status, admiration, or a place above others.

He wishes to be seen and treated as an equal, just as we all wish to be.

It's a powerful reminder that true greatness often lies in humility, in the ability to live without ego, and in the insistence on equality in every interaction.

I have had the immense privilege of meeting Billy not once, but twice.

Each encounter left a deep impression on me, more than I can fully express in words.

Just being in his presence is enough to sense a deep reservoir of wisdom, a quiet strength, and a clarity that resonates far beyond the moment.

He doesn't need to speak loudly to be heard, his very being communicates a truth that touches the psyche.

It is in his presence that I truly understood what it means to live with purpose, compassion, and balance.

And so, with all the sincerity in my heart, I end this book with a message of thanks: Thank you, Billy, for being my teacher, my example, and my inspiration.

From the deepest part of my being, from the source of my creation energy, I am, and always will be, forever grateful.